To
Steve,
from

7 May 2006

Trade Marks at the Limit

Trade Marks
at the Limit

Edited by

Jeremy Phillips

*Intellectual Property Consultant, Slaughter and May,
and Professorial Fellow, Queen Mary Intellectual Property
Research Institute, University of London, UK*

Edward Elgar
Cheltenham, UK • Northampton, MA, USA

Published by
Edward Elgar Publishing Limited
Glensanda House
Montpellier Parade
Cheltenham
Glos GL50 1UA
UK

Edward Elgar Publishing, Inc.
136 West Street
Suite 202
Northampton
Massachusetts 01060
USA

A catalogue record for this book
is available from the British Library

ISBN-13: 978 1 84542 738 2
ISBN-10: 1 84542 738 6

Typeset by Cambrian Typesetters, Camberley, Surrey
Printed and bound in Great Britain by MPG Books Ltd, Bodmin, Cornwall

Contents

Biographical notes

THE EDITOR

Jeremy Phillips

After graduating from Cambridge University and taking a doctorate at the University of Kent, Jeremy held lecturing posts at Trinity College Dublin, the University of Durham and Queen Mary before he assumed the editorship of *Trademark World*, *Patent World*, *Copyright World* and later *Managing Intellectual Property*. A Professorial Fellow at the Queen Mary Intellectual Property Research Institute, he has been Intellectual Property Consultant to London solicitors Slaughter and May since 1994.

A writer and lecturer on many aspects of intellectual law, Jeremy currently edits the *Journal of Intellectual Property Law and Practice* (Oxford University Press), the *European Trade Mark Reports* and the *European Copyright and Design Reports* (Sweet & Maxwell). Since 2003 he has been joint blogmeister of the IPKat weblog, which provides up-to-date news and commentary on a wide range of legal and commercial developments in the intellectual property field. His books include *Trade Mark Law: a Practical Anatomy* (Oxford University Press, 2003).

THE AUTHORS

Anthony P. Alden

Anthony is an associate in the Los Angeles office of Quinn Emanuel Urquhart Oliver & Hedges, LLP. He earned his BA, BS and JD degrees from Monash University in Melbourne, Australia, and an LLM from the Columbia University School of Law in New York.

Frank Azzopardi

Frank Azzopardi is an associate in Davis Polk & Wardwell's Corporate Department, specializing in intellectual property and in mergers and acquisitions. He joined Davis Polk in 2001, having previously been an associate in the Intellectual Property and Technology Department of Australian firm Allens Arthur Robinson. He has extensive transactional experience overseeing intellectual property issues arising from corporate transactions including mergers, asset sales, reorganizations, spin-offs, licensing arrangements, joint ventures and other collaborations.

Frank advises private equity, media, information technology, bio-pharmaceutical and other clients on a variety of intellectual matters, including patents, trade secrets, trade marks, copyright, mask works, domain names, rights of privacy, rights of personality and related common law rights. He also has litigation experience involving intellectual property disputes in the area of design patents, trade marks, copyright, cyber-squatting, passing off and personality merchandising. Frank holds Bachelors degrees in Law and Commerce from the University of Melbourne, Australia. He is admitted to practice in New York as well as in the Supreme Court of Victoria, Australia, and is a Registered Australian Trade Mark Attorney.

Mark Bezant

Mark Bezant is a Managing Director in the London office of LECG Corporation, a global expert services firm providing expert analysis, testimony, authoritative studies and strategic advisory services to clients. He specializes in intellectual property matters, business valuations and litigation support and his work covers the valuation of all forms of intangible assets.

Mark has acted in a number of high-profile IP matters and he is particularly interested in the interaction between the economics of intangible assets and the legal rights afforded to intellectual property, in both commercial and regulatory (accounting, tax, litigation, anti-trust) environments. He has presented and published extensively on IP and related valuation matters and is the author of *The Use of Intellectual Property as Security for Debt Finance*, published by the Intellectual Property Institute, London.

Thierry Calame

Thierry is a partner in Lenz & Staehelin, Switzerland, specializing in intellectual property law. He represents clients in patent, trade mark and other IP-related litigation and arbitration, advising on a wide range of IP-related commercial matters and licensing. His significant contentious practice includes numerous patent, trade mark and copyright infringement actions in various Swiss courts and the Federal Supreme Court.

Thierry holds a degree in Chemistry from the Swiss Federal Institute of Technology and a Doctorate in Law from the University of St Gallen, Switzerland. A visiting scholar at the Max-Planck Institute in Munich, Germany in 1996, he held a similar position at the University of Santa Clara Law School in the USA in 1998. Thierry is currently Assistant to the Rapporteurs General of the International Association for the Protection of Intellectual Property (AIPPI) and a member of the Board of Directors of the Swiss group of AIPPI. He is a regular lecturer on intellectual property issues and has written on a wide range of intellectual property topics, notably in patent and trade mark law.

Karin Cederlund

Joining the firm in 1994, Karin has been a partner in Mannheimer Swartling Advokatbyrå in Stockholm since 2001, specializing in intellectual property and advertising law. A member of the firm's practice group for litigation and arbitration, she also has extensive experience of litigation and transactions involving all forms of intellectual property rights.

Karin has in-depth knowledge of a number of business sectors, focusing particularly on biotech and pharmaceutical companies, media and publishing companies and collecting societies. A member of the board of the Swedish Association for the Protection of Industrial Property Law, she was admitted to the Swedish Bar Association in 1998, holding an LLM from the University of Stockholm and an MBA from the Stockholm School of Economics. She is a guest lecturer at the Faculty of Law, University of Stockholm, and at the Riga Graduate School, the LLM program.

Lasse A. Søndergaard Christensen

Lasse, a partner in the Danish law practice Gorrissen Federspiel Kierkegaard, is head of the firm's IP/Technology Group. He is also Associate Professor at the University of Aarhus, where he teaches intellectual property law and unfair marketing practices law.

Lasse received his law degree from the University of Aarhus in January 1991 and his LLM from the New York University School of Law in 1995. He has received further education at City University of Hong Kong. Admitted to the bar in 1994 and the High Court in 1996, Lasse joined Gorrissen Federspiel Kierkegaard in January 2002. Before that he worked for the Danish Ministry of Justice and as a partner in a law firm.

Lasse has authored numerous articles and book contributions on intellectual property-related matters in Danish and international publications and is the Danish correspondent to the *European Copyright and Design Reports*.

Lewis Clayton

Lew is a partner in the Litigation Department and co-chair of the Intellectual Property Litigation Group at Paul, Weiss, Rifkind, Wharton & Garrison LLP. He has chaired the Committee on Intellectual Property of the Commercial and Federal Litigation Section of the New York State Bar Association and contributes regular columns on intellectual property litigation to the *New York Law Journal* and the *National Law Journal*.

Lew has counselled clients and handled major litigation, both for plaintiffs and defendants, in a broad range of patent, copyright, trade mark and unfair competition matters across a wide spectrum of industries. He successfully enforced Revlon's patent on its ColorStay lipstick, and represents Gillette in its patent infringement litigation against Schick. He has won federal court injunctions for Castrol Inc. against the continued broadcast of competitors' nationwide advertising campaigns. Lew has also handled major trade mark litigation for such companies as Unilever and Revlon, successfully representing Unilever in a groundbreaking trade secret dispute with Procter & Gamble. In addition, he represented CBS in copyright litigation concerning CBS's reality television programme 'Survivor'.

Nicolas Dontas
Nicolas heads the IP department of Dontas Law Offices, a Greek business law firm established in 1922 by the late Nicholas A. Dontas. He graduated in Law with First Class Honours from the Law School of the University of Athens and was awarded a Merit in his LLM from the London School of Economics and Political Science. He regularly advises clients on matters involving trade mark, design and copyright protection, licensing and information technology agreements and unfair competition law claims; his litigation experience covers all these areas, with particular emphasis on trade dress infringement and trade mark dilution cases.

Nicolas has been included in the Euromoney guide, *The World's Leading Trademark Law Practitioners*, and has written and lectured widely on intellectual property matters. An active member of the International Trademark Association, he has made presentations to its meetings on a variety of trade mark-related topics.

Dawn Franklin
Dawn studied modern languages before joining Hertz to work for several years in UK sales, international sales and marketing. She later joined the service and finance division within Mars Confectionery before transferring to the parent company, Mars Incorporated, where she held roles in legal, personnel, risk management and site management. She subsequently became Marketing Property Manager, Europe, with responsibility for marketing properties in the pet-care and human foods businesses. Dawn left Mars after 21 exciting years to set up her own brand protection consultancy, Brandright, in 1996. She now works with a number of small, medium-sized and multinational companies in the development and management of their brand portfolios in fields as diverse as biotechnology, design, food and drink manufacture, chemicals, toiletries and publishing.

Dawn has served on the Board of Directors of the International Trademark Association, as a consultant to the World Intellectual Property Organization in Geneva and was a founder member of the British Brands Group. She is

currently Chairman of the trade mark committee of AIM (the European Brands
Association) based in Brussels and remains passionate about the benefits of
brands and the importance of best branding practice.

Luca Giove

A lawyer with leading Italian law firm Bonelli Erede Pappalardo since 2004,
Luca was admitted to the Venice bar in 2002. He holds a law degree from the
University of Padua (where he now teaches patent law) and an LLM from the
School of Oriental and African Studies, University of London.

Luca's practice is centred on IP litigation in disputes involving patents in
various fields (pharmaceuticals, chemicals, electronics, mechanical engineering), trade marks, copyright, advertising and unfair competition issues. He
also handles transactional work on a wide variety of IP/IT non-contentious
matters for Italian and international companies operating in the media, entertainment, publishing, pharmaceutical, chemical, software, medical devices,
mechanical engineering, luxury and fashion and consumer products sectors.

Charles H. Googe, Jr

Charles, a partner in the Entertainment and Corporate Departments of Paul,
Weiss, Rifkind, Wharton & Garrison LLP, leads the Intellectual Property
Group which focuses on all aspects of intellectual property, including copyright, trade mark and patent, trade secret and internet law. His experience
covers a broad range of industries, specialties and deal sizes.

Charles's special expertise encompasses all forms of transactional work
involving intellectual property and technology such as IP audits, developing and implementing prosecution strategies, licensing and due diligence.
He possesses specific experience in software, information technology and
entertainment content development, acquisition and distribution over the
internet and other media. Charles works closely with Paul, Weiss lawyers
on structuring the intellectual property aspects of highly sophisticated
transactions, as well as addressing the intellectual property needs of numerous medium-sized and start-up enterprises. In addition, he represents many
notable individuals and companies involved in every aspect of the entertainment, new media and publishing industries.

Janne Britt Hansen

Janne is an associate in the Danish law practice Gorrissen Federspiel
Kierkegaard. She is a member of the firm's IP/Technology Group and the head
of its intellectual property right registration department. Janne focuses on the
areas of trade marks, design and counterfeit. Her practice primarily includes
trade mark prosecution, protection, licensing and enforcement, litigation
including trade mark, design and copyright disputes as well as advertising and

marketing law. She also advises clients on international strategy and management of intellectual property portfolios.

Janne received her law degree from the University of Copenhagen in January 2000. She joined Gorrissen Federspiel Kierkegaard in October 2002 and was admitted to the Danish bar in January 2005. Between April 2000 to October 2002 she was head of section in the Danish Ministry of Justice and in the Danish Patent and Trade Mark Office.

Petra Hansson

Petra joined Mannheimer Swartling in 2000 after serving as a junior judge in Swedish District and Appeal Courts. She advises clients within a number of business sectors, including IT, entertainment and media, focusing primarily on intellectual property law.

Petra holds two LLM degrees. The first is from the University of Lund; the second is in Intellectual Property from Queen Mary and Westfield College, University of London. She is a guest lecturer in copyright law at the Faculty of Law, University of Stockholm, and is one of two editors of the Mannheimer Swartling intellectual property newsletter.

Rainer Hilli

Rainer is a partner in the law firm of Roschier Holmberg, based in Helsinki. He heads the firm's technology, media and communications group. He is experienced in both contentious and non-contentious intellectual property matters.

Rainer has litigated several landmark intellectual property cases before the national courts in Finland and has also appeared before the European Court of Justice (ECJ). He represented Gillette before the ECJ in a reference for a preliminary ruling which was discussed in his chapter. Rainer is also President of the Finnish AIPPI Group.

Philippe de Jong

Philippe is an associate at the Altius law firm, based in Brussels, Belgium. Having previously studied at the universities of Antwerp and Lausanne, he obtained an LLM Masters degree in intellectual property law from the University College London (UCL) and is currently a member of the Brussels bar.

Philippe specializes mainly in patent and trade mark law and has developed substantial knowledge of the regulatory regime for pharmaceuticals. He has published a number of articles in various leading European legal journals with regard to specific topics in intellectual property litigation.

Wolfgang Kellenter

Wolfgang is a partner in the German law firm of Hengeler Mueller, Düsseldorf, where he is co-head of the Intellectual Property Practice Group.

Wolfgang studied law at the universities of Erlangen and Bayreuth where he graduated and received a PhD in law. He subsequently obtained an LLM degree at the London School of Economics, where he specialized in intellectual property law. Wolfgang was admitted to the German bar in 1990 and as solicitor of England and Wales in 1992. He also currently lectures in Intellectual Property and Internet Law at the Heinrich Heine University in Düsseldorf. His main areas of practice are trade mark litigation, patent litigation and intellectual property licensing.

Susie Middlemiss
Susie is a partner and head of the Intellectual Property and Information Technology practice of the law firm Slaughter and May. She has extensive experience of a wide range of intellectual property matters involving all forms of intellectual property rights. Susie's litigation practice covers the High Court, the Patents County Court and the European Patent Office; she also advises in multi-jurisdictional disputes, particularly concerning patents and trade marks. Her practice encompasses strategic advice on the protection and enforcement of portfolios of trade marks and other IP rights. Her non-contentious experience includes advising on licences, distribution agreements, franchises and the intellectual property aspects of a range of other transactions.

Susie holds degrees in genetics and biological sciences and in law, both from the University of Sydney. She has considerable experience in acting for clients in the pharmaceutical, biotechnology and healthcare fields on a range of transactions and contentious matters and is a member of the editorial board of the *Bioscience Law Review*. Susie is also Chair of the European Sub-Committee of the International Trademark Association's Amicus Committee, which files briefs in cases raising significant issues of trade mark law before European National courts and the European Court of Justice.

Montiano Monteagudo
Montiano is a partner in the Barcelona office of Uría Menéndez. Since 1993 he has been a Professor of Commercial Law at the Universitat Pompeu Fabra (Barcelona). A regular speaker at other universities in Spain and abroad, he also participates in law seminars and conferences. He is the author of several books and articles regarding trade mark and unfair competition law.

Montiano's practice focuses on advising national and multinational companies on matters relating to intellectual property, unfair competition, competition law, contract law, information technology and corporate law. He also regularly advises multinational pharmaceutical companies and other innovative foreign and domestic businesses in sectors such as electronics and microelectronics, software, food, textile, homecare products and education. He represents clients before regulatory bodies and courts in proceedings for the protection of patents, trade marks, industrial designs, copyright, know-how and other intellectual property rights. He counsels market leaders in the telecommunications, pharmaceutical, electronics, financial services and food and drinks sectors in both contentious and non-contentious matters regarding unfair competition and advertising, including passing-off, misleading practices, protection of trade secrets, misappropriation of trade marks and trade dress.

Jackie O'Brien
Jackie is a partner in Allens Arthur Robinson in the Intellectual Property, Communications & Technology department, practising from its Sydney office. Jackie has practised IP for over 20 years, advising clients across a variety of industries including entertainment, eCommerce, clothing, pharmaceutical and luxury goods. She also advises on brand protection, registration and maintenance for some of the world's highest profile companies.

Jackie has developed anti-piracy programmes for numerous clients, using copyright and trade mark rights in combination with working with Australian Customs. She has also handled a number of domain name disputes and undertakes clearance work for advertising and promotional campaigns. Jackie advises extensively in relation to comparative advertising, specifically in sectors experiencing rapid growth and competition. Her considerable experience spans advising in relation to co-branded products and services and the legal issues surrounding product placement and promotion.

Núria Porxas
Núria is a lawyer in the Barcelona office of Uría Menéndez. Joining the firm in 1997, she became a senior associate in January 2005. She has lectured on intellectual property law and advertising law on several Master's programmes. Her practice covers all areas of copyright and intellectual property law, focusing on trade marks, unfair competition and advertising. In particular, she deals with know-how and IP licensing, and in creating strategies for developing, managing and protecting IP portfolios.

Núria regularly advises national and multinational companies regarding intellectual property rights, unfair competition and advertising. Her experience includes passing off, protection of company secrets and the misappropriation of trade marks. Núria participates in proceedings before regulatory bodies, Spanish courts and alternative dispute resolution bodies, particularly self-regulatory advertising associations. She is a member of the editorial team of Uría Menéndez in charge of comments and updates on intellectual property issues and unfair competition.

Bruce Proctor
Bruce began his career as an intellectual property litigator in his native New

York with the law firm of Wyatt, Gerber, Shoup, Scobey and Badie. He then worked in industry, joining the Bristol-Myers Squibb Company where he handled IP matters. Subsequently Bruce joined Unilever United States where he managed Unilever's New York Trademark function and also handled general corporate matters, with an emphasis on acquisitions and diverstitures. Bruce then joined The Coca-Cola Company as their Global Head of Trademarks, managing all of Coke's trade mark and related issues. In 2002 he moved to London, where he now works as Global Head of Intellectual Property for Diageo, managing a team located in both the US and the UK.

David W. Quinto
David W. Quinto is a partner in the Los Angeles office of Quinn Emanuel Urquhart Oliver & Hedges, LLP. The author of *Law of Internet Disputes* (Aspen, 2003), he has long represented numerous clients in trade mark matters. He is principally responsible for protecting the rights of the Academy of Motion Picture and Sciences in the OSCAR statuette and ACADEMY AWARDS telecasts and has been called upon to protect Mattel's BARBIE doll and HOT WHEELS toys, the America's Cup marks, the EMMY and numerous other intellectual properties. In 2004 he was retained to represent the government of the Russian Federation in an effort to recover for Russia the rights to STOLICHNAYA and other vodka trade marks.

David earned his BA degree from Amherst College, in Massachusetts, and his JD from the Harvard Law School.

Christian Schumacher
Christian is a junior partner at Schönherr Attorneys-at-Law, Vienna, Austria. Admitted to the Bar in 2003, he specializes in intellectual property law, unfair competition law and media law. Christian holds Master of Law and Doctorate degrees from the University of Vienna and a Master's degree from the New York University School of Law; he has also studied at the Université Paris II Panthéon-Assas.

Christian has authored a monograph on *Media Coverage and Protection of Personality Rights* (Manz, 2001) and contributed to the trade mark commentary entitled *marken.schutz* (Manz, to be published 2005). He regularly publishes articles and comments on recent court decisions in the Austrian law review entitled *ecolex* (Manz).

Grace Smith
Grace was admitted as a solicitor in Ireland in 1985 and as an attorney in the State of New York in 1989. She is also a Community trade mark attorney and has completed the WIPO workshop for Mediation in Intellectual Property Disputes.

Joining McCann FitzGerald, one of Ireland's leading law firms, in 1989, Grace became a partner in the Dispute Resolution & Litigation Group in 1994. For the past decade she has specialized in intellectual property law and now heads the firm's Intellectual Property Group. Grace has acted in most of the significant IP cases in Ireland over the last few years including *Guinness v Kilkenny; Monsanto v Merck; B&S v Autotrader; EMI v Gormley* and *Merial v Virbac*. Her practice includes contentious and non-contentious aspects of intellectual property including protection of knowhow, goodwill, trade marks, patents, copyright and designs. Her extensive experience includes advising on the legal issues arising from advertising and on the regulatory framework applicable to pharmaceutical products.

Grégoire Triet

Grégoire is a partner in Gide Loyrette Nouel's Intellectual Property, Technology & Electronic Communications Department. A specialist in patent and trade mark law, he has wide-ranging experience in patent infringement and validity disputes and in working on behalf of national and international clients. He also deals with copyright and unfair competition cases.

Having joined Gide Loyrette Nouel in 1983, Grégoire has been a partner since 1990. He is the author of a study commissioned by the Ministry of the Economy, Finance and Industry (2000), 'Comparative survey on the cost of litigation connected with industrial property in France, Germany, England, the United States, Spain and the Netherlands'. The President of AAPI (the French Association of Intellectual Property Lawyers), Grégoire is a member of the editorial boards of both the *European Trade Mark Reports* and the *European Copyright and Design Reports*.

Steven Warner

Steven joined Slaughter and May in 2000 and has been an associate solicitor in that firm's Intellectual Property Department since 2002. His practice covers both contentious and non-contentious matters relating to all aspects of intellectual property, including patents, trade marks, passing off, copyright and the protection of trade secrets and other confidential information.

Before moving into law, Steven obtained a Bachelor of Arts degree (Philosophy, Politics and Economics) and a DPhil degree (Political Theory) from the University of Oxford.

Steven Weiner

Steven, a partner in Davis Polk & Wardwell, spearheads the firm's corporate intellectual property practice. He advises clients on business-critical IP matters including assessment and resolution of IP threats, patent analysis and strategy, copyright fair use analysis, negotiation of IP licences, participation in technology standards and the complex IP aspects of mergers and acquisitions, divestitures, and other corporate transactions. His clients include technology and media industry leaders such as Yahoo! and Comcast, investment and financial services firms and new ventures and non-profits at the cutting edge of research and development.

Before joining Davis Polk in 2002, Steven served as Vice President for Intellectual Property and Strategic Planning at SRI International, as Senior Intellectual Property Counsel at SGI and as an intellectual property litigation associate at Irell & Manella. He graduated, *summa cum laude*, from the University of Pennsylvania in 1985, receiving a Master's degree in electrical engineering and computer science from MIT in 1987 and a J.D., *cum laude*, from Harvard Law School in 1990. He is a registered US patent attorney and is admitted to the bar of California.

Preface

To the best of my knowledge this is the first book on the subject of permitted but unauthorized uses of the trade marks of others. Working without an obvious model to which reference may be made or from which inspiration may be drawn, we have had to draw on our own ideas – an exciting and stimulating experience.

The launch of this volume at the May 2006 International Trademark Association Meeting is to the credit of its many authors, whose unstinting efforts, trade mark expertise, enthusiasm and ability to work under pressure have turned the project from dream to reality.

Particular credit is due to my friend and colleague, Susie Middlemiss, who heads the Intellectual Property Group at Slaughter and May. Susie's participation in this book at every level cannot be understated. Her expert professional knowledge, tact and humour have each been invaluable assets and I have shamelessly made demands upon all three of these assets when necessary.

Luke Adams also deserves a special mention, together with his team at Edward Elgar Publishing. Luke cannot have faced a team of contributors that was more determined to get a title out on time: the sprint to print has been fraught with difficulties but Luke has seen it through with admirable cool.

Jeremy Phillips
Temple Fortune, April 2006

Introduction: Permitted but unauthorised use

Jeremy Phillips

WHAT IS MEANT BY 'PERMITTED BUT UNAUTHORISED USE'?

Trade mark law confers upon the proprietor of a registered trade mark a very wide power over other traders who use his trade mark. Put simply, if that use is without the proprietor's permission, the proprietor has the power to prohibit it by bringing a legal action against the user for infringement. If however that use is with the proprietor's permission, he may make that use conditional upon such terms as he seeks to impose.

The reality is less simple. This is because there is a category of use that the trade mark owner is powerless to prevent: use which, while lacking the proprietor's authorisation, is nonetheless permitted by the law. More accurately, there are several different categories of use that the law tolerates, whatever the feelings of the trade mark owner. Some of these uses are based on commercial imperatives, such as a retailer's need to be able to inform consumers about the goods he sells; others are based on political imperatives, such as the exercise of the human right of freedom of speech; others again are based on considerations of honesty or fairness, such as where a trader seeks to trade under his own name even though that name is the same as, or similar to, an earlier registered trade mark.

STRIKING A BALANCE

In each of the instances in which the law permits the use of a trade mark even where that mark's owner does not authorise it, it is plain that the law has sought to establish a balance between the interests of the trade mark owner and those of others. In some cases the balance is sought between the trade mark owner and a direct competitor; in other cases it may be sought between him and those whose business interests lie downstream of his own (such as distributors and retailers), the consumer of his goods or even the public at large.

Wherever a balance is sought, it is necessary to identify the point at which the competing or conflicting interests are in equilibrium. Too much protection for the trade mark owner may mean that others cannot refer to the mark when critically comparing products sold under it with those of other products; too little protection may mean erosion of the trade mark's ability to provide consumers with a confident guarantee that its use indicates the identity of the origin of goods or services for which it is used.

The technique provided by legislators the world over is the same. Since it is impossible to predict the precise circumstances in which the valuable role of a trade mark is threatened, and it is equally impossible to anticipate the circumstances in which its enforcement may be oppressive, general principles are enacted into law. It is then left to the courts or other tribunals to interpret those general principles in the light of specific sets of facts in which the interests of trade mark proprietor and unauthorised user collide.

THE TENSIONS OF TRADE MARK LAW

It is now no longer doubted that the right conferred by trade mark registration is a property right. This is something that is explicitly stated in the trade mark legislation of most countries and which has been backed by a ruling of the European Court of Human Rights in 11 October 2005 in Case 73049/01 *Anheuser-Busch Inc. v Portugal.*

Many property rights are vulnerable to exceptions or limitations in favour of third parties, even where the property right owner withholds his authorisation. Thus, in respect of real property such as land, the right to exclude others may be exercised against casual acquaintances or passers-by, but will not enable the rights owner to bar access to, for example, the police authorities or the emergency fire services. Other third party users may include members of the public who have a right of way. The enforcement of intellectual property rights is likewise diminished by the ability of third parties to 'invade' the rights owner's intellectual estate and to do so against his will. Patent, trade mark and copyright law make ample provision for such use.

The analogy between real property and intellectual property is however an imperfect one. This is because the unauthorised but permitted use of land or other real property is unlikely to destroy its value completely while, in the case of a trade mark, permitted third party use can result in the goodwill in the mark being wiped out (as where one branded product is compared highly unfavourably with another). Nor does the analogy with land convey the risk that a trade mark will cease to be able to inform consumers of the origin of goods or services marketed under it (as happens where the honest use of a confusingly similar mark cannot be restrained). The vulnerability of trade

marks to diminution of their value or their power may be more fully appreci-
ated when one considers the very wide range of uses to which a trade mark
may be put and which do not even fall within the scope of trade mark infringement at all. For example, it is not an infringement of a trade mark for a large
number of consumers to opt to refer to their vacuum cleaners as hoovers or for
the media and the medical profession to describe acquired immune deficiency
syndrome as AIDS, thus rendering commercially useless several trade marks
for slimming products. But these uses lie outside the scope of this volume.

THIS BOOK

Trade Marks at the Limit examines the points at which trade mark rights reach
the limits of their enforceability. In doing so, it seeks to set out the general
framework within which the balance of competing interests is attained.
Subsequent chapters consider areas in which specific problems arise, also
contrasting the European approach with those of the United States and
Australia. Finally, the book addresses some broader issues. One is theoretical
(is it in some way better for a business not to rely upon the unauthorised but
permitted use of the marks of others) and two are practical (how does third
party use affect a trade mark's valuation and what steps can a trade mark
proprietor take to minimise any unwanted effects of such use?).

This book is not intended to be a text book or a practitioners' manual. At
one level it is a collaborative snap-shot of the law and practice as it stands, as
viewed from the perspective of a band of authors who all work extensively
within the field of trade mark law and branding practice and who care greatly
about how the system works. Yet it is also more than that: the chapters treat
their appointed topics to a greater deal of in-depth analysis than most judges,
authors of textbooks and professional treatises are able to justify when
addressing trade mark law as a whole. Speculative issues are investigated as
well as matters of persistent concern. Questions are asked even when there is
no easy answer – or no answer at all.

In this book the reader may find more questions asked than answers given,
but that should be viewed as a positive advantage. Particularly in European
law, where the norms of a relatively newly-approximated system are still
'bedding down', uncertainties are bound to remain unresolved. Some of these
uncertainties are being addressed by references made to the Court of Justice of
the European Communities. Other uncertainties are being left unresolved (for
example the interplay of the trade mark right and the rights of political and
commercial free speech) because many businesses may be content to live with
the flexibilities that uncertainties present than an adverse result in their resolution.

In publishing this collection of essays, the editor and authors join in hoping that they will at least have done something to sensitise readers to some of the complexities of the issues that are involved when delineating the limit beyond which a trade mark owner may not interfere with the use that others make of his trade mark. This is an area in which further debate is inevitable. We all hope that this debate will be well-informed and that we will, through the medium of this book, have contributed to it.

PART ONE

The legal background

1. Permitted use under international law

Nicolas Dontas

Developed to facilitate international commerce and to bring down the trade
barriers that result from the principle of territoriality of trade mark protection, the international law on trade marks establishes a general legal framework with which national and regional jurisdictions should comply.
Consequently, several international treaties have been signed to facilitate the
international protection of trade marks, from the Paris Convention of 1883[1]
to the World Trade Organization's TRIPs Agreement.[2] Specifically, the international legal framework on trade marks is based upon the following international treaties:

The Paris Convention of 1883
The Paris Convention on the Protection of Industrial Property is the oldest and
most important treaty with respect to industrial property rights. It is based on
a set of principles that were intended to secure and protect trade mark rights in
international trade. The Paris Convention required signatory states to implement the well-known principle of territoriality,[3] the national treatment principle,[4] the principle of independence of rights[5] and the *telle-quelle* principle,[6]
which created a solid basis for the future development and evolution of international trade mark law.

---

[1] Paris Convention for the Protection of Industrial Property of 20 March 1883,
as revised to 14 July 1967 and amended on 28 September 1979.
[2] Agreement on Trade-Related Aspects of Intellectual Property Rights,
Annex 1C of the Marrakech Agreement Establishing the World Trade Organization,
signed in Marrakech, Morocco on 15 April 1994.
[3] The principle that intellectual property rights are territorial in nature: see
Articles 4, 4*bis*.
[4] National treatment, the principle of giving others the same treatment as one's
own nationals, is provided for under Article 2 of the Paris Convention and also now in
TRIPs Article 3.
[5] Arts 4*bis*, 6.
[6] Under Article 6*quinquies* A(1), the 'telle-quelle' doctrine requires that a trade
mark be 'accepted for filing and protected' in another country based on registration in
the applicant's country of origin.

The Madrid Agreement of 1891
The Madrid Agreement Concerning the International Registration of Marks[7]
simplifies international registration procedures for the acquisition of trade
mark rights by providing for a single international application system.

The Trademark Registration Treaty of 1973
Under the auspices of the World Intellectual Property Organization (WIPO),
the Trademark Registration Treaty was unsuccessful in overcoming the objections of the United States to the Madrid Agreement and it is now ratified only
by the Russian Confederation and four African countries.[8]

The Madrid Protocol of 1989
Like the Trademark Registration Treaty, the Madrid Protocol aimed at gaining
the approval of those countries that had refused to sign the Madrid Agreement.
The Protocol is a new treaty, introducing new procedures for international
registration, and is linked to the Madrid Agreement by means of a common
implementing regulation.

The Trademark Law Treaty of 1994
While the initial intention of the negotiators was to compile a legal text regulating all aspects of trade mark protection, the Trademark Law Treaty's scope
is limited to the harmonization of administrative procedures relating to
national registration.

*Agreement on Trade-Related Aspects of Intellectual Property Rights of 1994
(TRIPs)*
The TRIPs Agreement was negotiated in the World Trade Organization (WTO)
as part of the Uruguay Round of Negotiations, which were concluded on 15
April 1994. TRIPs deals with copyright and related rights (that is, rights of
performers, producers of sound recordings and broadcasting organizations),
geographical indications, including appellations of origin, industrial designs,
integrated circuit layout-designs, patents, including the protection of new varieties of plants, trade marks and undisclosed or confidential information,
including trade secrets and test data. TRIPs also specifies enforcement procedures, remedies, and dispute resolution procedures. Rules for the protection of
trade marks are laid down in Articles 15 to 21. These provisions deal with the
conditions and content of protection, but only in a general way, endorsing

---

[7]   Madrid Agreement Concerning the International Registration of Marks of 14
April 1891, as revised to 14 July 1967 and amended on 28 September 1979.
[8]   This Treaty is now of such minor importance that its text has not been made
available on the WIPO website.

certain general principles that the signatory countries must enforce. According to its preamble, the purpose of TRIPs is to 'reduce distortions and impediments to international trade' by 'taking into account the need to promote effective and adequate protection of intellectual property rights', while at the same time ensuring that 'measures and procedures to enforce intellectual property rights do not themselves become barriers to legitimate trade'.

This evolution of the framework of international trade mark law over the decades is significant: while principally regulating trade mark registration issues, in an effort to reconcile the principle of territoriality with the need for uniform registration procedures, national jurisdictions have today moved forward, seeking to harmonize the law not only as regards the acquisition of trade mark rights but also its exercise. In other words, international law has extended its regulatory activity to ensure the development of uniform rules regarding the enforcement of the exclusive character of trade mark rights in the course of their use in the market place.

LIMITATION TO THE EXCLUSIVE CHARACTER OF INTELLECTUAL PROPERTY RIGHTS (IPRs) IN INTERNATIONAL LAW

Exclusivity in the use of a trade mark by its owner is not an inflexible privilege. There are limits to the absolute protection and the monopolistic character of trade mark rights; these limits are imposed for the sake of more effective competition. As products and services become increasingly interrelated and the number of trade mark registrations increases, the use of another's trade mark often becomes a necessity. Accordingly, the limits to absolute trade mark protection are justified by the public interest, which dictates a balancing approach as regards the conflicting interests of the trade mark owners and those of third parties.

The idea of the public interest prevailing over the interests of intellectual property owners does not apply only as regards trade mark rights. Within the framework of other intellectual property rights (IPRs), international treaties contain a number of provisions authorizing their signatory states to limit, under certain circumstances, the rights of the beneficiaries of IPRs. A typical example is the general exception concerning reproduction rights of authors in copyright law, introduced under the Berne Convention.[9] According to Article 9(2) of that convention, three conditions must be complied with before an

---

[9]   Berne Convention for the Protection of Literary and Artistic Works 1886, as amended to 1979.

exception relating to the author's reproduction rights can be justified. First, the reproduction must be for a specific purpose: it is allowed only 'in certain special cases'. Secondly, the reproduction must 'not conflict with a normal exploitation of work'. Thirdly, the reproduction should 'not unreasonably prejudice the legitimate interests of the author'.

Similarly, limitations to IPRs were introduced under the TRIPs Agreement. Article 13 of TRIPs on copyrights and related rights provides that 'members shall confine limitations or exceptions to exclusive rights to certain special cases which do not conflict with a normal exploitation of the work and do not unreasonably prejudice the legitimate interests of the right holder'.

A balance of interest through limitation of IPRs can also be found in Article 26(2) of the TRIPs Agreement, which covers industrial designs:

> Members may provide limited exceptions to the protection of industrial designs, provided that such exceptions do not unreasonably conflict with the normal exploitation of protected industrial designs and do not unreasonably prejudice the legitimate interests of the owner of the protected design, taking account of the legitimate interests of third parties.

Finally, Article 30 of the TRIPs Agreement, applying the same test to patents, provides that:

> members may provide limited exceptions to the exclusive rights conferred by a patent, provided that such exceptions do not unreasonably conflict with a normal exploitation of the patent and do not unreasonably prejudice the legitimate interests of the patent owner, taking account of the legitimate interests of third parties.

PERMITTED USE OF TRADE MARKS

Under Article 16 of the TRIPs Agreement, the exclusive nature of the right of the trade mark holder is recognized. A minimum standard of exclusive rights is thus conferred on the proprietor of a registered trade mark: all WTO members must guarantee this minimum standard under their domestic legislation. Article 17 of the TRIPs Agreement was adopted to regulate the permitted use of a trade mark by a third party. It provides that 'Members may provide limited exceptions to the rights conferred by a trade mark, such as fair use of descriptive terms, provided that such exceptions take account of the legitimate interests of the owner of the trade mark and of third parties'.

The above wording makes clear that Article 17 is a non self-executing provision. This means that no private party involved in a dispute may invoke it to establish any rights. Nevertheless, a non self-executing provision is not a useless provision. Any regional or national legislation should comply with Article 17. A national court, presuming that it has jurisdiction to declare the provisions of national law incompatible with international law, should not apply any rules which run contrary to the TRIPs Agreement.

The question of interpreting the exceptions and limitations to trade mark protection, as provided under Article 17, has not yet been addressed to a WTO Panel. From a first reading, one might already observe that Article 17 is less strict than the exceptions and limitations provided by Articles 13 and 30 of TRIPs, in connection with copyright and patent rights. In particular, Article 17 does not provide that exceptions or limitations must be limited to 'certain special cases'. It only states that Member States may provide 'limited exceptions' to the rights conferred by trade marks. Moreover, Article 17 does not provide that the exceptions may 'not conflict with the normal exploitation' of a product or service in relation to which a trade mark has been registered. On the other hand, however, Article 17, unlike Article 13, does not limit its scope to the rights of trade mark holders but also takes into account the 'interests of third parties' (for example, licensees).

LIMITED EXCEPTIONS

TRIPs does not support or endorse unlimited or unjustified exceptions to trade mark protection. Exclusivity is essential in protecting the function and value of the trade mark right as an intellectual property asset. Article 17 is the outcome of the balance between preserving the trade mark rights of the owner against the necessity of allowing third parties a reasonable use of someone else's mark. Therefore, only *limited exceptions* are justified, that is, exceptions that do not affect the core of the rights conferred by a trade mark.

The notion of *limited exceptions* was to some extent interpreted and applied in the dispute between Australia and the European Union before the WTO.[10] In that case, Australia raised arguments against European Union legislation concerning prior rights in a trade mark that may contain a reference to a term which is subsequently registered as a geographical indication. The WTO Panel agreed with Australia that the European Union's regime was inconsistent with its obligations under Article 16 of the TRIPs Agreement, because it failed to grant to the owners of validly registered, pre-existing trade marks the right to prevent confusing use of geographical indications registered under the relevant EC Regulation.[11] However, the Panel considered that Article 17 allows

---

[10]   In this regard see Complaints by the United States (WT/DS174) and Australia (WT/DS290).

[11]   Council Regulation (EEC) No 2081/92 of 14 July 1992 on the protection of geographical indications and designations of origin for agricultural products and foodstuffs.

the European Union to establish some limitations on the rights to be granted to a trade mark owner, as long as European Union legislation ensures the rejection of geographical indications that cause a relatively high likelihood of confusion.

USE OF DESCRIPTIVE TERMS

Article 17 indicates *fair use of descriptive terms* as being one of the possible exceptions to trade mark protection. In the absence of any case law interpreting Article 17, Article 6 of Directive 89/104[12] could facilitate the deeper understanding of this TRIPs provision. Article 6 of the Directive, entitled 'Limitation of the effects of a trade mark', provides in its paragraphs 1(b) and (c) that:

> The trade mark shall not entitle the proprietor to prohibit a third party from using, in the course of trade ... (b) indications concerning the kind, quality, quantity, intended purpose, value, geographical origin, the time of production of goods or of rendering of the service, or other characteristics of goods or services; (c) the trade mark where it is necessary to indicate the intended purpose of a product or service, in particular as accessories or spare parts; provided he uses them in accordance with honest practices in industrial or commercial matters.

Examining Article 17 in conjunction with Article 6 of the Directive, it may be argued that 'descriptive terms' is a notion including all types of indications listed under paragraph 1(b) of Article 6 of the Directive. Having this in mind, the European Court of Justice in *Anheuser-Busch Inc v Budejovicky Budvar*[13] made specific reference to Article 17 of TRIPs and ruled that:

> The exceptions provided for in Article 17 of the TRIPs Agreement are intended to enable a third party to use a sign which is identical or similar to a trade mark to indicate his *trade name*, provided that such use is in accordance with honest practices in industrial or commercial matters (emphasis added).

THE LEGITIMATE INTERESTS OF THE OWNER OF THE TRADE MARK AND OF THIRD PARTIES

The permitted use of descriptive indications is not unlimited. The notions of *fair use* and *respect of the legitimate interests of the owner and third parties*

---

[12]   First Council Directive 89/104 of 21 December 1988, to Approximate the Laws of the Member States Relating to Trade Marks (OJ EC No L 40 of 11.2.1989, p. 1).
[13]   Case C-245/02 [2005] ETMR 27.

are employed as the criteria of judging whether the use may be permitted or not. The terms 'fair use' and 'respect of the legitimate interests of the owner of the trade mark and of third parties' will, most probably, be interpreted as the duty to protect the core of the trade mark rights, that is, as the obligation to avoid any use that will not be in accordance with honest practices in industrial and commercial matters. Such would be the case if, for example, the third party use gives the impression that there is a commercial connection between the third party and the trade mark owner, or affects the value of the trade mark by taking unfair advantage of its reputation, or it amounts to the denigration of that mark.

CONCLUDING REMARKS

Article 17 seeks to reconcile the fundamental interests of trade mark protection with those of free movement of goods and freedom to provide services in the global market. It reflects the recognition of the fact that the strong monopolistic characteristics of trade mark rights are often in conflict with the needs of a globalized economy. As pointed out by Advocate General Tizzano in *Gillette*, the limitation of trade mark rights seeks to balance the owner's interest in the trade mark 'being able to perform to the full its function of guaranteeing the product's origin against the interest of other traders in having full access to the market, but leaving the door open for other interests too to come into play'. Together with the strong regional legislations of the European Union and the NAFTA Agreement,[14] which includes an almost identical provision (Article 1708 para. 12), Article 17 serves as a guarantee that the essential function of trade mark rights is protected, while competition and third parties' rights are equally preserved.

---

[14] North American Free Trade Agreement between the Government of Canada, the Government of the United Mexican States and the Government of the United States of America.

2. Permitted use under European law: the framework

Susie Middlemiss

NON-INFRINGING ACTS

Most defences to trade mark infringement actions revolve around the elements which must be present to establish infringement. Attention focuses on issues such as the analysis of nuances in spelling and pronunciation of the trade marks or signs of competing parties in order to assess their identity or similarity, comparison of the goods or services for which they are used and the likelihood of confusion between them. There are also defences or exceptions to infringement which do not centre on the comparison of marks, goods or services. These defences focus instead on the nature of use of a trader's sign, where specific categories of use are expressly permitted.

Under European law, there are broadly four varieties of use which are tolerated in certain circumstances:

- descriptive use (in particular references to the characteristics or use of the goods or services);
- use in relation to genuine goods (most frequently falling under the ambit of the doctrine of 'exhaustion');
- comparative advertising and
- use in the face of acquiescence and use of earlier rights (these arise in rather specific circumstances).

The first group of defences may be conveniently referred to as 'descriptive defences', since they broadly revolve around the descriptive use of a sign. These exceptions allow a trader, for example, to refer to the trader's own name or to the characteristics or intended purpose of goods or services without infringing another's trade mark. European legislation provides for these defences, through Article 6 of the Trade Marks Harmonisation Directive ('Harmonisation Directive')[1] and Article 12 of the Community Trade Marks

---

[1]   First Council Directive 89/104 of 21 December 1988 to approximate the laws of the Member States relating to trade marks.

Regulation ('CTM Regulation').[2] This provides that the following will not infringe another's trade mark:

- use of one's own name;
- use of indications concerning the characteristics of the goods or services, including the kind, quality, value, geographical origin or time of production of the goods;
- use which is necessary to indicate the intended purpose of the goods or services, in particular as accessories or spare parts.

The second category of defence relates to use in relation to genuine goods. By this defence, the use of another's trade mark in relation to goods that have already been put on the market by its proprietor or with the proprietor's consent will not infringe the rights in that trade mark under the doctrine of exhaustion of rights. This defence, which is now embodied in both national and Community legislation,[3] is subject to exceptions in certain specific circumstances.

The third category of defences is provided under the Comparative Advertising Directive,[4] in respect of certain kinds of advertising which involve use of others' trade marks.

The fourth category of defence relates to acquiescence and earlier rights. As a result of Article 9 of the Harmonisation Directive, a proprietor who has acquiesced in the use of a later mark in particular circumstances cannot assert infringement. Also, under Article 6(2), a proprietor cannot take action against use of an earlier right arising in a particular locality. There are no equivalent provisions under the CTM Regulation.

This chapter provides an overview of these defences based on 'non-infringing acts' and looks at a number of issues which are common to the different descriptive defences. Later chapters will focus on particular defences and the cases that have considered them.

THE DESCRIPTIVE DEFENCES

Broadly speaking a defence will arise when a trade mark is used descriptively, provided the use is fair. A number of issues recur in the case law:

---

2   Council Regulation 40/94 on the Community trade mark.
3   Harmonisation Directive (Article 7) and the CTM Regulation (Article 13).
4   EU Council Directive 84/450 as amended by Directive 97/55.

i.   is the use in accordance with honest practices? All of the descriptive
      defences are subject to this requirement;
ii.   what is the nature of the use? Is it descriptive use or trade mark use? and
iii. does the use fall within the defence because it is a permissible variety of
      use – for example relating to characteristics of, or the purpose of the
      goods or services?

Honest Practices

Absence of honest practices amount to unfair competition

The concept of a standard of 'honest practices in industrial and commercial
matters' against which conduct is judged derives from unfair competition law.
The Paris Convention provides that 'any act of competition contrary to honest
practices in industrial or commercial matters constitutes an act of unfair
competition'.[5] In the Paris Convention, unfair competition is defined in terms
of activity which is contrary to honest practices. This definition is accompanied by a non-exhaustive list of activities that are unacceptable. While the
Paris Convention does not have direct effect in all national jurisdictions, by
implication it would seem that any specific descriptive use will only escape
infringement if it does not amount to unfair competition. This is echoed by the
European Court of Justice (ECJ) in cases concerning the descriptive defences
which establish that honest practices amount to a 'duty to act fairly in relation
to the legitimate interests of the trade mark owners.[6] In *Gerolsteiner*[7] the ECJ
held that the national court was required, taking account of all the circumstances of the case, to assess whether the defendant 'might be regarded as
unfairly competing'.

In short, descriptive use is acceptable provided that in execution it does
not amount to unfair competition. The legislation is not however expressed in
such broad terms and a defendant seeking to rely on the descriptive defences
must show that a use falls within one of the permitted types of use discussed
later.

Whose 'practices' are relevant?

In principle the reference to 'honest practices' suggests a comparison with
behaviour which is

---

[5]   Paris Convention on the Protection of Industrial Property 1883, as amended
to 1979, Article 10*bis*.
[6]   *Bayerische Motorenwerke AG (BMW) and BMW Nederland BV v Deenik*
Case C-63/97 [1999] ETMR 339, [1999] ECR I-905, para 61.
[7]   *Gerolsteiner & Brunnen GmbH & Co. v Putsch GmbH* [2004] ETMR 40,
paragraph 26.

- usual or established in the particular trade or
- actually found in that trade, rather than merely being desirable.

The concept is therefore variable depending on the particular trade, the particular circumstances and the time that a practice is assessed. The variable nature of the concept raises the question of whether the relevant practices are those in the particular country concerned or are judged on a European-wide or international basis. This issue has yet to be addressed by the ECJ.

Commentators suggest[8] that there should be a minimum objective standard on the basis that local standards are too limited and there may not always be relevant international standards. This approach is consistent with the Opinion of the Attorney General in *Hölterhoff*[9] who maintained that 'there is a large and clear shared concept of what constitutes honest conduct in trade'. This prevents an otherwise dishonest activity being sanctioned just because it is widely adopted within a particular trade. On this basis, the question whether use accords with honest practice should be an objective test and the state of mind of the defendant should be irrelevant. The English courts have taken this approach in interpreting this wording in a slightly different context.[10] Even if it is not relevant to the issue of liability for trade mark infringement, the defendant's state of mind may have an impact on awards of damages.

When is a practice honest?
The question whether a party is acting in accordance with honest practices must be answered on the basis of a global assessment of all the circumstances.[11] The ECJ, having considered a range of cases relating to different types of descriptive use, has indicated that it will not regard certain activities as being in accordance with honest practices, though this list is not apparently exhaustive.

In *Budvar*[12] the ECJ identified three relevant factors for establishing whether use was in accordance with the duty to act fairly. These are

---

8   See for example Christopher Wadlow, *Law of passing off – unfair competition by misrepresentation*, 3rd edition (London: Sweet & Maxwell, 2004), paras 2–27.
9   *Hölterhoff v Freiesleben* Case C-2/00 [2002] ETMR 917, [2002] ECR I-4187.
10   The English courts have not considered the meaning of honest practices in Article 6. However, the UK's Trade Marks Act 1994, s.10(6) is an additional provision, not reflected in the Directive, which uses the same wording and essentially provides a specific defence for use in relation to genuine goods and services. See for example *Barclays Bank plc v RBS Advanta* [1996] ETMR 199; *Levi Strauss & Co v Tesco Stores Ltd* [2002] ETMR 95; *R v Johnstone* [2003] ETMR 1; *O2 Holdings Ltd and another v Hutchinson 3G UK Ltd* [2005] ETMR 61, 62.
11   *Bayerische Motorenwerke*, para 61.
12   *Anheuser-Busch Inc. v Budejovický Budvar, národní podnik*, Case C-245/02 [2004] ECR I-0000, [2005] ETMR 27, para 83.

- the extent to which the sign suggests a link;
- the extent to which the party using the sign should have been aware of that;
- whether the mark has 'a certain reputation' from which the defendant might profit.

These factors emphasise that the analysis will vary with the nature of the particular marks and, in particular, with the extent to which they are descriptive or distinctive, how similar they are and how well-known. One result, for example, may be that an unauthorised use of a famous mark is less likely to be regarded as an honest practice than the same use of a newly registered mark.

While its guidance is not exhaustive, the ECJ has given some examples of use which will not be in accordance with honest practices. These are

- use which gives the impression of a commercial connection between the parties;
- use which affects the value of a trade mark by taking unfair advantage;
- use which entails discrediting or denigrating a trade mark;
- presentation of a product as an imitation or replica of the trade mark owner's product.

These examples, which track the wording found in the Comparative Advertising Directive, are instances of comparisons that will not be acceptable under that Directive.

Use as a Trade Mark[13]

Another issue of central importance to trade mark infringement generally, and to the descriptive defences, is the relevance of use 'as a trade mark'. Trade mark use (use as an indication of origin) is often contrasted with descriptive use. It is often said that a sign must be used *as a trade mark* before infringement may be established. However, the position is not entirely clear.

In *Arsenal*[14] the ECJ was specifically asked whether the fact that the use complained of does not indicate trade origin constitutes a defence to an action

---

[13]   On trade mark use see Jeremy Phillips and Ilanah Simon (editors), *Trade Mark Use* (Oxford University Press, 2005), especially Robert Sumroy and Carina Badger, 'Infringing "in the course of trade": trade mark use and the essential function of a trade mark'.

[14]   *Arsenal Football Club plc v Reed*, Case C-206/01 [2002] ECR I-10273, [2003] ETMR 19.

for infringement. The ECJ did not answer the question directly, but reconfirmed that the essential function of a trade mark is to guarantee the origin of goods or services, thus allowing the proprietor to distinguish its goods or services from those of others.

According to the ECJ, a proprietor may not prohibit use of a sign identical to the trade mark for identical goods if that use cannot affect his own interests as proprietor, having regard to its function. The court continued, 'thus certain uses for purely descriptive purposes are excluded' because they do not affect any of the interests the provision aims to protect, and do not therefore fall within the concept of 'use'.[15]

The ECJ distinguished *Hölterhoff* on the basis that the factual situation in *Arsenal* was completely different: in the latter case the dispute arose in the context of sales to consumers and was obviously not intended for purely descriptive purposes. In *Hölterhoff* a trade mark was used orally in a transaction between two jewellery dealers, for the purpose of indicating the style and cut of a diamond that the defendant sought to sell. However in *Arsenal* the defendant's use of the sign created the impression that there was a material link between the goods and the trade mark proprietor, though it might also be seen as a badge of allegiance to the Arsenal football club. As a consequence of the misuse, the Arsenal sign did not convey the guarantee of origin as required by the case law in that not all goods sold under the mark came from a single undertaking. On that basis, the use of an identical sign the effect of which is liable to jeopardise the guarantee of origin (which constitutes the essential function of the mark) is a use that the proprietor may prevent. Once this is found to be the case, it is immaterial that the sign is also perceived as a badge of support, loyalty or affiliation.

The ECJ's conclusion in *Arsenal* still seems to leave open the possibility that a defendant's use of a mark, particularly in a descriptive context, may affect the ability of that mark to function as a guarantee of origin without itself being a use 'as a trade mark'. For example, excessive use of a mark by a third party might dilute its impact and ultimately its ability to indicate the trade mark owner, though in the short term it is not used by the defendant to indicate the origin of the defendant's goods. On the *Arsenal* test such use should amount to infringement but the point awaits a further ECJ reference.

Irrespective of whether trade mark use is a condition precedent to a use falling within the scope of infringing acts, the issue arises again specifically in relation to the descriptive defences, but here the question is whether the defences merely allow a defendant to use a sign in a descriptive way or whether the defendant is also entitled to use his sign as a trade mark.

---

[15] See *Hölterhoff*, para 16.

In *Windsurfing* [16] the ECJ indicated that the descriptive defences do not confer a right to use a name as a trade mark but merely guarantee a right to use it descriptively. More recently, however, the ECJ in *Gerolsteiner* [17] ruled that the question whether there has been trade mark use by the defendant is irrelevant to the question of whether the genuine use exceptions apply: the only relevant question is whether the use is in accordance with honest practices. This approach is consistent with that taken by the Court of Appeal for England and Wales in dealing with *Arsenal* after the ECJ decision, a judgment which can also be explained on the basis that a mark may be capable of being used in more than one way.[18] In *Arsenal* the claimant's trade mark was used by the defendant both as a badge of allegiance and as a trade mark (since some consumers would think that the goods were connected with Arsenal). A later chapter discusses the implications of *Gerolsteiner*.[19]

The Harmonisation Directive does however acknowledge that there may be use of a trade mark in a manner which is not trade mark use; indeed it specifically allows Member States to retain provisions controlling that use. Article 5(5) provides that certain provisions relating to the protection of a sign other than for the purposes of distinguishing goods or services are not affected by the infringement provisions of the Directive. The implication is that the directive is not solely concerned with trade mark use.

The Nature of the Descriptive Use

Those cases in which the ECJ has been required to rule on the descriptive defences have concerned a variety of categories of use and a diverse range of signs and marks, some more similar than others. Although it is possible to glean some general principles from the cases, it is not clear that each of these general principles will apply across all categories of allegedly infringing use.

Use of one's own name and address
A trade mark proprietor is not entitled to stop a third party using its own name or address, again subject to the proviso of Article 6(1)(a) that the use be in accordance with honest practices. The provision refers to use in the course of trade. By implication, use which is not in the course of trade falls outside the scheme for infringement.

---

[16]   *Windsurfing Chiemsee Produktions- und Vertriebs GmbH (WSC) v Boots- und Segelzubehör Walter Huber*, Joined Cases C-108/97 and C-109/97 [1999] ECR I-2779, [1999] ETMR 585.
[17]   *Gerolsteiner*, paras 19 and 24–26.
[18]   *Arsenal Football Club plc v Reed* [2003] ETMR 73 (CA).
[19]   Chapter 11, Grace Smith, 'Honest commercial use in the light of the ECJ's *Gerolsteiner* ruling'.

There are no ECJ decisions on this provision. The application of the proviso is likely to be important since it has the effect of preventing a trader adopting a name as its own in order to benefit from its similarity to a registered mark. There is some uncertainty as to whether corporations or organisations are entitled to benefit from this provision. The non-binding Annex to the Community Trade Mark Regulation states the view of the Council and Commission that the reference to use of 'his own name' in this context only applies to natural persons. There is some logic in this suggestion in that the choice of a corporation's name is within its own control. Although there may be circumstances where that choice is made without knowledge of a mark, there is a good argument that the company should bear the risk in relation to marks on a public register, where for example it is expanding into a new area of business and comes into conflict with an existing mark. The question has been considered by the English House of Lords[20] which indicated that the 'better view is that a company can claim the protection of this provision' but that the matter was not *acte clair* and therefore remains a question for the ECJ.

Indications of the characteristics of the goods

Many descriptive uses of a sign have the potential to escape infringement on the basis that the sign is simply used to indicate some characteristic of the goods, such as their quality or geographical origin. The key question in cases of descriptive use (according to the ECJ in *Gerolsteiner*[21]) is whether words are used as an indication of one of the characteristics of the goods. It is irrelevant that the indication may also be used in another way, for example where the use of a trade mark is to indicate the origin of another's goods.

As discussed above, the court must look at the allegedly infringing use in all the circumstances when deciding whether an unauthorised user of another's mark has complied with its duty to act fairly or is unfairly competing. This approach is again consistent with the Paris Convention, which provides that acts which mislead the public as to the nature, the manufacturing process, the characteristics, the suitability for their purposes or the quantity of the goods will amount to acts of unfair competition (though only some of these will also amount to an Article 6 defence).

In assessing the circumstances, relevant factors include consideration of what efforts have been made to distinguish the respective parties' goods or services, whether there is a suggestion that the goods are the same or of equivalent quality, and whether there are similarities of packaging (for example in

---

[20]   *Scandecor Developments v Scandecor Marketing* [2001] 2 CMLR 30, [2001] ETMR 74, paras 54 and 65(8).
[21]   *Gerolsteiner*, para 27.

the shape and labelling of bottles). The ECJ has indicated that it is permissible to use a mark to lend an aura of quality to the defendant's goods.[22]

An issue arises as to whether a sign may be used as an indication of characteristics of the goods where confusion is likely to result. Use which suggests a connection between the trade mark proprietor and the defendant has been held to be not in accordance with honest practices.[23] On that basis, a car dealer was held entitled to use the BMW mark to indicate that he specialised in the repair and maintenance of BMW cars, provided that he did not give the impression that there was a commercial connection between his business and BMW. This case is discussed in a following chapter.[24]

Going apparently further, use which suggests a 'link' between the defendant and the proprietor has also been found to be not in accordance with honest practices.[25] 'Link' is also the word used by the ECJ[26] to describe the effect a sign must have to establish infringement under Article 5(2) (by establishing a link between the sign and the mark) of the Harmonisation Directive, where unfair advantage is taken of, or detriment is caused to, a mark with a reputation. In that context 'link' means something less than confusion, being perhaps more akin to the concept of 'association'.[27] It was originally suggested that the concept of confusion for the purposes of infringement under the Harmonisation Directive was broader than confusion as to origin as required by Article 5(1)(b) and encompassed in the Benelux concept of 'association'. The ECJ rejected this view but suggested that some lesser connection or 'links' would suffice for Article 5(2).[28] It remains to be seen whether, and how, the concept of 'link' differs from 'connection' in relation to honest practices. This position in any event sits uneasily with the more recent approach of the ECJ in *Gerolsteiner*.[29] The ECJ held there that an Article 6 defence might be established *despite* confusion, though the defendant is still required to make efforts to avoid confusion. This result suggests that confusion on its own is not sufficient to result in a use not being in accordance with honest practices. It is difficult to reconcile this position with the principle that suggestion of a 'connection' or 'link' will be a basis for lack of honest practices.

---

22   *Bayerische Motorenwerke*, para 53.
23   Ibid.
24   Chapter 9, Montiano Monteagudo and Núria Porxas, 'Repairs and other specialist services: the ECJ's *BMW* ruling'.
25   *Anheuser-Busch*, para 83.
26   *Adidas-Salomon AG & Adidas Benelux BV v Fitnessworld Trading Ltd*, Case C-408/01 [2004] ETMR 10, 38–42.
27   On the meaning of 'association' and its place within European trade mark law see *SABEL v Puma* Case C-251/95 [1997] ECR I-6191, [1998] E.T.M.R. 1.
28   *Adidas-Salomon*, para 42(2).
29   *Gerolsteiner*, para 25.

The ECJ's more recent liberal approach to resultant confusion also seems to be inconsistent with both the Comparative Advertising Directive and the Paris Convention. The Comparative Advertising Directive provides that certain comparisons are permitted, provided they do not cause confusion between advertisers and competitors and/or their trade marks or goods. It would seem odd if use of a mark was unacceptable as a comparative advertisement under the Directive on the basis that it caused confusion but did not amount to infringement. Further, under the Paris Convention, actions which create confusion may be prohibited as unfair competition.

It is suggested that the correct analysis is that there is a two-stage test: there must be (i) confusion *and* (ii) lack of honest practices, since an act that causes confusion alone, but which does not result from the absence of an honest practice, is insufficient to incur liability for trade mark infringement, given the scope of Article 6.

Use to indicate intended purpose

Special principles apply where a sign is used to indicate the intended purpose of goods or services. To establish a defence, the defendant's use of a trade mark must be *necessary* to indicate the intended purpose. In other words, use is only permitted where either the information cannot be communicated without that use, or it is the only practical way of communicating the information.[30] The scope of the requirement of 'necessity' has yet to be clarified but is likely to vary with the particular circumstances of the case.

Spare parts and accessories are examples of use to indicate intended purpose that are specifically given in the Directive. However, the defence is not limited to these categories of goods.[31] The cases relating to this provision are discussed in later chapters which consider use in relation to spare parts, repairs and refills.[32]

EXHAUSTION

The principles of exhaustion generally prevent a trade mark owner from relying on its trade mark rights so as to prevent the resale of goods that have been

---

[30]   *Gillette Company and another v LA-Laboratories Ltd Oy*, Case C-228/03 [2005] ETMR 67.
[31]   Ibid., para 32.
[32]   See Chapter 8, Rainer Hilli, 'Compatibility of products: the ECJ's *Gillette* ruling'; Chapter 9, Montiano Monteagudo and Núria Porxas, 'Repairs and other specialist services: the ECJ's *BMW* ruling'; Chapter 10, Wolfgang Kellenter, 'Refills, recharged batteries and recycled products'.

put on the market by the trade mark proprietor or with his consent. In these circumstances a third party is effectively entitled to use the mark descriptively when referring to genuine goods. However, the proprietor can rely on his trade mark rights where he nonetheless has legitimate reasons to oppose further commercialisation, especially where the condition of the goods is changed or impaired. While the Directive and the Regulation do not give an exhaustive list of legitimate reasons, as the use of the term 'especially' suggests and case law has confirmed, it is difficult to establish other grounds. Later chapters examine the extent to which trade mark owners can control goods at the border between countries[33] and object to repackaging (a practice which has been the subject of a large volume of case law).[34]

Consent

To establish the defence, consent must be given by the proprietor or any member of its group. The question whether consent has been given is an objective test, to be assessed in all the circumstances. Consent is normally express but may be implied, though where a proprietor is said to be giving up its rights (by giving its consent), the intention to do so must be unequivocally demonstrated. Before a third party can safely trade in goods bearing a trade mark, the consent must have been given not merely in general but must relate to the actual batch of goods concerned, since consent to the marketing of one batch of goods does not apply to other batches of goods of the same description.

Legitimate Reasons for Opposing Resale

Physical condition of the goods
Many cases have focused on the legitimate reasons given in the Directive, that the physical condition of the goods has been changed or impaired. A large number of cases concern the extent to which repackaging (usually carried out by an importer reselling in one country goods that have been sold at a cheaper price in another country) will fall within this definition and provide a basis for enforcing trade mark rights.

To avoid infringement, repackaging must be *necessary*, which requires rules or practices (in the territory of importation) which provide that a product can only be sold in a particular size or presentation. Repackaging, though not essential, may be reasonably required for effective access to a market because

---

[33]   Chapter 7, Luca Giove, 'Controlling third party use at the border'.
[34]   Chapter 6, Christian Schumacher, 'Use of trade marks on repackaged and relabelled pharmaceutical goods – the view from private practice'.

of consumer resistance to other presentations. This requirement will not be satisfied if alternative, less invasive methods such as overstickering of the original manufacturer's label are used.

Damage to a trade mark

In addition to the specific example of an activity which has an effect on the physical condition of the goods, the ECJ has recognised that certain uses of a trade mark may form a legitimate reason for prohibiting descriptive use and overriding the principle of exhaustion. The general rule is that, once a trade mark right is exhausted, third parties may sell and also advertise these goods without infringement. However, this is not permitted where the use is liable to damage, to a significant extent, the reputation of a trade mark for luxury goods, including its image.[35]

COMPARATIVE ADVERTISING

A further category of trade mark use which may fall outside trade mark infringement is comparative advertising. Once again, one trader is typically using another's mark in order to refer to the latter's goods or services, so as to persuade relevant consumers to purchase the goods of services of the advertiser and not those of the trade mark owner.

The factors which are specifically recognised as taking a comparative advertisement outside the permissible scope of use of another's trade mark reflect elements identified as being objectionable in relation to unfair competition. Certain kinds of comparative advertising are specifically permitted under the Misleading and Comparative Advertising Directive.[36] While these have issues in common with the defences to trade mark infringement, they are different. It appears possible, on the face of the Directive, that a use of another's trade mark that is permitted as a comparative advertisement may nonetheless be prohibited by the provisions of trade mark law. The Comparative Advertising Directive appears however to prevent this as it provides essentially that a comparison that is acceptable under that Directive will not amount to a trade mark infringement. This is dealt with in the recitals to the 1997 Amendment which do not however have legal force. If an advertisement which is acceptable under the Comparative Advertising Directive can not amount to trade mark infringement, in effect this adds another defence to the provisions of the Trade Mark Directive. In contrast, conceivably, though a

---

[35]   *Parfums Christian Dior SA* v *Evora BV*, Case C-337/95 [1998] ETMR 26, para 45.

[36]   Council Directive 84/450, as amended by Directive 97/55.

comparison may not amount to infringement, it may be unacceptable under the Comparative Advertising Directive.

There is considerable overlap between the defences to trade mark infringement and the provisions relating to comparative advertising involving the use of others' trade marks, though they are drafted in different terms. Comparative advertising will be permitted only where certain conditions are met and those relevant to trade marks are that:

- it does not create confusion in the marketplace between the advertiser and a competitor or between the advertiser's trade marks, trade names, other distinguishing marks, goods, services, activities and those of a competitor;
- it does not discredit or denigrate the trade marks, trade names, other distinguishing marks, goods, services, activities or circumstances of a competitor;
- it does not take unfair advantage of the reputation of a trade mark, trade name or other distinguishing marks of a competitor or of the designation of origin of competing products;
- it does not present goods or services as imitations or replicas of goods or services bearing a protected trade mark or trade name.

Comparative advertising in the context of trade marks has been seldom considered by the ECJ. The existing cases are discussed elsewhere in this book.[37]

ACQUIESCENCE AND PRIOR USE

Acquiescence

This defence is of rather narrow application and differs from the others in not relating to descriptive use. The proprietor of an earlier mark falling within Article 4(2) of the Harmonisation Directive (broadly CTMs, EU national marks, international and famous marks) may not assert infringement in respect of (or apply to invalidate) a later registered mark (as a result of Article 9) where

- the proprietor has acquiesced for 5 successive years in the use of the later mark
- unless the later registration was applied for in bad faith.

---

[37]   Chapter 5, Philippe de Jong, 'Comparative advertising in Europe'.

However, the proprietor of the later registered mark is not entitled to oppose the use of the earlier right, despite the fact that the earlier right can not be invoked against the later one. There are no ECJ cases on this provision.

Use of Earlier Rights Applying Only in a Particular Locality

Under the Harmonisation Directive, a proprietor may not prohibit a third party from using in the course of trade an earlier right which applies only in a particular locality (Article (6)(2)). However, this only applies if the right is recognised in the relevant Member State and the defence will only apply within that territory. This is likely to be of limited application and a potential defendant will usually oppose the mark in the first place. The provision was apparently introduced to address a particular situation that arises under German law. It has not been considered by the ECJ.

CONCLUSION

Under European law, a range of different defences give traders the ability to use others' marks in a descriptive sense and in referring to the proprietor's original goods. The defences are carefully defined and limited. There also remains the possibility that, outside these specific legislative defences and the whole trade mark scheme, there may be scope for resisting an infringement claim on the basis that its enforcement would amount to an unacceptable fetter on other human rights, in particular the right to freedom of expression. This is considered in a later chapter which addresses the tension between critical comment and trade mark rights.

Law within the EU seeks to strike a balance between two competing interests: the desire to achieve free movement of goods within the Community and the rights conferred by the trade mark system. Trade marks represent monopoly rights which present a danger of partitioning the market. However, they also serve to promote competition by allowing customers to identify and distinguish the goods and services of consumers. The essential function of the trade mark, to act as a guarantee of origin, is said to justify a derogation from the prohibition on quantitative restrictions on imports.

The descriptive defences limit the trade mark monopoly with a view to eliminating factors likely to distort competition. Exhaustion also sets boundaries to trade mark rights, preventing a proprietor from using a mark to partition markets and encourage price differentiation between member states. This is regarded as an acceptable limitation because the trade mark owner has already marketed the goods.

The attempt to strike this balance between the desire to promote competition and to protect trade mark rights will continue to occupy the ECJ and the rules can be expected to vary with the circumstances of each case, and over time as practices within particular industries develop.

3. Comparative advertising in the United States

Charles H. Googe, Jr and Lewis Clayton

While European law is sceptical of comparative advertising, US law embraces it. As long as it does not confuse or deceive the public, an American advertiser has a good deal of freedom to use a competitor's trade name, trade mark, or other distinctive features in comparative ads. While American statutory and common law prohibits false advertising, it is not considered unfair to analyse or criticize another's product as long as it is done truthfully. In fact, the Federal Trade Commission and US courts encourage truthful comparative advertising, and truthful advertising is considered commercial speech that is entitled to protection under US constitutional law.

THE ROOTS OF US COMPARATIVE ADVERTISING LAW

The differences between American and European treatment of comparative advertising law arise in part from different conceptions about the role of trade marks. US law encourages competition, while the EU takes a more cautious approach to comparative claims. With respect to comparative advertising, even now that the EU is moving in the American direction with its Misleading and Comparative Advertising Directive,[1] the ability to engage in comparative advertising in Europe is limited. Comparative advertising must 'objectively compare one or more material, relevant, verifiable and representative features of those goods and services . . .'.[2] Aside from the fact that this subject matter restriction is difficult to interpret, it inhibits advertisers from comparing product attributes that may be important to consumers but simply a matter of opinion or preference. The EU comparative advertising law also specifically

---

[1] Council and Parliament Directive 97/55, Amending Directive 84/450 concerning misleading advertising so as to include comparative advertising, 1997 OJ (L 290) 18, available at http://europa.eu.int/comm/consumers/cons_int/safe_shop/mis_adv/index_en.htm#directive (follow Directive 97/55 hyperlink).

[2] Ibid. at Art. 3a(1)(c).

disallows advertisements that present a product as an imitation of the goods or services bearing the protected trade mark, which discourages manufacturers from making cheaper copies of expensive products.

Two additional important threads that have been woven into US trade mark law are an accent on economic growth and an emphasis on providing consumers maximum choice for minimal cost. American trade marks, unlike patents and copyrights, are intended to protect consumer choice rather than to encourage or protect creative commercial activity. Trade marks are meant to reduce the time and energy consumers must devote to shopping (their 'search costs') by providing recognizable symbols that quickly communicate that the product they see on the shelf is of comparable quality as ones with that mark purchased in the past. The mark allows consumers to develop brand preferences that help them make product choices. Trade marks also allow consumers to fix blame for poorly constructed purchases, encouraging manufacturers to produce goods with consistently high quality.

American law demands that a trade mark owner's interest in maximizing the value of a mark be offset by interests in consumer protection, consumer choice and economic development. Accordingly, the limited rights conferred by trade mark ownership provide no monopoly and no shield against comparative advertising.

Moreover, American trade mark law generally places the burden on the trade mark holder to prove infringement or dilution of a mark. Similarly, US false advertising law requires that the plaintiff prove that the advertising at issue is false or misleading to a significant number of consumers.

FAIR USE OF TRADE MARKS

As the scope of trade mark protection is limited, there are several ways to use another's trade mark without liability for infringement. First, anyone is entitled to make 'fair use' of descriptive terms, even if they are trade marked. The Lanham Act creates a so-called 'classic' or 'statutory' fair use defence to trade mark infringement claims,[3] which prevents trade mark holders from appropriating useful words for themselves. It defines fair use as using a term 'fairly and in good faith, only to describe the goods or services of the [advertising] party, or their geographic origin'.[4] For instance, Apple Computers has a trade mark registration for the word APPLE in the context of computer hardware, but it cannot prevent a farmer from making fair use of the word 'apple' to describe

---

[3]   See 15 USC §1125(c)(4).
[4]   15 USC §1115(b)(4).

his produce. That is not really a trade mark 'use' at all – if the farmer's use of
the word 'apple' does not create an association between the fruit and the
computer company in consumers' minds, it is beyond the scope of the trade
mark owner's rights over the word.

Advertisers may also use trade marks *nominatively* – to name the plaintiff's
actual trade marked product, not their own. The nominative fair use defence,
unlike the statutory fair use defence described above, is judicially created.[5]
While the outlines of the doctrine are still not well-developed, under one test[6]
it is satisfied where (1) the defendant could not identify the plaintiff's product
without using its mark, (2) the defendant used only so much of the mark as
was necesssary and (3) the defendant's use of the mark does not suggest sponsorship, endorsement, or other unauthorized affiliation.

In a leading case invoking the doctrine, the newspaper *USA Today*
conducted a survey about the 1980s boy band New Kids On The Block, asking
readers 'which of the five is your fave?' The readers voted by calling a 900
number, for which they were charged. The band sued the paper claiming that
it had made wrongful commercial use of its trade name. The court found for
USA Today because (1) it is impossible to refer to the New Kids except by
using the band name; (2) *USA Today* used the trade mark no more than necessary, refraining from using the band's distinctive logos and (3) the poll did not
mislead consumers into thinking that the band sponsored the poll. The court
instructed that the band's trade mark did 'not entitle them to control their fans'
use of their money . . . to channel their fans enthusiasm (and dollars) only into
items licensed or authorized by them'.[7]

For the same reason, in another case, a court allowed a model to identify
herself on her website and in advertisements as 'Playboy Playmate of the
Year', making nominative use of the trade marked terms 'Playboy' and
'Playmate'. The court found that the defendant used the trade marked terms
only to identify herself and her accomplishments, not to imply Playboy's sponsorship.[8]

COMPARATIVE ADVERTISING AS FAIR USE

Comparative advertising can be considered a form of nominative fair use. It
allows an advertiser to name its competitor's product in order to compare it to

---

5   *New Kids on the Block v News Am. Publ'g., Inc.*, 971 F.2d 302 (9th Cir. 1992).
6   Ibid. at 308.
7   Ibid. at 309.
8   *Playboy Enter., Inc. v Terri Welles, Inc.*, 78 F. Supp. 2d 1066, 1089 (S.D. Cal.
1999), *aff'd in part, rev'd on other grounds*, 279 F.3d 796 (9th Cir. 2002).

its own. From an economic perspective, one of the main benefits of comparative advertising is in overcoming consumer brand preferences. Although brand
preferences make it easier and more efficient to shop, they may also lead shoppers to unknowingly make poor choices, like ignoring higher-quality, lower-
priced competitive products. That mistake is rational – it may not be worth the
risk to try to buy something new and cheaper, only to find that you get what
you pay for. Comparative advertising allows advertisers to use competitors'
marks to identify the competitors' products and to compare and contrast them
with their own. That increases consumers' knowledge and encourages them to
try new products.

Comparative advertising does not conflict with American trade mark laws
because the object is to educate, not deceive, the consumer. Invoking this principle, a court approved of a competitor's advertisement that its product was
'Equivalent to METAMUCIL'.[9] Use of the METAMUCIL mark was permissible 'so long as it does not contain misrepresentations or create a reasonable
likelihood that purchasers will be confused as to the source, identity, or sponsorship of the advertiser's product'.[10] The Court ensured that clarity by requiring the competitor to print the word 'equivalent' in at least as large of letters
as the mark METAMUCIL, to place a trade mark symbol next to the term
METAMUCIL, and to state that the makers of METAMUCIL did not make or
endorse the competitor.[11]

Thus, US law will protect the non-misleading use of a trade mark to
promote a copycat product, marketed as a cheaper alternative to the trade mark
holder's offering. For example, an American 'smell alike' perfume manufacturer may copy the unpatented scent of a fancy perfume and proclaim on the
box, 'If you like CHANEL NO. 5, you'll love SECOND CHANCE'.[12]

However, the comparative advertising slogan used for another perfume, 'If
you like OPIUM you'll love OMNI' was prohibited.[13] It was banned as 'a
deliberate attempt to have the consumer identify the OMNI product as originating from the same source as OPIUM'. The advertisement aimed to mislead,
rather than educate, consumers, and so the court enjoined the makers of OMNI
from using the slogan. The OMNI-makers attempted to resolve the dispute by
changing their slogan to

---

[9] See *G.D. Searle & Co. v Hudson Pharm. Corp.*, 715 F.2d 837 (3rd Cir. 1983).
[10] Ibid. (quoting *SSP Agricultural, Etc. v Orchard-Rite Ltd.*, 592 F.2d 1096, 1103
(9th Cir. 1979)).
[11] See *G.D. Searle & Co*, 715 F.2d at 839, 843 (upholding the lower court's
injunction).
[12] *Smith v Chanel, Inc.*, 402 F.2d 562, 563 (9th Cir. 1968).
[13] *Charles of the Ritz Group Ltd. v Quality King Distrib.*, 832 F.2d 1317 (2d Cir.
1987).

If You Like OPIUM, a fragrance by Yves Saint Laurent, You'll Love OMNI, a fragrance by Deborah Int'l Beauty. Yves Saint Laurent and Opium are not related in any manner to Deborah Int'l Beauty and Opium.

The court ordered injunctive relief against that slogan too. The court was moved by the fact that the words OPIUM and OMNI were printed much larger than the rest of the disclaimer, and the whole paragraph was printed on a part of the box that is usually hidden from customers' view due to the way stores display the product. In context, this was a misleading, rather than pro-competitive, use of a trade mark.

THE FIRST AMENDMENT

Attempts to restrict advertising face an additional hurdle in the United States – the Constitution. The First Amendment of the United State Constitution protects commercial speech, such as advertisements, in addition to personal and political speech. The Constitution affords commercial speech less protection than other kinds of speech, but judicial injunctions or governmental regulations that attempt to curtail such speech require a strong showing that the restriction is necessary and narrowly-drawn. If the speech is lawful and not misleading, the government may only regulate it if the regulation directly advances a substantial governmental interest and is no more extensive than necessary to serve that interest. Or, as one court put it, 'in the First Amendment area, the State cannot use a shotgun to kill a fly'.[14]

In the case of comparative advertising commercial speech, injunctions or regulations aimed at false commercial speech that would also restrain some forms of truthful comparative advertising are unlikely to pass constitutional muster because the governmental interest in protecting the value of individual trade marks is unlikely to be considered important enough to justify silencing speech and depriving consumers of information.

On the other hand, it is important to remember that *false or misleading* comparative advertising itself receives no statutory or Constitutional protection. In order to establish that a comparative advertisement is false or misleading, a trade mark holder has to comply with relatively demanding standards of proof under the Lanham Act. Unless the explicit words of the advertisement are clearly and plainly false – are false 'on their face' – a plaintiff ordinarily is required to obtain a consumer survey showing that consumers actually understand the advertisement to convey a false message.[15] Moreover, some courts

---

[14]   *Metpath, Inc. v Myers*, 462 F. Supp. 1104, 1109 (N.D. Cal. 1978).
[15]   See, for example *Schering Corp. v Pfizer Inc.*, 189 F.3d 218 (2d Cir. 1999).

have developed a set of rules governing the kinds of non-leading questions that may be asked in a survey, the minimum size of a sample, and the use of controls and other techniques of social science research.

For example, the makers of a product named 'BreathAsure', which did not actually improve bad breath, did not engage in literally false advertising because their slogan made no overt claims about the product's breath-freshening capabilities. However, the court found that the name of the product itself misled consumers and enjoined use of the 'BreathAsure' trade mark.[16]

When false advertising is wrapped up with completely truthful comparative advertising, courts face a difficult decision about how to excise the false portion without inhibiting protected speech. As a rule, remedies against false advertising must be tailored to impose no more of a restraint on commercial speech than is reasonably necessary to prevent false advertising. For example, an appeals court reversed an injunction against a dog food manufacturer that was making questionable claims about the comparative medical benefit of its formulation, because the injunction would have required court supervision over the future debate on the medical theory underlying the manufacturer's representations. Such an injunction was not sufficiently tailored to restrict only the defendant's deceptive commercial speech, and stay out of the constitutionally protected veterinary debate.

INTERNET ADVERTISING: A TRADE MARK FRONTIER

The limits of the wide scope of comparative advertising allowed by US courts have recently been tested in a number of trade mark and unfair competition disputes based on internet advertising. Courts are still struggling to define trade mark 'use' in the context of highly technical and still-developing advertising techniques. In addition, it is unclear how exactly to determine 'likelihood of confusion' in this fast-changing arena.

A series of cases involving a company that advertises through internet 'pop-up' ads has arguably expanded the scope of comparative advertising. A software company called 'WhenU.com' distributes a computer program that monitors the user's internet activity and opens pop-up windows that target advertisements based on the user's internet surfing habits. For instance, when a computer user goes to the website for 1-800 Contacts, an online contact lens retailer, the WhenU program opens a pop-up advertisement for a competing company called Vision Direct. Companies like Vision Direct pay WhenU to target their ads in this manner.

---

[16]   See *Warner-Lambert Co. v BreathAsure, Inc.*, 204 F.3d 87 (3d Cir. 2000).

1-800 Contacts argued that WhenU was infringing its trade mark by misleading customers into believing that WhenU's ads were related to the 1-800 Contacts' website, rather than trying to lure customers away from it. To support their claim, plaintiffs conducted a survey that found that over half of the respondents believed that the website owners themselves placed WhenU's competing pop-up ads on the website, or at least 'pre-screened and approved' them.

The US Court of Appeals for the Second Circuit recently found that WhenU does not 'use' 1-800 Contacts' trade mark within the meaning of the Lanham Act because WhenU's pop-up advertisements do not include 1-800 Contacts' trade marks or even reference 1-800 Contacts.[17] WhenU only uses the trade marked terms in internal software code that is not accessible to the computer issue. The issue of consumer confusion was therefore moot. The court likened WhenU's advertising to retail store product placement, in which a retailer places its store brand generic product next to the name-brand item it imitates. Another court further decided that even if WhenU does use others' trade marks in its advertisements, it does so as part of legitimate, non-confusing comparative advertising because WhenU's pop-ups are separate windows, distinct from the competitor's webpage.[18] The fact that WhenU's pop-ups engage in no actual comparison between their product and their competitors', but rather create an entirely new advertisement on top of the competitors' websites, demonstrates how far US courts can stretch comparative advertising doctrine.

GOOGLE AD WORDS

Internet search engines have taken comparative advertising a step farther – selling ads based on others' trade marks. The search engine sells advertising space on its webpage and displays advertisements in response to user queries that include the purchased terms. For example, Google might sell the Pepsi Cola company advertising space linked to the word 'Coke' so that when a user searches for 'Coke', a Pepsi advertisement appears next to the search results. Such advertisements typically appear in a separate, smaller section of the search result page to the right of the actual search results under the title 'Sponsored Links'.

As in the pop-up advertising previously discussed, trade mark holders who

---

[17] *1-800 Contacts v WhenU.com*, 414 F.3d 400 (2d Cir. 2005); *accord U-Haul Int'l, Inc. v WhenU.com, Inc.*, 279 F. Supp. 2d 723 (E.D. Va. 2003).

[18] See *Wells Fargo & Co. v WhenU.com, Inc.*, 293 F. Supp. 2d 734 (E.D. Mich. 2003).

challenge Google's advertising practices in the US typically must show (1) that Google uses their trade marks in commerce within the meaning of the Lanham Act and (2) that the use confuses consumers. Litigation is still at its early stages, but so far Google has claimed tentative victories in US and German courts, while French courts have strongly rejected its practices.

In the first US decision on the issue, *Government Employees Insurance Company (GEICO) v Google*, a federal district court found that Google does make commercial use of others' trade marks when it sells sponsored links keyed to trade marked terms.[19] However, it further held that the use does not necessarily confuse consumers, and even if it does, Google may not be liable. Dismissing GEICO's broadest claims, the court found that there was no evidence that consumers were confused by sponsored ads that made no direct reference to GEICO. However, the Court did find that consumers were confused by ads that included GEICO's trade marks, and that those ads therefore violated trade mark law.

Before the court could decide whether Google, in addition to the advertisers themselves, was liable for the infringing advertisements, the parties settled the case. A German court following similar reasoning as the *GEICO* court answered that question in Google's favour, holding that Google cannot be held liable for advertiser's trade mark infringement.[20] It agreed with a previous Munich district court ruling[21] that it would not be feasible for Google to analyse every advertising purchase for trade mark violations due to the large number of ads it sells, the legal and linguistic complexity of determining whether particular words violate trade mark rights, and its inability to know about possible licensing agreements between trade mark holders and advertisers.

Reflecting their traditional hostility to comparative advertising, French courts, without considering the practical arguments that formed the basis of the German court's decision, have found that Google is liable for allowing advertisers to select trade marked terms as keywords.[22] In the case of the hotel

---

[19] No. 1:04cv507 *(LMB)*, 2005 US Dist. LEXIS 18642 (E.D. Va. 8 Aug. 2005).

[20] *Metaspinner GmbH v Google Deutschland* (Hamburg District Court, Case 312 O 321/04) (reversing a preliminary injunction against Google), available only in German at http://www.linksandlaw.de/urteil77-adwords-haftung-suchmaschine-google.htm.

[21] *Nemetschek AG v Google* (Case 33 O 21461/03), available only in German at http://www.linksandlaw.de/urteil76-adwords-haftung-markenverletzung.htm.

[22] *Hotels Méridien v Google France* (Nanterre Court (TGI), Emergency Order, 16 December 2004), translated into English at http://www.juriscom.net/jpt/ visu.php?ID=631. See also *Société Viaticum and Société Luteciel v Société Google France* (Versailles Court of Appeal, 10 March 2005), available at http://www. legalis.net/jurisprudence-decision.php3?id_article=1415 and reported at [2004] ETMR 63.

chain Le Méridien, a court even enjoined Google from selling ads for the word *meridien*, a dictionary-defined word meaning, most commonly the circle on the surface of the earth passing through the North and South poles. Read literally, this decision could yield the absurd result of prohibiting Google from selling ads keyed to the word *meridian* to, for instance, a cartography website.

These cases reveal both the flexibility of trade mark law in adapting to new media and the importance of remembering its fundamental principles and underlying purposes when applying it in new situations. The American and German Google cases are based on an understanding that the purpose of trade mark law is to avoid consumer confusion, not to grant trade mark holders unlimited rights to trade marked words. The French courts, on the other hand, have focused on fairness to trade mark holders without appearing to make a serious evaluation of their decisions' impact on businesses or consumers.

More than 25 years ago, the United States Federal Trade Commission published a brief *Statement of Policy Regarding Comparative Advertising*.[23] The Commission acted in order to express its disapproval of industry codes and standards that discouraged comparative advertising. The Guidelines declare that

> comparative advertising, when truthful and non-deceptive, is a source of important information to consumers and assists them in making rational purchase decisions. Comparative advertising encourages product improvement and innovation, and can lead to lower prices in the marketplace.[24]

The Commission noted that it had criticized industry codes against 'disparagement' because they may have the effect of discouraging comparative advertisements. As one Commission decision put it, a comparative advertisement 'may have the effect of disparaging the competing product, but we know of no rule of law which prevents a seller from honestly informing the public of the advantages of its products as opposed to those of competing products'. Those principles continue to animate American trade mark law today.

---

[23]   16 CFR §14.15 (1979) (revised as of 1 January 2005), available at http://www.ftc.gov/bcp/policystmt/ad-compare.htm.

[24]   16 CFR §14.15(c).

4. A contrast with trade mark law: the permitted use of geographical indications

Lasse A. Søndergaard Christensen and Janne Britt Hansen

INTRODUCTION

Trade marks and geographical indications (GI) have much in common in that they create links between the product and the consumer. Just as a trade mark communicates to consumers concerning the source and quality of goods bearing the mark, a GI provides consumers with assurances that the goods were produced, processed or prepared in a certain place and as a result have certain characteristics. Furthermore, GIs are often chosen and used as trade marks. Similarities between the functions of trade marks and GIs suggest that they are treated more or less identically with regard to their scope of protection. However, this assumption is far from reality.

Where a trade mark is not always easy to obtain and where the proprietor of a trade mark must accept limitations in his monopoly through third party rights to use his mark, at least some GIs (specifically within EU) seem worryingly easy to obtain and provide an almost absolute monopoly, leaving almost no room for third party usage. This is a paradox.

PROTECTION FOR GIs

Various ways of protecting GIs exist under multilateral and bilateral treaties and national law. GIs can also be protected by unfair competition provisions and by registration as collective trade marks or certification marks.

The TRIPs Agreement requires World Trade Organization (WTO) members to provide certain basic minimum protections for GIs. In general, WTO members must enable interested parties to prevent (1) the use of a GI in a manner which misleads the public as to the geographical origin of the good and (2) any use which constitutes an act of unfair competition. The TRIPs

Agreement provides enhanced protection for GIs that identify wines and spirits.[1]

At Community level, a separate register has been established with Council Regulation 2081/92 of 14 July 1992 on the protection of geographical indications and designations of origin for agricultural products and foodstuffs. That Regulation distinguishes between two categories of protected names: designations of origin (PDOs) and geographical indications (PGIs). A PDO describes foodstuffs which are produced, processed and prepared in a given geographical area. For a PGI, the geographical link must occur in at least one of the stages of production, processing or preparation, or the link may consist simply in the reputation of the product. This means that all PDOs are PGIs and, in this chapter, the term PGI will generally be used for both PDOs and PGIs.

The Regulation creates a system under which registration and protection cover all Member States within the Community. Products may be marked with a Community symbol indicating PGI or PDO status. According to its preamble, the Regulation primarily pays regard to the interests of producers and consumers. Thus its protection is designed to promote product quality, promote rural development and the production of diversified products, to increase the competitiveness of products identifiable by quality labels and to ensure their protection by preventing substitutes or imitations undermining the reputation of those products as well as ensuring proper product information for the consumer.

Since the adoption of the Regulation in 1992, more than 775 names have been registered as PGIs and PDOs. Most of the products concerned are cheeses, fresh meat, meat-based products, fruit and vegetables.

REGISTERING A PGI

An application to register the name of a geographical area must be sent, along with a technical specification of the product that is to bear the name, to the appropriate authorities in the Member State where that area is located. Applications are made in the name of producer groups: farmers, producers, processors.[2]

If the national authority finds that the requirements of the regulation are satisfied and that registration of the name as a PGI or PDO is appropriate, it

---

[1]   Cf. Articles 22–24 of the Agreement on Trade-related Aspects of Intellectual Property Rights (TRIPs).

[2]   Article 4 concerns the product specification. The Regulation also provides for the registration of PDOs and PGIs related to areas located outside the Community, cf. Article 12.

forwards the application to the European Commission, which must verify within six months that the application includes all the particulars required and that the name qualifies for protection.[3]

Generic terms are expressly excluded from registration by Article 3 of Regulation 2081/92. 'Generic term' means the name of an agricultural product or foodstuff which, although it relates to the place or the region where this product or foodstuff was originally produced or marketed, has become the common name of a product.

If an application meets registration requirements, it will be published in the *Official Journal of the European Communities*. Within six months from the date of publication, statements of objection – by a member state, WTO members or recognised third countries – may be transmitted to the Commission. Typically, statements of objections come from manufacturers who *use* the designation for which protection is sought. If no statement of objection has been received within six months, the name is entered in the register of PDOs and PGIs. The annex to Commission Regulation 1107/96 contains all registrations and is amended in accordance with each subsequent registration. The countries' governments are the official owners of the registrations – Italy and France being the top scorers with approximately 150 each.

PROTECTION/TOLERATED USE OF PGIs IN THEORY

Registration gives producers the exclusive right to use a registered name for their products. A specific feature of the right is that it belongs not only to the producers who made the application but to all producers in the geographical area defined who comply with the conditions of production laid down in the specification. This exclusive right does not prevent the possibility of registering homonymous names, if they do not mislead the public into believing that products originate from another territory. Specific rules are given in Articles 6(6) and 12(2) of the Regulation.

PGIs enjoy, in the Community market, the protection specified in Article 13. In short, registered PGIs are legally protected against any misuse or false or misleading indication.

Article 13(1) reads:

---

[3]   Within six months of the entry into force of the Regulation, Member States had the option to inform the Commission which of their legally protected names, or which names established by usage, they wished to register under the Regulation. The 'simplified procedure' (formerly Article 17) was revoked by Regulation 692/2003.

1. Registered names shall be protected against

(a) any direct or indirect commercial use of a name registered in respect of products not covered by the registration in so far as those products are comparable to the products registered under that name or insofar as using the name exploits the reputation of the protected name;
(b) any misuse, imitation or evocation, even if the true origin of the product is indicated or if the protected name is translated or accompanied by an expression such as 'style', 'type', 'method', 'as produced in', 'imitation' or similar;
(c) any other false or misleading indication as to the provenance, origin, nature or essential qualities of the product, on the inner or outer packaging, advertising material or documents relating to the product concerned, and the packing of the product in a container liable to convey a false impression as to its origin;
(d) any other practice liable to mislead the public as to the true origin of the product.

Where a registered name contains within it the name of an agricultural product or foodstuff which is considered generic, the use of that generic name on the appropriate agricultural product or foodstuff shall not be considered to be contrary to (a) or (b) in the first subparagraph.

As Article 13(1) indicates, the powers available to holders of the right are extensive. The prohibition covers all practices that refer in any way to a PGI or a PDO so as to take unjustified advantage of its reputation. This wording gives room for a strict limitation of others' use of PGIs. Further powerful protection is found in Article 13(3), which states that protected names may not become generic, regardless of whether producers defend their rights.

Since obtaining a PGI is fairly simple but the monopoly conferred by a PGI is comprehensive, what use must right owners of the PGI tolerate? Tolerated use of a PGI is regulated by Article 13(4), which provides for possible transitional periods for the phasing-out of the registered name for products which do not comply with the specification. For instance, where registration of the proposed name would jeopardise the existence of an entirely or partially identical name or trade mark, or the existence of products which have been legally on the market for at least five years preceding the application's date of publication, a maximum transitional period of five years may be granted to use the name. However, before a company is allowed to continue to market a product under a PGI for a transitional period of a maximum five years, an admissible statement of objection must be filed.

Tolerated use of a PGI is also regulated by Article 13(5), which provides for an extended legal period of coexistence between a registered name and an unregistered name for a maximum of 15 years, if the unregistered name has been in legal use consistently and fairly for at least 25 years before the Regulation's entry into force and if the purpose of its use was not to profit from the reputation of the registered name.

Finally, Article 14 is designed to solve the conflicts between trade marks that include geographical names and PGIs. Under Article 14(1) any application for a conflicting trade mark for the same type of product made *after* the date of application for protection of the geographical name at Community level will be refused. In this case, the Regulation gives priority to the geographical name.

Article 14(2) provides for coexistence in certain cases, where the use of a trade mark engenders one of the situations indicated in Article 13. However, a conflicting trade mark may only continue to be used, in accordance with Community law, if it was applied for, registered or established by use in good faith before either the date of protection in the country of origin or the date of submission to the Commission of the PGI application.

In general, registration of a conflicting trade mark does not prevent registration of the geographical name. Only in one circumstance, referred to in Article 14(3), is the application to register the geographical name refused. This is when, in the light of the trade mark's reputation and the length of time it has been used, registration of a geographical name would be liable to mislead the consumer as to the true identity of the product. In all other cases, the name may be registered notwithstanding the existence of the registered trade mark.

PROTECTION/TOLERATED USE OF TRADE MARKS IN THEORY

Article 17 of TRIPs entitles WTO members to provide limited exceptions to the rights conferred by a trade mark, such as an exception for the fair use of descriptive terms, provided that they take account of the interests of the trade mark owner and of third parties. Council Directive 89/104 of 21 December 1988 to approximate the laws of the Member States related to trade marks (the trade mark directive) provides for various such exceptions. Article 5 defines the rights conferred by a trade mark, while Articles 6 and 7 contain rules on the limitation of the effects of a trade mark.

Under Article 5(1) the registered trade mark confers an exclusive right on its owner. By Article 5(1)(a) the holder of that exclusive right may prevent all third parties not having his consent from using in the course of trade any sign which is identical with the trade mark in relation to the goods or services which are identical with those for which the trade mark is registered. Article 5(3) sets out in a non-exhaustive way the types of use which the owner may prohibit.

Article 6 reconciles the fundamental interests of trade mark protection with those of free movement of goods in the common market. First, according to Article 6(1), the trade mark owner may not prohibit a third party from using

(a) his own name or address or (b) indications concerning the kind, quality, intended purpose, value, geographical origin, the time of production of goods or of rendering of the service, or other characteristics of goods or services. Secondly, the trade mark owner may not prohibit a third party from using the mark in trade where it is *necessary* to indicate the intended purpose of a product or service, cf. Article 6(1)(c).

Use must be in accordance with honest practices in industrial or commercial matters before it is tolerated by Article 6.

Apart from these limitations, a third party has limited access to use others' trade marks in connection with comparative advertising (see Directive 84/450, as amended by Directive 97/55).

Article 7 of the trade mark directive regards the exhaustion of the rights conferred by a trade mark. It provides that the trade mark does not entitle the proprietor to prohibit its use in relation to goods put on the market in the Community under that trade mark by the proprietor or with his consent except where there exist legitimate reasons for him to oppose further commercialisation of the goods, especially where the condition of the goods is changed or impaired after they have been put on the market.

COMPARISON OF PGI AND TRADE MARK PROTECTION/ TOLERATED USE IN THEORY

PGIs are similar to, but not identical with, registered trade marks. Essentially, the former protect the names of products (or rather the products as such), whereas the latter protect the sources from which they are produced. Regulation 2081/92 bans the direct or indirect use of PGIs by anyone other than the designated producers and thus gives absolute protection of the name for all legitimate producers. Since the PGI is a collective exclusive right, the tolerated use of a PGI by new producers in the geographical zone cannot as such be compared with the use of a registered trade mark or with the use of ordinary intellectual property rights. Thus, with regard to its contents, the registration system for GIs is a separate system of intellectual property rights although it does bear some similarities to registered collective marks.

To qualify for registration, a geographical name need only to fulfil the definition of a PDO or a PGI and be accompanied by a detailed specification. It need not be capable of distinguishing the goods of one undertaking from those of other undertakings, as is required for trade mark registration. In practice, while initially PGIs seemed to comprise proud and well-known regions, later years have witnessed a tendency to obtain PGIs for less well-known products and places. Further, unlike a registered trade mark, a PGI is guaranteed against 'genericity' and the right continues to exist even if the name is not used.

Thus trade mark registrations face numerous obstacles that PGIs do not encounter. Adversely, and paradoxically, the PGI enjoys a broader scope of protection.

Superficially GIs and trade marks are treated similarly in regard to generic terms, such terms being ineligible for registration. However, the similarity stops when it comes to the territorial scope of the assessment. Thus, in the system of GIs, a Community-wide decision is taken as to whether a term is generic whereas, for trade mark registration, there is scope for individual perceptions by Member States.[4] In consequence, unlike trade marks, a GI may be registered in the Community although it is regarded a generic term in one or more Member States. Often, consumers in one Member State will share the perception as to whether a given term is generic. In other words, the scope of protection of a PGI in those Member States has enormous dimensions, if a certain term suddenly changes from being a common expression for a type of product to becoming a term enjoying exclusivity.

PGIs are broadly protected against misuse, imitation and even evocative uses, including cases where the true origin of the product is indicated or where the protected name is accompanied by an expression such as 'in the style of' or 'imitation'. By way of example, in comparison with the concepts of similarity of marks and goods in the trade mark directive, it will be interesting to see the scope of protection given by the interpretation of the Regulation of the term 'comparable products' in Article 13(1)(a), and 'evocation' in Article 13(1)(b). Further, the wording regarding the *exploitation of the reputation* in Article 13(1)(a) seems to offer wide protection of products equivalent to the protection afforded to well-known trade marks.

In 13(1)(b), the wording 'even if the true origin of the product is indicated' also provides a broad scope of protection to PGIs compared to the protection of trade marks, in that use is not permitted despite the use can be said to be in accordance with honest practice (cf. Article 6(1) of the trade mark directive). Finally Article 13(1)(d) offers a broad scope of protection (cf. the statement that PGIs enjoy protection against 'any other practice liable to mislead the public as to the true origin of the product'). From the wording, the protection of a PGI against unfair competition is much wider – and more absolute – than the protection afforded by the trade mark directive.

As can be seen, registration of PGIs has major legal repercussions in terms

---

[4]   If a trade mark consists exclusively of signs or indications which have become customary in the current language or in the bona fide and established practices of trade, this is an absolute ground for refusal, cf. Article 3(1)(d) of the trade mark directive. In this respect, examiners will consult standard dictionaries in all languages of the Community, cf. OHIM's examination guidelines.

of producers' rights and in terms of the type and extent of protection of the registered name. The permitted use by third persons seems limited.

A type of tolerated use that only exists with regard to PGIs and not to trade marks, however, is the right of temporarily continued legal use of a PGI (the system of derogation). However, instead of designating this use 'tolerated use', 'confiscation' of an earlier right to use a certain geographical indication may seem more appropriate. The fact is that EU takes back the name that it regards as having a particular need for GI protection even if the name in question is currently being used in a legal manner.

In theory, if conflicts arise between a trade mark and a geographical name, the balance between the two types of intellectual property right appears clearly to favour the PGI. Thus, as a general rule, where a prior trade mark exists, the trade mark and GI are permitted to coexist. It seems to be the general Community position that PGIs will be superior to trade marks.[5]

As previously stated, the background to the protection of GIs and the protected object as such is different from and thus not comparable with trade marks. However, as the different rights conflict with each other, the different treatment – especially with regard to the strength and scope of protection – is likely to create problems in the ordinary system of protection of intellectual property rights characterised by the principle of territory and the traditional 'first-in-time, first-in-right' principle.

There now follows a review of case-law exemplifying different types of use of PGIs, regarding the interpretation of the Regulation and thus on the extent of protection/tolerated use of PGIs.

PROTECTION/TOLERATED USE OF PGIs IN PRACTICE

Existing case law on tolerated use of PGIs primarily regards disputes as to (1) objections to registration as PGIs, i.e. actions for annulment, (2) the scope of protection of PGIs, and (3) the proper use of PGIs in accordance with its specifications.

In *FETA*, the ECJ found that the word FETA should be allowed to remain on the register of PDOs.[6] The governments of Denmark and Germany

---

5   For example, in the Opinion of the Economic and Social Committee on the 'Proposal for a Council Regulation amending Regulation 2081/92-2002/0066', the Committee considered that 'although priority must be given to the general and public interest represented by PGI/PDO, both forms of intellectual property deserve proper protection as they both provide a means of addressing such issues as unfair competition or misleading advertising'.

6   Cases C-465/02 and C-466/02, [2006] ETMR 16. Denmark and Germany challenged Commission Regulation 1829/2002 of 14 October 2002 which declared

objected on the grounds that FETA was not a geographical indication but a generic term. Many companies in these countries have produced cheese called FETA for ages – though using production methods different from the traditional Greek method. A consumer survey made by the Commission in 1994 showed that 63 per cent of Danish consumers found that FETA was a common name for a type of cheese.

Although FETA does not refer to a specific location, the ECJ found that it fulfilled the requirements for protection as a PDO, since the cheese's quality and characteristics derived from the geographical environment in which it was produced. Taking into account the factors mentioned in Article 3(1) of the Regulation (one of these being 'the existing situation in other Member States'), the ECJ concluded that the term FETA was not generic, due to the predominant consumer perception in the Community of this word's link with Greece.

PARMESAN[7] concerned the registered PDO of the Italian Republic, PARMIGIANO REGGIANO. An Italian company produced a dried, grated pasteurised cheese in powder form, made from a mixture of several types of cheese of various origins, which did not comply with the specification for the PDO PARMIGIANO REGGIANO. The cheese, sold with a label bearing the word PARMESAN, was marketed exclusively outside Italy. The Parmigiano Reggiano Consorzio complained, maintaining that the Italian company's use of the word PARMESAN was a misleading indication. The ECJ stated that the Italian company was not entitled to use the word PARMESAN with reference to the system of derogation[8] since that to allow the continued use of that name under certain conditions and within certain limits, applied *only* to products not originating in the state of the PDO. The German government argued that the reference for a preliminary ruling was inadmissible, since the designation PARMESAN had become the common name of a foodstuff within the meaning of Article 3(1). Furthermore, since only the name PARMIGIANO REGGIANO had been registered, Community protection was confined to that name and only covered that precise formulation of the name registered.

FETA a PDO for Greece. PDO protection of FETA was first applied by Greece in 1994 in accordance with the simplified procedure in former Article 17 and was granted by Regulation 1107/96. By Regulation 1070/1999 FETA was deleted from the list of PDOs. The ECJ based its annulment of the registration on the fact that the Commission, when registering the name FETA, took no account of the fact that the name had been used for a considerable time in certain member states other than Greece. Following the Commission's re-examination, in 2002 FETA was again declared a PDO.

[7]   Case C-66/00, [2003] ETMR 55.
[8]   Cf. former Article 13(2) of Regulation 2081/92.

The AG opined that, since assessment of whether a name is generic in terms of the Regulation falls within the remit of the Commission, it is not for the Court to assume the task of the Commission on that question.[9]

According to the Italian Government, the designation of origin PARMI-GIANO REGGIANO referred to parmesan originating in a particular place (the town of Parma and its surroundings) and in a particular region (Emilia-Romagna). The AG concluded that the names PARMESAN and PARMI-GIANO REGGIANO were equivalent, since the term PARMIGIANO was the essential component of the PDO.

The ECJ stated that it is far from clear that the designation PARMESAN has become generic. Moreover, all the governments that submitted written observations contended that the French designation PARMESAN was the correct translation of the PDO PARMIGIANO REGGIANO. On this basis, the ECJ found the questions referred admissible for a preliminary ruling.

'*Evocation*' in Article 13(1)(b) was interpreted in *GORGONZOLA*.[10] GORGONZOLA was registered as a PDO in June 1996.[11] Thirteen years earlier, the Austrian trade mark CAMBOZOLA was registered for cheese. To decide whether CAMBOZOLA fell within Article 13, the ECJ stated that 'evocation' as referred to in Article 13(1)(b) covers a situation where the term used to designate a product incorporates part of a protected designation so that, when the consumer is faced with the name of the product, the image triggered in his mind is that of the product whose designation is protected.[12] Further, the ECJ stated that a protected designation may be evoked where there is no like-lihood of confusion between the products concerned and even where no Community protection extends to the parts of that designation that echo the term or terms at issue. Use of the name CAMBOZOLA could therefore be deemed, for the purpose of Article 13(1)(b) to evoke the protected PDO, GORGONZOLA, irrespective of the fact that the packaging indicated the product's true origin.

With regard to the question of proper use of a PGI, two decisions concern-ing subsequent product processes should be mentioned. In *PROSCIUTTO DI PARMA*,[13] a chain of British supermarkets sold genuine Parma ham[14] which was sliced and packaged in the UK. *GRANA PADANO*[15] concerned a French

---

9   Cf. para. 40.

10   Case C-87/97, [1999] ETMR 135.

11   Regulation 1107/96, 12 June 1996.

12   Case C-87/97, para. 25.

13   Case C-108/01, [2004] ETMR 23.

14   PROSCIUTTO DI PARMA was listed as a PDO, cf. Regulation 1107/96, 12 June 1996.

15   Case C-469/00, [2004] ETMR 22.

company marketing GRANA PADANO cheese under the designation 'Grana Padano freshly grated'.[16]

In each case the Regulation contained reference to or requirement in respect of subsequent processes such as slicing and grating. The only reason given for requiring slicing and packaging of Parma ham to take place in Parma was to help ensure that the product was genuine. It was not however disputed that the product sold was the genuine product. Since the condition in question had not been mentioned in Regulation 1107/96, it was disproportionate to require the ham to be sliced and packaged in Parma. Accordingly the Consorzio could not prevent the use of the PDO.

In both cases, the ECJ concluded that Regulation 2081/92 must be interpreted as not precluding the use of a PDO from being subject to the condition that operations such as the slicing and packaging of the product take place in the region of production, where such a condition is laid down in the specification.[17]

Both cases also concerned the free movement of goods – whether imposing conditions that grating/slicing/packaging operations should be carried out in the region of production constitute a measure having equivalent effect to a quantitative restriction on exports within the meaning of Article 29 of the EC treaty. The ECJ concluded that such steps could be justified under Article 30 and thus compatible with Article 29.

PROTECTION/TOLERATED USE OF TRADE MARKS IN PRACTICE

A short review of relevant case law regarding permitted use of trade marks can be given by referring to *BMW, GEROLSTEINER* and *GILLETTE* (Article 6) and *DIOR* as well as decisions in the field of repackaging of trade marked products (Article 7).

In *BMW*[18] the ECJ ruled that Articles 5 to 7 of the trade mark directive do not entitle a trade mark proprietor to prohibit a third party from using the mark for the purpose of informing the public that he carries out repair and maintenance of goods covered by that trade mark and put on the market under that mark by the proprietor or with his consent, or that he specialises in the sale or the repair and maintenance of such goods, *unless* the mark is used in a way as to create the impression that there is a commercial connection between the

---

[16]   GRANA PADANO was a registered PDO as of 21 June 1996, under Regulation 1107/96.
[17]   Case C-108/01, para. 50. Case C-469/00, para. 83.
[18]   Case C-63/97, [1999] ETMR 339.

other undertaking and the trade mark proprietor, in particular that the reseller's business is affiliated to the trade mark proprietor's distribution network or that there is a special relationship between the two.

The ECJ held that the mere fact that the reseller benefits from using the trade mark in advertisements for the sale of goods covered by the mark, which are in other respects honest and fair but lend an aura of quality to his own business, was not seen as an infringement. The court said it had to reconcile the fundamental interests of trade mark protection with those of free movement of goods in such a way that trade mark rights are able to fulfil their essential function, to guarantee origin such that there is no possibility of confusion.

In *GEROLSTEINER*[19] an Irish company's use of the term KERRY SPRING on labels on soft drinks allegedly infringed Gerolsteiner's trade mark GERRI for mineral water. The KERRY SPRING drinks were manufactured and bottled in Ireland using water from a spring called Kerry Spring: that name was included in the list of mineral waters recognised by Ireland. Although the marks were found confusingly similar, the owner of the GERRI mark had to accept the Irish company's use of the word KERRY for identical goods (mineral water) – provided it was in accordance with honest practices – since use of the word KERRY was justified by its referral to a geographical indication: see Article 6(1)(b).

GILLETTE[20] concerned a Finnish company's use of the trade marks GILLETTE and SENSOR on a sticker bearing the words 'All Parason Flexor and Gillette Sensor handles are compatible with this blade' on the packaging of its razor blades. The ECJ concluded that the legality of the use of the trade mark depends on whether that use is necessary to indicate the intended purpose of a product. Use of the trade mark by a third party who is not its owner is necessary in order to indicate the intended purpose of a product marketed by that third party where such use in practice constitutes the only means of providing the public with comprehensible and complete information on that intended purpose in order to preserve the undistorted system of competition in the market for that product.

Further, the ECJ stated that the condition of 'honest use' in Article 6(1) constitutes in substance the expression of a duty to act fairly in relation to the legitimate interests of the trade mark owner. The use of the trade mark will not be in accordance with honest practices in industrial and commercial matters if, for example, it is done in such a manner as to give the impression that there is a commercial connection between the third party and the trade mark owner.[21]

---

[19] Case C-100/02, [2004] ETMR 40.
[20] Case C-228/03, [2005] ETMR 67.
[21] Case C-228/03, paras 40–45.

In *DIOR*,[22] the scope of exhaustion of Article 7 was interpreted. ECJ stated that, within the concept of exhaustion (when a product has been put on the market in the Community under that trade mark by its proprietor or with its consent), a trade mark proprietor may not prohibit the reseller's use of the trade mark unless it is established that, under the circumstances, the use of the trade mark for that purpose seriously damages the trade mark's reputation. As the ECJ mentioned in paragraphs 44–45, a balance must be struck between the legitimate interest of the trade mark owner in being protected against resellers using its trade mark for advertising in a manner which could damage the reputation of the trade mark and the reseller's legitimate interest in being able to resell the goods in question by using advertising methods which are customary in its sector of trade.

COMPARISON OF PGI AND TRADE MARK PROTECTION/TOLERATED USE IN PRACTICE

The picture illustrated by the practice for PGIs and trade marks not only confirms the impression under the comparison of use in theory but strengthens the impression that third party use of a trade mark appears to be much more likely to be tolerated than use of a PGI.

First there is a major difference between the registration systems with regard to the grant of protection. For instance, a name can be afforded protection as a PGI in the Community even though it is perceived as a generic term in one or more Member States. As shown in *FETA*, registration as a PGI is not precluded even if the name is perceived as a generic term in a Member State.

In *PARMESAN* the ECJ refused to examine the German Government's arguments that PARMESAN had become, in general, a name which on its own refers to a grated cheese, stating that it was far from clear that the designation PARMESAN had become generic. Nor was the argument that Community protection was confined to the name PARMIGIANO REGGIANO, since only that precise formulation was registered. Considering the possible various local perceptions of the term, the protection of PARMIGIANO REGGIANO was granted a wide scope of protection – without substantial examination.

Where there is a conflict between a prior mark and a later GI, the differences in the scope of permitted use are well illustrated by *GORGONZOLA* and *GEROLSTEINER*. These cases somehow reflect diametrically opposite situations and, in both, the GI enjoys a broader protection than the trade mark. With regard to the PDO GORGONZOLA it was stated that use was not permitted by a third party of a name, even if this name was *not* confusingly similar with

---

22   Case C-337/95, [1998] ETMR 26.

the PGI and thus did not cause any confusion among the public. In contrast, in *GEROLSTEINER*, the owner of the trade mark GERRI could not prevent use of the GI KERRY for identical products, *although* the mark and GI were found confusingly similar.

In *GORGONZOLA* the ECJ endorsed the view that 'evocation' does not require likelihood of confusion. In contrast, in disputes concerning trade marks, where there is merely an association of ideas, this does not amount to a likelihood of confusion. Further, the interpretation of 'evocation' was extremely broad, in that the packaging for CAMBOZOLA indicated that it was produced in Germany.

The protection of a trade mark stops at the stage where the purpose of the mark is fulfilled, i.e. when the consumer is able to distinguish the goods of one undertaking from those of other undertakings. The protection of PGIs goes further.

As a general principle in the trade mark directive, a third party's use of a trade mark is tolerated where the use is in accordance with honest practices. As can be seen in *BMW* and *GILLETTE*, a number of subjective criteria can be set up for tolerated use of a trade mark and the decision whether use is tolerated is subject to a very concrete assessment. In contrast, in decisions on tolerated use of PGIs, reference is made to objective and absolute criteria and does not appear to pay much attention to the conflicting interests of opposing parties.

The balance referred to in *BMW* and *DIOR*, between the legitimate interest of the trade mark owner and the third party's legitimate interest in using the trade mark, does not seem to take place or cannot be transferred to disputes concerning use of PGIs.

A number of similarities with regard to the permitted use of a PGI/trade mark may be found in the PGI cases concerning slicing/grating and the cases regarding repackaging of trade marked products. However, it is apparent from both the wording and the structure of Regulation 2081/92 that the specification constitutes the instrument which determines the extent of the uniform protection given by that regulation within the Community. Thus, from a PGI owner's point of view, there seems to be an easy 'solution', in that operations can be prohibited to third parties outside the region of production if a condition is expressly provided for in the specification. In other words, if detailed specifications are filed, the protection of a PGI will be correspondingly detailed. Moreover, it is possible to change product specifications along the way – and thus in reality to extend the protection.

CONCLUSIONS/EVALUATIONS

As can be seen, special challenges exist in regard to the protection of GIs –

especially with regard to their interaction with trade marks. Even within the Community, harmonisation is difficult, not least because of the imbalance in the number of GIs from different Member States and because there is no common perception as to whether a GI has become a generic term. GI protection goes beyond trade mark protection and sometimes even extinguishes the prior rights of trade mark owners. Having regard to regional and international differences, the broad scope of protection and limited permitted use of PGIs seems even more thought-provoking.

The protection of PGIs is designed to promote product quality, to prevent substitutes or imitations from undermining the reputation of these products and to ensure that the consumer receives proper information about products. Territorially, however, the definition of 'quality' should be a relevant issue to reach agreement upon, before a GI is afforded protection. Danish methods of manufacturing white salted cheese (FETA) may appeal – as a quality product – to Danish consumers to a larger extent than Greek FETA. In Denmark the word FETA is a generic name within the meaning of Article 3(1) of Regulation 2081/92 in the sense that the name is not linked to production in a particular place but only to characteristics of the product itself. Danish producers' use of the name FETA scarcely undermines the reputation of Greek FETA. In the light of this specific case, we believe that there are product names for which it is too late to afford protection, where a link to the geographical origin does not exist, or no longer exists, in the minds of the consumers.

The Regulation has a major economic impact, since only producers from the relevant geographical areas will be able to use a name once it is registered. With reference to principles of prescriptive rights and passivity, it does seem problematic suddenly to forfeit a right to use a name. In this context it is pertinent to ask whether protection of GIs and the phasing-out of current use will be of any value. In Denmark, the ECJ's decision in *FETA* implies that this term cannot be used by the Danish producers of the salted white cheese as from 2007. The case received comprehensive media coverage and Danish consumers hardly understand the reasonableness behind the change of name of this cheese product. In future, the 'demanding and quality-oriented' consumer may even wish to prefer the Danish cheese and thus boycott the Greek FETA – which was hardly the idea behind the PGI system.

Moreover, in practice, to 'force' a generic term to become a protected term is an impossible task. In comparison, a degenerated trade mark can never regain its main function – a guarantee of the identity of origin of the marked goods – once the name has become descriptive of the goods in question.

Names for new products from foreign places are particularly vulnerable to implementation in local language. In our opinion, apart from the barrier of different local perceptions of GIs, it is extremely difficult to regulate tolerated use of GIs due to the great differences in the various types of GIs. In this respect, a GI consisting only of a geographical term is very different from a GI consisting of a geographical term combined with a generic term designating the type of the product. Obviously a GI consisting of a geographical term alone risks becoming a common term for the product and is likely not to be perceived as a GI at all (the consumer cannot be said to be misled as to the origin of the product: when a geographic designation is identified with a type of product rather than with a geographical area, it no longer suggests that the product originated in the particular region).[23]

One can ask whether sufficient protection for the consumers already exists. Regulation 2081/92 refers to increasing consumer demand for greater emphasis on quality and information as regards the nature, method of production and processing of foodstuffs and their special characteristics. Consumers undoubtedly need product transparency and accurate information about food products, especially in relation to their origin. However, the safeguarding of accurate consumer information as regards the origin and identity of a product referred to by a traditional name is ensured by Directive 2000/13 on labelling, presentation and advertising of foodstuffs.[24]

Moreover, Directive 84/450 on misleading advertising aims to improve consumer protection. Article 3 provides that, in determining whether advertising is misleading, account must be taken of any information it contains concerning the geographical or commercial origin of goods. Does this leave the main purpose of Regulation 2081/92 as being producer and product protection?

Producers as well, however, already have the possibility of protecting certain quality marks through the system of collective Community trade marks. An exception to the general rules on absolute registrability of Community trade marks is made for certain geographical marks as collective marks. Thus any sign or indication which may serve, in trade, to designate the geographical origin of the goods or services, may constitute a collective mark. Such a sign would give rise to objection as being non-distinctive if registration was sought as an ordinary Community trade mark. This system's object of protection is identical with the PGI system. However, the protection of a

---

[23] Apparently because of difficulties, the Commission has still not completed a non-exhaustive list of generic and thus unregistrable names as required by Article 3 in Regulation 2081/92.

[24] Directive 2000/13 is the consolidated version of Directive 79/112 on the labelling of foodstuffs and its subsequent amendments. Article 2 of that directive provides that the labelling and methods used must not be such as could mislead the purchaser as to the characteristics of the foodstuff and, in particular, the origin or provenance of that foodstuff. A name or indication in the labelling referring to a specific region would therefore be admissible only if the foodstuff was actually produced in that region.

geographical collective mark is not as broad as is the PGI protection. For example, if the proprietor has not taken reasonable steps to prevent misuse of the collective mark, revocation may result.

It is a principle of European law that Community action must be proportionate to its objectives. One could argue that individualisation of GIs is possible by using fewer intervening tools, letting the producers of the 'original' product market their product as such – either by using some sort of indication (for example collective and certification mark) or simply by skilled marketing.

Considering consumer awareness today (which seems to be one of the reasons for the need for Regulation 2081/92) – it seems most expedient to market products such as PARMESAN and FETA (which will undoubtedly be considered types of product by some) internationally, using entirely new kinds of quality marks.

Consequently, is Regulation 2081/92 nothing but a convenient tool for the EU, its real purpose being protection of the local economy? If that is so, some countries have been more active in getting trade protection for their local companies than others. Remember Italy and France have around 150 PGIs each, while the Baltic States have none.

According to the New World, the notion of trade protection rather than consumer protection is not far from the truth. In the eyes of countries such as the US and Australia, the EU is seen as having a special commercial interest in the agricultural products the Regulation covers, wishing to maintain its privileged position for that group of products and preventing the new countries from using terms which are now generic in their territories.

With regard to the interaction between the systems of protection of GIs and trade marks, completely different approaches exist in the WTO debate. On one side it is stated that, although complementary, trade marks and GIs are different legal concepts, express different interests and therefore need to be treated differently. The other side represents the view that GIs should be treated in the same way as trade marks and other IP rights, with conflicts being resolved on the basis of the established intellectual property principles of territoriality, exclusivity and priority.

A compromise solution seems inevitable. Unfortunately, however, for a long period of time, this will probably not make the instrument of GI protection less blurred and the issue 'GIs versus trade marks' less controversial.

PART TWO

Specific issues

5. Comparative advertising in Europe

Philippe de Jong

1. INTRODUCTION

The purpose of the present chapter is to give a concise overview of the co-existence of comparative advertising and trade mark legislation. Reduced to one
question, the title of this chapter reads: to what extent is comparative advertising tolerated as a fair use of another's trade mark? First, the relevant legal
provisions will be briefly examined. Secondly, the case law giving guidance
on the interpretation of these provisions will be given more extensive treatment.

2. TRADE MARK LAW

In 1988 the European Community undertook the first initiative to harmonise
the often diverging trade mark laws of the EU Member States. The aim of this
initiative was to approximate these laws rather than to harmonise them fully.
This initiative led to the Trade Mark Directive (TMD)[1] of 21 December 1988.

2.1 The Exclusive Rights of the Trade Mark Proprietor

According to the TMD[2] a registered trade mark confers upon its proprietor the
exclusive right to prevent all third parties without his consent from using in the
course of trade[3]

(a) any identical sign in relation to goods or services identical with those for
which the trade mark is registered;

---

[1] First Council Directive 89/104 of 21 December 1988 to approximate the laws
of the Member States relating to trade marks, OJ L 40, 11 February 1989, p. 1.
[2] As well as to the Community Trade Mark Regulation (Council Regulation
40/94 of 20 December 1993 on the Community Trade Mark, OJ L 11, 14 January 1994,
p. 1), which contains identical provisions.
[3] Article 5(1), (2) TMD.

(b)   any sign where, because of its identity with, or similarity to, the trade mark and
      the identity or similarity of the goods or services covered by the trade mark and
      the sign, there exists a likelihood of confusion on the part of the public, which
      includes the likelihood of association between the sign and the trade mark.

With regard to well-known marks, a further provision was included, allowing
the trade mark proprietor to prevent the unauthorised use of

(c)   any sign which is identical to, or similar to, the trade mark in relation to goods
      or services which are (dis)similar[4] to those for which the trade mark is regis-
      tered, where the latter has a reputation and where use of that sign without due
      cause takes unfair advantage of, or is detrimental to, the distinctive character
      or the repute of the trade mark.

A trade mark proprietor can thus prevent a third party from making use of his
trade mark as a trade mark, that is for the purpose of distinguishing goods or
services. 'Trade mark use' constitutes, *inter alia*:[5]

(a)   affixing the sign to the goods or to the packaging thereof;
(b)   offering the goods – including putting them on the market or stocking them for
      the purpose of offering them – under that sign, or offering or supplying
      services under the sign;
(c)   importing or exporting the goods under the sign;
(d)   *using the sign* on business papers and *in advertising*. (emphasis added)

In addition to protection against 'trade mark use', many EU Member States
offer the trade mark proprietor protection against so-called 'non trade mark
use', that is protection against the use of a sign other than for the purposes of
distinguishing goods or services. The conditions for such protection are (i) that
the sign is used without due cause and (ii) that it takes unfair advantage of, or
is detrimental to, the distinctive character or the repute of the trade mark.[6]
However, such protection has not been harmonised by EU law.[7]

2.2   Limitations to the Exclusive Trade Mark Right

Several limitations apply to the effects of the exclusive rights of a trade mark
proprietor. More precisely, a trade mark does not entitle its proprietor to
prohibit a third party from using, in the course of trade

---

    [4]   *Davidoff & Cie SA, Zino Davidoff SA* v *Gofkid Ltd* Case C-292/00 [2003]
ECR I-389, [2002] ETMR 99.
    [5]   Article 5(3) TMD.
    [6]   Article 5(5) TMD.
    [7]   *Robelco NV v Robeco Groep NV* Case C-23/01 [2002] ECR I-10913, [2003]
ETMR 52.

(a) his own name or address;

(b) indications concerning the kind, quality, quantity, intended purpose, value, geographical origin, the time of production of goods or of rendering of the service, or other characteristics of goods or services; or

(c) the trade mark where it is necessary to indicate the intended purpose of a product or service, in particular as accessories or spare parts.

These limitations apply on condition that the third party concerned uses the trade mark in accordance with honest practices in industrial or commercial matters.[8]

3. THE LAW ON COMPARATIVE ADVERTISING

Before harmonisation of the law on comparative advertising, this practice was frowned upon in many EU Member States. Some states possessed stringent legislation banning comparative advertising as a sort of unfair trade practice; in others, harsh court rulings deterred companies from engaging in any comparative advertising campaigns.

Thirteen years after the passage and implementation by Member States of the Misleading Advertising Directive[9] (MAD), the Commission decided that legislation was needed which was specifically tailored to create uniform laws on comparative advertising throughout the different EU Member States.

The general idea behind this new initiative was that comparative advertising should be allowed. Thus it happened that, on 6 October 1997, the MAD was amended by Directive 97/55 of the European Parliament and of the Council amending Directive 84/450/EEC concerning misleading advertising so as to include comparative advertising. The MAD thus became the 'Misleading and Comparative Advertising Directive' (MCAD).[10]

In addition to the existing definitions of 'advertising' and 'misleading advertising', 'comparative advertising' was defined as 'any advertising which explicitly or by implication identifies a competitor or goods or services offered by a competitor'. The MCAD permits comparative advertising, as far as the

---

[8] Article 6 TMD. For a clarification of this provision see *Gillette v LA Laboratories* Case C-228/03 [2005] ETMR 67 and *Arsenal Football Club plc v Reed*, Case C-206/01 [2002] ECR I-10273, [2003] ETMR 19.

[9] Council Directive 84/450 of 10 September 1984 relating to the approximation of the laws, regulations and administrative provisions of the Member States concerning misleading advertising.

[10] In turn, this Directive has recently, to a very limited extent, been amended by Article 13 of Directive 2005/29 of 11 May 2005 concerning unfair business-to-consumer commercial practices in the internal market.

comparison is concerned,[11] provided that the following cumulative conditions are met:[12]

(a) the comparative advertisement is not misleading;
(b) it compares goods or services meeting the same needs or intended for the same purpose;
(c) it objectively compares one or more material, relevant, verifiable and representative features of those goods and services, which may include price;
(d) it does not create confusion in the market place between the advertiser and a competitor or between the advertiser's trade marks, trade names, other distinguishing marks, goods or services and those of a competitor;
(e) it does not discredit or denigrate the trade marks, trade names, other distinguishing marks, goods, services, activities, or circumstances of a competitor;
(f) for products with a designation of origin, it relates in each case to products with the same designation;
(g) it does not take unfair advantage of the reputation of a trade mark, trade name or other distinguishing marks of a competitor or of the designation of origin of competing products;
(h) it does not present goods or services as imitations or replicas of goods or services bearing a protected trade mark or trade name.

Although comparative advertising, including the fair use of another's trade mark, was now in principle allowed in all EU Member States, several of the criteria and definitions set out in the MCAD did not appear to be as clear as expected since, to the author's knowledge, on three[13] occasions since the coming into force of the MCAD, the European Court of Justice (ECJ) was called upon to give further guidance.

In essence, the ECJ was asked to give guidance on, among other things, the following issues:

• does comparative advertising require that the advertisement contains a comparison, or does a mere reference to a competitor suffice?

---

[11] This clause, which has triggered confusion, is intended to indicate that the advertisement also has to comply with all other advertising legislation. In other words, even if the advertisement is allowed according to the MCAD, it may well be impermissible for other reasons.

[12] Article 3a(1) MCAD.

[13] Fourth and fifth rulings are expected in the course of 2006/2007 (see the References for a preliminary ruling by the Brussels Commercial Court (Rechtbank van Koophandel) of 29 July 2004 in *Lidl Belgium GmbH & Co. KG v NV Etablissmenten Franz Colruyt*, Case C-356/04, 2004 [O.J.] C-273/12) and by the Brussels Court of Appeal by decision of 13 October 2005 in *De Lantsheer v Comite Interprofessionel du Vin de Champagne and Veuve Clicquot Ponsardin*, docket number 2005/6480, 2006 [O.J.] C-381/05.

- when does a comparative advertiser take unfair advantage of his competitor's reputation and does it matter whether the comparative advertisement is directed towards a specialised public or the public at large?
- can an advertiser compare two different branded products without mentioning the origin of the compared products? and
- can an advertiser randomly choose the products included in the (price) comparison?

These cases have become known as *Toshiba*, *Pippig* and *Karner*. The first two will be discussed further below. The relevance of the latter is limited in the context of this chapter since it deals with the permissibility of stricter national rules on *misleading* advertising and will therefore not be dealt with here. Two further pending cases will be discussed briefly where relevant.

4. TOSHIBA

The first case concerned a dispute before the Düsseldorf Landgericht, Germany, between the German companies Toshiba Europe GmbH (Toshiba Europe), a subsidiary of the Japanese Toshiba Corporation, and Katun.[14]

4.1 The Facts

Toshiba Europe, the official European distributor of Toshiba photocopiers, also distributed spare parts and consumable items for those photocopiers. In its advertisements and communications to customers, Toshiba Europe used particular model references, such as 'Toshiba 1340', in order to identify its different photocopier models. For the same purposes it also used distinguishing marks ('product descriptions') and each product had an order number or 'product number'.

Katun sold spare parts and consumable items which were suitable for use in, *inter alia*, Toshiba photocopiers. In its catalogues, Katun listed Toshiba spare parts and consumable items in categories of products specific to a group of particular models of Toshiba photocopiers: thus reference would be made to Katun product X for Toshiba photocopier 1340.

Each list of spare parts and consumable items was made up of four columns. The first, headed 'OEM ('Original Equipment Manufacturer') product number', contained Toshiba Europe's order number for the corresponding

---

[14]   Case 112/99, [2001] ECR I-7945.

product sold by Toshiba Europe; the second, headed 'Katun product number', contained Katun's order number; the third column a description of the product and the fourth referred to the number of the particular model or models for which the product was intended.

In proceedings before the Landgericht, Toshiba Europe complained solely of the fact that Katun's catalogues contained Toshiba Europe's own product numbers, appearing alongside Katun's product numbers. It did not object to the use of any Toshiba trade mark as such. Toshiba Europe contended that the indication of its own product number was not necessary in order to explain to customers the possible use of products offered by Katun in Toshiba products: Katun could have just referred to the corresponding models of Toshiba photo-copiers. By using Toshiba's OEM product numbers in its catalogues, Katun was taking unfair advantage of Toshiba's reputation.

Katun counter-argued that its advertising was directed exclusively at specialised traders, who were quite aware that the products offered were not those of the original manufacturers. Furthermore, in view of the large number of spare parts and consumable items involved in a photocopier model, a refer-ence to the OEM product number was objectively necessary in order to iden-tify the products. Katun contended that it could not indicate the actual product being compared if it could not use Toshiba Europe's product numbers and had to refer only to the corresponding photocopier model, there being numerous, mutually indistinguishable accessories and spare parts for different photo-copier models. Finally Katun argued that the parallel indication of Toshiba Europe's product number and the Katun product number allowed customers to compare the prices of the original manufacturer and those of a competing supplier, which the MCAD explicitly permitted.

4.2   The Findings of the ECJ

4.2.1   Does a comparative advertisement need a comparison?

The ECJ considered first whether the indications of the OEM product numbers referred to in Katun's catalogue, but allocated to the spare parts and consum-able items by Toshiba itself, should be regarded as comparative advertising. Toshiba Europe submitted that listing the product numbers alongside each other is merely a generalised assertion that the products are equivalent, not an objective comparison of material, relevant, verifiable and representative features of those products. Thus Katun's advertisement was not a comparative advertisement.

Toshiba Europe's argument was drawn from a contradiction in the text of the MCAD: the fulfilment of the eight conditions outlined in Article 3a MCAD admittedly only rendered comparative advertising lawful 'as far as the comparison is concerned'. Consequently, a narrow, literal interpretation of

Article 2(2a) MCAD, read in conjunction with Article 3a, would render unlawful *any reference* enabling a competitor, or the goods or services which he offers, to be identified in a representation which did not contain an actual *comparison* of those goods or services or of the persons offering them. Against this backdrop, the mere mention of Toshiba Europe's trade mark(s) or of the reference numbers of the models for which the spare parts and consumable items are manufactured (for example the Toshiba 1340) would have to be unlawful.[15]

The ECJ disagreed with this narrow interpretation of 'comparative advertising'. In its view Article 6(1)(c) TMD and the existing ECJ case law on trade marks[16] acknowledged that the use of another person's trade mark may be legitimate where it is necessary to inform the public of the nature or the intended purpose of the products or services offered, in particular as accessories or spare parts. A narrow, literal interpretation of the MCAD would therefore result in a contradiction with the TMD. For those reasons the ECJ decided that the TMD should prevail over the MCAD, holding that the conditions required for comparative advertising must be interpreted in the sense most favourable to it. It is thus irrelevant whether an advertiser's goods or services are actually compared with those of the competitor, it being sufficient for a representation to be made in any form which refers, even by implication, to a competitor or to the goods or services which he offers.[17] However, *Toshiba* teaches that, when a comparative advertisement is limited to a mere reference, the *BMW* criteria must be fulfilled: the reference should be necessary to inform the public of the nature or the intended purpose of the products or services. Applied to the present case, there is comparative advertising when the necessary specification of Toshiba's product numbers alongside those of Katun enabled the public to identify precisely Toshiba's products to which Katun's products corresponded.[18] Such an indication

---

[15]   As indicated earlier, Toshiba Europe did not contest Katun's use of such marks or reference numbers, but only the use of the product numbers.

[16]   *Bayerische Motorenwerke AG (BMW) and BMW Nederland BV v Deenik* Case C-63/97 [1999] ETMR 339, [1999] ECR I-905, paras 58 to 60. See also ECJ, 17 March 2005, Case C-228/03, *Gillette v LA Laboratories* and *Arsenal v Matthew Reed*, [2002] ECR I-10273.

[17]   The ECJ confirmed this principle in *Pippig*, discussed below (Case C-44/01, para. 35).

[18]   The Belgian Supreme Court recently held that such identification should not be 'instant'. According to this Court, there will be comparative advertising even when the consumer, after further research, identifies or recognises the competitor later on (Belgian Supreme Court, 29 April 2004, [2004] T.B.H. 981; for a critical comment, see K. Daele, 'Vergelijkende reclame : overzicht van rechtspraak (2002–2004)', [2005] TBH 746 (750)).

constitutes a positive statement that the two products have equivalent technical features, that is to say, a comparison of material, relevant, verifiable and representative features of the products within the meaning of Article 3a(1)(c) MCAD.

4.2.2   How to take unfair advantage of a competitor's trade mark or other 'distinguishing marks'?

(i) What is a 'distinguishing mark'?   Before considering whether Katun's use of Toshiba's product numbers took unfair advantage of Toshiba's reputation, the referring German Court first asked whether Toshiba Europe's OEM product numbers were 'distinguishing marks' which could be unfairly taken advantage of under Article 3a(1)(g) MCAD. Relying on its established case law,[19] the ECJ questioned whether product numbers used by an equipment manufacturer to identify spare parts and consumable items would in themselves, when used alone without an indication of the manufacturer's trade mark or the equipment for which the spare parts and consumable items are intended, be identified by the public as referring to the products manufactured by a particular undertaking:

> They are in fact combinations of numbers or of letters and numbers and it is questionable whether they would be identified as product numbers of an equipment manufacturer if they were not found, as in the present case, in a column headed 'OEM product number'. Likewise, it may be wondered whether those combinations would enable the manufacturer to be identified if they were not used in combination with his trade mark.[20]

The ECJ left this question for the national courts to determine case by case but reiterated that, in order to determine whether product numbers or the like amounted to 'distinguishing marks' within Article 3(1)(g) MCAD, account should be taken of the perception of an average individual who is reasonably well informed and reasonably observant and circumspect[21] as well as of the type of persons at whom the advertising is directed. In *Toshiba* those persons appeared to be specialist traders who were much less likely than final consumers to associate the reputation of the equipment manufacturer's products with those of the competing supplier.

---

[19]   *Lloyd Schuhfabrik Meyer* Case C-342/97 [1999] ECR I-3819, [1999] E.T.M.R. 690, para. 22.

[20]   *Toshiba*, para. 51.

[21]   The *Gut Springenheide* criterion (Case C-210/96, *Gut Springenheide GmbH v OKS*, [1998] ECR I-4657).

(ii) When does comparative advertising take unfair advantage of the reputation of a competitor's brand? Next the ECJ indicated that, even assuming that the OEM product numbers were 'distinguishing marks', an advertiser cannot simply be considered as taking unfair advantage of the reputation attached to a competitor's distinguishing marks if effective competition in the relevant market depends on a reference to those marks. In other words, the mere mention of OEM product numbers does not necessarily take unfair advantage of a competitor's reputation in them, if there be any.[22] Only in specific circumstances can a third party's use of a mark be considered to take unfair advantage of the distinctive character or the reputation of the mark or be detrimental to it, for example by giving the public a false impression of the relationship between the advertiser and the trade mark owner.[23]

In assessing the existence of an unfair advantage, the question was therefore: 'could the indication of Toshiba Europe's OEM product numbers alongside Katun's product numbers cause the public to associate Toshiba Europe, whose products were those identified, with Katun, in that the public might associate the reputation of Toshiba Europe's products with the products of Katun?'

In making that determination, the overall presentation of the advertising in issue must be considered.[24] In this instance the ECJ admitted that Katun would have difficulty in comparing its products with those of Toshiba Europe if it did not refer to the latter's product numbers, which facilitated rapid comparison between the products' prices. Furthermore, the ECJ, going deeply into the

---

[22]   The Court referred to the 15th recital of the MCAD preamble, which states that the use of a trade mark or distinguishing mark does not amount to trade mark infringement where it complies with the conditions laid down by the MCAD, the aim being solely to distinguish between the products and services of the advertiser and those of his competitor and thus to highlight its objectivity.

[23]   Case C-63/97 *BMW* [1999] ECR I-905, para. 40.

[24]   Such overall assessment is not always easy. The court has suggested that account be taken of whether (i) the 'distinguishing mark' is only one of several indications in the advertisement relating to the original manufacturer and his products or if it is the only one and (ii) of whether the mark of the competing supplier and the specific nature of his products are highlighted in such a way that (no) 'confusion or association' is possible between the manufacturer and the competing supplier or between their respective products. With regard to this latter parameter, it is not entirely clear how 'confusion' or 'association' relate to each other. In any event, in view of the existing case law of the ECJ (*SABEL v Puma* Case C-251/95 [1997] ECR I-6191, [1998] ETMR 1 and *Marca Mode v Adidas AG and Adidas Benelux BV* Case C-425/98 [2000] ECR I-4861, [2000] ETMR 561, a likelihood of association cannot suffice to render comparative advertising unlawful. It has been correctly pointed out by leading scholars that this would deprive comparative advertising as such of every meaning (see J. Stuyck, 'Concurreren, vergelijken, aanhaken: het kruispunt van het handelspraktijkenrecht met het merkenrecht', [2002] TBH 272 (277–278)).

facts of the case, found that the adduced examples of Katun's lists of spare parts and consumable items clearly evidenced that a distinction had been made between Katun and Toshiba Europe, so that no false impression was given concerning the origin of Katun's products.

5. PIPPIG

The second important case referred to the ECJ concerned a dispute before an Austrian court between the Austrian companies Pippig and Hartlauer.[25] Pippig marketed spectacles through three specialist opticians' shops which it operated in Linz. It obtained its supplies from around 60 different manufacturers and had a representative assortment of the collection of each of its suppliers. Hartlauer, a commercial company, had branches throughout Austria with optical shelves where two types of spectacles were sold. Hartlauer sold spectacles of little-known brands at low prices, these comprising the vast majority of Hartlauer's products. Hartlauer also sold spectacles of better-known brands. Unlike Pippig, Hartlauer did not obtain these spectacles directly from the suppliers of opticians, but acquired them outside normal distribution channels, particularly through parallel imports.

In 1997 Hartlauer circulated an advertising leaflet throughout Austria which contained various statements. First it stated that 52 price comparisons for spectacles carried out over six years had revealed a total price differential of 204 777 Austrian Shilling (ATS), or ATS 3900 on average per pair of spectacles, between the prices charged by Hartlauer and those of traditional opticians. The leaflet claimed in particular that, for a clear Zeiss lens,[26] opticians made a profit of 717 per cent. Secondly, the leaflet contained a direct comparison between the price of ATS 5785 charged by Pippig for Titanflex Eschenbach spectacles with Zeiss lenses and the price of ATS 2000 charged by Hartlauer for spectacles of the same model but with lenses of the Optimed brand.

The same price comparison was made in advertisements on various Austrian radio and television channels in which, by contrast with the advertising leaflet, it was not stated that the spectacles compared had lenses of different brands. Hartlauer's television advertisements showed Pippig's shop front, displaying the sign 'Pippig'.

The preparation of this comparative advertising campaign included the carrying out of a test purchase in which an employee of Hartlauer visited a

---

25 ECJ, 8 April 2003, Case C-44/01, [2003] ECR I-3095.
26 Zeiss is one of the most established high quality brands in the market.

Pippig shop and ordered Titanflex Eschenbach spectacles with Zeiss lenses. Those spectacles were then photographed. This photograph was used twice in the advertising leaflet distributed by Hartlauer: once to illustrate Pippig's offer for those spectacles and once to illustrate Hartlauer's offer for spectacles of the same model with Optimed lenses.

Pippig sued Hartlauer before the Austrian Oberster Gerichtshof, demanding that Hartlauer cease its comparative advertising campaign on the grounds that such advertising was (i) misleading and (ii) discrediting. It also sought damages against the defendants and the publication of the judgment at their expense.

5.1 Findings of the ECJ

5.1.1 What happens if comparative advertising is also misleading?

The first issue addressed by the Court concerned yet another difficulty in the text of the MCAD and related to the interpretation of Article 7(2) MCAD. Article 3a(1)(a) MCAD states that comparative advertising should not be 'misleading according to [. . .] Article 7(1)' MCAD. This provision (which was part of the original MAD) states that EU Member States may retain or adopt provisions ensuring more extensive protection, with regard to *misleading* advertising, for consumers, persons carrying on a trade, business, craft or profession, and the general public. This aspect of the MCAD was discussed in *Karner*, mentioned earlier.[27]

However, Article 7(2) of the MCAD, which was inserted by the amending Directive, provides that Article 7(1) MCAD does not apply to *comparative* advertising as far as the comparison is concerned. Thus a strange situation arose where one of the conditions required of comparative advertising, that is that it cannot be misleading (Article 3a(1)(a) MCAD), explicitly refers to a provision (Article 7(1) MCAD), which, by virtue of another provision (Article 7(2) MCAD), could not apply to comparative advertising.

The ECJ circumvented this anomaly as follows. Reiterating the principle set out in *Toshiba* that the conditions required of comparative advertising should be interpreted in the sense most favourable to it, the ECJ declared that stricter national provisions on protection against misleading advertising cannot be applied to comparative advertising as regards the form and content of the comparison.[28] The text of Article 7(2) left no room for different interpretations.

---

[27] Case C-71/02, *Herbert Karner Industrie-Auktionen GmbH/Troostwijk GmbH* [2004] ECR I-3025.

[28] The ECJ stipulated that there is no need to establish distinctions between the various elements of the comparison, that is statements concerning the advertiser's offer, statements concerning the competitor's offer and the relationship between those offers (§§36–37 of the ruling).

Although we appreciate the difficulty of the question referred to the ECJ, it is hard to see how this solution is to be applied in practice. In our opinion, there is no reason why misleading advertising should, at the national level, be treated more strictly outside of a comparison than in the context of a comparison. A better solution, as the Austrian Government suggested, may be to allow a stricter criterion of deception to be applied to Article 3a(1)(a) MCAD, but not to Article 3a(1)(b) to (h). The present interpretation may leave Article 3a(1)(a) devoid of any meaning.

5.1.2   Can an advertiser compare two different brands without mentioning the origin of the products compared?

The second major issue before the Court was the permissibility of a comparison of products of different brands where the names of the manufacturers, which are not identical, are not mentioned in the advertisement[29] (Hartlauer compared Pippig spectacles containing Zeiss lenses with identical Hartlauer spectacles containing Optimed lenses, without mentioning that the lenses were from different brands). At the outset the ECJ reiterated that an advertiser can, in principle, state the trade mark of a competitor in the context of comparative advertising.[30] The same applies to the reproduction of a competitor's logo as well as a picture of its shop front.[31] In this case, however, the ECJ went further, holding that the omission of a competitor's trade mark in an advertising message involving a comparison might deceive, or at least be capable of deceiving, the persons to whom it is addressed, thereby making it misleading within the meaning of Article 2(2) MCAD. The ECJ added that, where the brand name of the products may significantly affect the buyer's choice[32] and the comparison concerns rival products whose respective brand names differ

---

[29]   The original question of the referring Court was whether the comparison of the price of a brand-name product with the price of a no-name product of equivalent quality is permitted where the name of the manufacturer is not indicated. However, as both products in the main proceedings (that is Zeiss lenses and Optimed lenses) were branded products, the ECJ rephrased the question.

[30]   In support of this statement, the ECJ referred to the 14th recital of the MCAD preamble, Article 3a(1)(d), (e) and (g) MCAD and its earlier *Toshiba* ruling (para. 34).

[31]   Pippig had argued that it was not indispensable for Hartlauer to appear triumphantly before Pippig's shop and that depicting its shop front including its logo, in addition to citing its name, was discrediting within the meaning of Article 3a(1)(e) MCAD. This finding of the court has been criticised by legal scholars in that it does not comply with recital 15 of the Amending Directive (see K. Daele, 'Vergelijkende reclame: overzicht van rechtspraak (2002–2004)', [2005] TBH 746 (761)).

[32]   Referring to its earlier case law in *Estee Lauder* (Case C-220/98 [2000] ECR I-117, paras 27 and 30), the ECJ reiterated that the buyer's choice should be assessed against the backdrop of the presumed expectations of an average consumer who is reasonably well informed and reasonably observant and circumspect.

considerably in the extent to which they are known, omission of the better-known brand name *is* misleading and thus makes the comparative advertisement unlawful.[33]

Against this backdrop, it must be asked whether a comparative advertisement which refers to a famous type of product (for example 'Champagne'), is unlawful when this reference does not allow a specific competitor (for example one specific manufacturer of Champagne) or the goods he offers to be identified.[34]

Notwithstanding this, it was held irrelevant that the compared products had been acquired through different distribution channels, that is the one through an official distribution network, the other through parallel imports. On this point, the ECJ agreed with Hartlauer that spectacles of a given brand remained the same branded product, regardless of whether they were official or 'grey' products.[35]

Finally, contrary to Pippig's contentions, the ECJ found it equally irrelevant that, at the date of its test purchase, Hartlauer had not yet offered for sale the product that would subsequently be compared with the one involved in the test purchase. According to the ECJ, Article 3a MCAD does not preclude an advertiser from carrying out a test purchase with a competitor before his own offer has even commenced, provided all of the conditions for comparative advertising are met.

5.1.3 Which products or services should be included in the comparison?

The final question was whether a price comparison entails discrediting the competitor and is therefore unlawful for the purposes of Article 3a(1)(e)

---

[33]   The European Commission, in our opinion, quite rightly observed that there is nothing in the MCAD to prohibit the comparison of branded products with 'unbranded' (that is with a less known brand) ones (§33 of the ruling). However, in the case of spectacles for example, the fact that they have lenses of a famous brand might be a characteristic increasing their quality and thus their price. Therefore, the presence or absence of such lenses in the spectacles being compared for price should be mentioned in order to prevent the advertising from being misleading. This reasoning should probably apply to other products composed of multiple elements, for example cars, computers, and so on. See also the *Pippig* and *Toshiba* case note of J.G. Van Olst, 'Napraten over vergelijkende reclame' [2003] Mediaforum 186 (192).

[34]   This is one of the questions referred to the ECJ by the Brussels Court of Appeal in the ruling of 13 October 2005 in *De Lantsheer*.

[35]   In this context, Hartlauer also contended that comparative advertising concerning products of the same brand can, moreover, take place only between a parallel importer and an official distributor, since official distributors habitually comply with the sale prices recommended by manufacturers, thereby eliminating competition on price.

MCAD when the products are chosen in such a way as to obtain a price difference greater than the average price difference and/or the comparisons are
repeated continuously, creating the impression that the competitor's prices are
excessive. The ECJ took the view that comparing rival offers, particularly as
regards price, is in the very nature of comparative advertising. Price comparison cannot in itself therefore entail the discrediting or denigration of a
competitor who charges higher prices.

   The choice as to the number of comparisons which the advertiser wishes to
make between the products which he is offering and those offered by his
competitors falls within the exercise of his economic freedom. Any obligation
to restrict each price comparison to the average prices of the products offered
by the advertiser and those of rival products would be contrary to the objectives of the MCAD. However, the ECJ added, the main aim of comparative
advertising being to help demonstrate objectively the merits of the various
comparable products, such objectivity implies that the persons to whom the
advertising is addressed are *capable* of knowing the actual price differences
between the products compared and not merely the average difference
between the advertiser's prices and those of its competitors.

   Further questions with regard to the permissibility of global price comparisons have been referred to the ECJ by the Brussels Commercial Court in a
dispute between the supermarket chains Lidl and Colruyt.[36] Although Lidl's
claim in the main proceedings also concerned the alleged unfair advantage
obtained by Colruyt in using Lidl's trade mark and trade name in its advertisements, the questions referred to the ECJ only deal with Colruyt's statements that it is cheaper overall by reference to a price index.[37]

---

   [36]   Brussels Commercial Court, 29 July 2004, *Lidl Belgium GmbH*, VS 3722/
2004, unpublished.
   [37]   The five following (extensive) questions have been referred to the ECJ (2004
[O.J.] C-273/12):

   1. Must Article 3a(1)(a) MCAD be construed as meaning that the comparison of
       the general price level of advertisers with that of competitors, in which an
       extrapolation is made on the basis of a comparison of the prices of a sample of
       products, is impermissible inasmuch as this creates the impression that the
       advertiser is cheaper over its entire range of products, whereas the comparison
       made relates only to a limited sample of products, unless the advertisement
       makes it possible to establish which and how many products of the advertiser,
       on the one hand, and of the competitors used in the comparison, on the other,
       have been compared, and makes it possible to ascertain where each competitor
       concerned by the comparison is positioned in the comparison and what its prices
       might be in comparison with those of the advertiser and the other competitors
       used in the comparison?
   2. Must Article 3a(1)(b) MCAD be construed as meaning that comparative

6.   THE *CHAMPAGNE* CASE

In a recent decision of 13 October 2005 the Brussels Court of Appeal has stayed proceedings in a comparative advertising case brought before it and has, as indicated earlier, referred several questions to the European Court of Justice on the interpretation of the MCAD. The claim was initially brought by the Comité Interprofessionnel du vin de Champagne (CIVC) against a Belgian brewer. The CIVC controls the protected appellation of origin Champagne, the use of which is subject to stringent criteria.

The Belgian brewer marketed a beer, MALHEUR BRUT RESERVE. Both its packaging and its bottle were reminiscent of Champagne. In addition, the leaflet which was attached to the bottle's neck stated:

> Malheur Brut Réserve is an exclusive beer, with 11% alcohol volume. It has been bottled in the traditional 'Champagne bottle' ('bouteille champenoise') and, like the vineyards of Reims and Epernay, the brewer has succeeded in gathering the yeast close to the cork prior to removing the sediment during the traditional disgorgement ('dégorgement') and prior to installing the final cork. The end result is an exceptionally refined and elegant beer.

Furthermore, the brewer had referred to the beer as 'Champagne Beer' ('Bière Champenoise').

The court at first instance granted CIVC's claim that (i) the references to the geographical indication 'Reims-France', (ii) the mention 'La première bière brut au monde' (the first brut beer in the world), (iii) the mention

---

advertising is allowed only if the comparison relates to individual goods or services that meet the same needs or are intended for the same purpose, with the exclusion of product selections, even if those selections, on the whole and not necessarily in regards to every sub-division, meet the same needs or are intended for the same purpose?

3.   Must Article 3a(1)(c) MCAD be construed as meaning that comparative advertising in which a comparison of the prices of products, or of the general price level, of competitors is made will be objective only if it lists the products and prices of the advertiser and those of all the competitors in the comparison that are being compared and makes it possible to ascertain the prices being charged by the advertiser and its competitors, in which case all products used in the comparison must be expressly indicated for each individual supplier?

4.   Must Article 3a(1)(c) MCAD be construed as meaning that a feature in comparative advertising will satisfy the requirement of verifiability in that Article only if that feature can be verified as to its accuracy by those to whom the advertising is addressed, or is it sufficient if the feature can be verified by third parties to whom the advertising is not addressed?

5.   Must Article 3a(1)(c) MCAD be construed as meaning that the price of products and the general price level of competitors are in themselves verifiable features?

'Méthode traditionnelle', (iv) the mentions 'like the Champagne farmers of Reims and Epernay' and 'like the vineyards of Reims and Epernay', (v) the mention 'its acidity is obviously reminiscent of Champagne', (vi) the mention 'it's brewed like Champagne although it remains beer' and (vii) the denomination 'Champagne Beer' amounted to an unfair trade practice. The brewer appealed.

On appeal, CIVC reiterated that the brewer's practices were unfair because the reference to the process of 'dégorgement' asserts or suggests that the beer is endowed with qualities similar to the viticultural characteristics of this 'dégorgement' (and 'remuage'). Furthermore, in the commercialisation of the beer a context had been created which was traditionally used for the promotion and commercialisation of sparkling wines, in particular the use of the look and feel of a bottle closely resembling the bottle used for the commercialisation of Champagne. According to CIVC, this type of advertising amounted to comparative advertising within the meaning of Article 2(2a) MCAD. This comparative advertisement was misleading, subjective and took unfair advantage of the repute of the appellation of origin 'Champagne'.

The Court of Appeal has asked the ECJ for further clarification on the notion of 'identification'. In particular, it wonders whether, for a competitor to be identified, it is sufficient that a reference is made to a group of companies (the manufacturers of Champagnes). In addition, the court wants to know which criteria should be taken into account in order to determine the level of competition between the advertiser and the company/companies referred to as well as the criteria to determine the substitutability of their products.

7.   CONCLUSION

The co-existence of trade mark law and the provisions on comparative advertising has proved to be a fine balancing act, which is not always easy to apply in practice. The harmonisation tools offered in the MCAD have often not been as helpful as one may have expected: five out of eight cumulative conditions required for comparative advertising to be lawful as well as the definition of comparative advertising itself have needed (or will need: see *Colruyt/Lidl* and *Champagne*) further interpretative guidance from the highest European Court.

Mentioning a competitor's trade mark in a comparative advertisement amounts to actionable 'trade mark use'. However, provided that all conditions required for a comparative advertisement are met, comparative advertising will give the advertiser due cause to use a competitor's trade mark, regardless of the fame or repute of that trade mark.[38]

---

[38]   'The protection of well-known marks in the European Union, Canada and the

It follows from *Toshiba* that such use will not be considered as taking an unfair advantage of a competitor's trade mark or other 'distinguishing marks'. The MCAD expressly allows the use of a third party's trade mark, trade name or other distinguishing marks – such as logos and shop fronts – in comparative advertising because it helps consumers identify the goods or services of the advertiser's competitor and thus enhances competition in the internal market. Such use is admittedly exempted from trade mark infringement only inasmuch as it is *solely* intended to distinguish and thus to highlight objectively the differences between the products or services of the advertiser and those of the third party competitor.[39] Use which goes beyond this intention may still amount to trade mark infringement. The fact that the advertisement is directed at a specialised public may make an infringement less likely.

Furthermore, it follows from *Pippig* that the use of a third party's (better known) trade mark may even be necessary, when its omission causes the comparative advertisement to be misleading. This will, in particular, be the case when the omitted brand name is better-known and may significantly affect the buyer's choice.

Finally, the *Toshiba* and *Pippig* rulings have made it clear that no actual comparison between an advertiser and his competitor or their respective products is needed for there to be comparative advertising. It is sufficient to make a representation which refers, even by implication, to a competitor or to the goods or services which he offers and which allows the consumer to recognise the competitor. However, it also follows from the ECJ's reference in *Toshiba* to its *BMW* ruling that, when the comparative advertisement does not contain a comparison as such, but merely a reference, such reference should be (i) necessary and (ii) used in accordance with honest practices in industrial and commercial matters.[40]

In *Champagne* the ECJ will need to clarify whether it is sufficient that an advertisement contains a reference to a type of product (for example Champagne) to claim that each of the companies offering or manufacturing this type of product has been identified.

In brief, comparative advertising is intended to benefit the consumer, not to

---

Middle East. A Country and Regional Analysis', prepared by the International Trademark Association ('INTA'), October 2004, para. 4.2(g) (available at http://www.inta.org/membersonly/downloads/ref_protection.pdf).

[39]   15th recital of the Amending Directive's preamble.

[40]   Paras 33–34 of *Toshiba*. See also the comments of leading Benelux commentator J. Stuyck, 'Concurreren, vergelijken, aanhaken : het kruispunt van het handelspraktijkenrecht met het merkenrecht' [2002] TBH 272 (277); see also the *Arsenal* and *Gillette* rulings, discussed elsewhere in this book.

harm a competitor unnecessarily. When a comparative advertisement does not mislead, deceive or confuse the consumer and if it does not discredit, disparage, denigrate or dilute a competitor's brand, comparative advertising is a welcome means of enhancing competition in the market place.

6. Use of trade marks on repackaged and relabelled pharmaceutical goods

Christian Schumacher

1. INTRODUCTION

Parallel imports of repackaged or relabelled pharmaceutical goods have provided the basis for a multitude of court proceedings in the EU Member States, in some of which the legal issues were referred to the European Court of Justice (ECJ) for a preliminary ruling. The now-settled case-law of the ECJ involving such cases provides an example of situations where the exclusive right of a trade mark owner to control the sale of trade marked goods is limited in order to ascertain that the free movement of goods between EU Member States is not prohibited.

Just as with other goods, the reason for parallel imports of pharmaceutical products is that significant price differences exist between EU Member States. Germany, Austria and Denmark have been identified in litigation as countries in which certain pharmaceutical products were sold for a significantly higher price than in the United Kingdom, France, Portugal, Spain or Greece. In the pharmaceutical market such price differences may result either from different price schemes applied by the trade mark owner for sales to different Member States or from factors over which trade mark owners have no control, such as divergent rules between the Member States as to the fixing of maximum prices, the profit margins of pharmaceutical wholesalers and pharmacies or the maximum amount of medical expenses which may be reimbursed under sickness insurance schemes.[1]

However, while products such as clothing, perfume or the like can very often simply be purchased in one Member State and resold in another Member State without any alteration, the free movement of pharmaceutical products is often hindered by specific national requirements imposed by Member States upon the sale of pharmaceutical products. Sales in different Member States may have to comply with different labelling requirements, in particular as to

---

[1]   *Bristol-Myers Squibb and others*, Cases C-427/93, C-429/93 & C-436/93, [1996] ECR 3457, [1996] ETMR 1, para. 46.

the language in which the labelling must be printed. Besides, other factors, even consumer expectations, might affect the practical ability of a parallel importer to resell pharmaceutical products, purchased in a low price country, at a profit in a high price country.

It is the declared goal of the legal regime of the European Union to overcome any artificial obstacles to the free movement of goods between EU Member States. Based on that goal, the concept of *exhaustion* of trade mark rights in Article 7(1) of the Trade Mark Directive provides for a general principle of the unrestricted resale within Europe of original goods that were first marketed within the European Economic Area (EEA).[2] As an exception to this general rule, Article 7(2) of the same Directive allows the trade mark owner to prohibit the resale of original goods if there are 'legitimate reasons' to oppose that resale, *inter alia* if the condition of the resold goods has been changed and the condition of the goods as resold does not therefore correspond to the condition under which the trade mark owner had originally chosen to market the product. The product in such a case will no longer be viewed as having been authorized for sale by the trade mark owner. Such sale may be prohibited by the trade mark owner in order to protect the identity of origin of all of the products sold under the mark.[3]

2. TYPICAL FACT SCENARIOS

Changes affecting the packaging of pharmaceutical goods in practice range from the creation of multi-packs, in which original packaging is tied together, and the overstickering of the original packaging, to wholly new external packaging into which the original inner packaging (blister packs, ampoules, and so on) is inserted (often called 'reboxing'). The original mark may be printed on new external packaging, or holes or transparent openings may allow the end user to see the trade mark that has been applied to the inner packaging. Sometimes the original trade mark is replaced with the mark used by the manufacturer in the country of importation; sometimes too the generic name is shown instead of the original mark. Translated information will usually be provided, in particular user information inserted in the language of the target market.

---

[2] Comprising the 25 EU Member States plus Iceland, Liechtenstein and Norway. For a case involving repackaging of a pharmaceutical product obtained within the EEA in Norway, see EFTA Court, 8 July 2003, E-3/02 – *Paranova*.

[3] See further Urlesberger, 'Legitimate Reasons for the Proprietor of a Trade Mark Registered in the EU to Oppose further Dealings in the Goods after They have been Put on the Market for the First Time', CML Rev. 1999, 1195.

Repackaging or relabelling is, however, not confined to pharmaceutical products. The original manufacturers of other products, for example alcoholic beverages, are also confronted with parallel imports of original products, of which the packaging has been altered. In *Loendersloot v Ballantine and others*[4] alcoholic drinks, particularly whisky, from which labels the identification numbers and the name of the importer approved by Ballantine had been removed, were parallel imported and then resold. In that case the ECJ applied the same legal standards as will be outlined below for pharmaceutical products, but with certain exceptions, which will be addressed when discussing their respective requirements.

3.   REQUIREMENTS FOR LAWFUL REPACKAGING AND RELABELLING

Where a change of the packaging is necessary for the resale of original products obtained in one Member State in another Member State, the fundamental freedom of movement of goods in the EU collides with another fundamental right, the right of protection of the industrial property of the trade mark owner. Article 30 EC allows derogations from the free movement of goods (Article 28 EC) only to the extent to which such exceptions are justified for the purpose of safeguarding the rights which constitute the specific subject-matter of the industrial property concerned. In relation to trade marks, regard must be had to the essential function of the trade mark, which is to guarantee the identity of the origin of the trade marked product to the consumer or ultimate user, by enabling him without any possibility of confusion to distinguish that product from products which have another origin. This guarantee of origin means that the consumer or ultimate user can be certain that a trade marked product which is sold to him has not been subject at a previous stage of marketing to interference by a third person, without the authorization of the proprietor of the trade mark, such as to affect the original condition of the product.[5]

On the other hand, the trade mark owner will not be allowed to exercise this right in such a manner as to constitute a disguised restriction on trade between Member States within the meaning of the second sentence of Article 30 EC. As the ECJ has pointed out, such a restriction might arise, *inter alia*, when the trade mark proprietor puts on to the market in various Member States an identical

---

[4]   *Loendersloot (Frits) v George Ballantine & Son*, Case C-349/95 [1998] ETMR 10, ECR I-6227.
[5]   *Hoffmann-La Roche*, Case C-102/77 [1978] ECR 1139, para. 7; *Boehringer Ingelheim and others*, Case C-143/00 [2002] ECR I-3759, [2002] ETMR 78, para. 12.

product in various packages while availing himself of his trade mark rights in order to prevent repackaging by a third person even if it were done in such a way that the identity of origin of the trade marked product and its original condition could not be affected.[6]

This is how Article 7 of the EU Trade Mark Directive is to be interpreted: ECJ case-law under Article 30 EC must be taken as the basis for determining whether a trade mark owner may oppose the marketing of products, which bear the trade mark but where the packaging has been changed, under Article 7(2) of the Trade Mark Directive.[7]

3.1 First Requirement: no Artificial Partitioning of the Markets between Member States

It is the goal of ECJ case-law on Article 30 EC to stop the trade mark owner exercising his trade mark rights in such a way that the markets between EU Member States would be *artificially partitioned*. The trade mark owner would artificially partition markets between Member States if he were to use his trade mark rights to prevent changes in the packaging even if those changes were *necessary in order to market the product in the Member State of importation.*[8] It does not matter whether the trade mark owner *intended* to partition the market artificially or not. What matters is whether his use of his trade mark rights serves to safeguard the essential function of the trade mark.[9]

Where the trade mark owner uses different trade marks in the Member State of origin and in the Member State of importation, even the *replacement of the trade mark* may be necessary in order to market the product in the Member State of importation.[10]

When is a change in the packaging *necessary* to market the product in the Member State of importation?

- When it enables *effective access* to the markets of the importing Member State.[11]
- When the size of the packet used by the owner in the Member State

---

[6]   *Hoffmann-La Roche*, para. 9.

[7]   *Bristol-Myers Squibb*, para. 41.

[8]   *Bristol-Myers Squibb*, para. 56; ECJ, 11 July 1996, Joined Cases C-71/94, C-72/94 and C-73/94, para. 46 – *Eurim-Pharm*; ECJ, 11 July 1996, Case C-232/94, para. 28 – *MPA Pharma*.

[9]   *Bristol-Myers Squibb*, para. 57; *Eurim-Pharm*, para. 47; *MPA Pharma*, para. 29.

[10]   *Pharmacia & Upjohn SA v Paranova A/S*, Case C-379/97 [1999] ETMR 937, paras 37–39.

[11]   *Pharmacia & Upjohn*, para. 43.

where the importer purchased the product cannot be marketed by reason of a rule authorizing packaging only of a certain size, a national practice to the same effect, sickness insurance rules making the reimbursement of medical expenses depend on the size of the packaging, or well-established medical prescription practices based, *inter alia*, on standard sizes recommended by professional groups and sickness insurance institutions.[12]

- When a trade mark is replaced and the rules or practices in the importing Member State prevent the product in question from being marketed under its trade mark in the exporting Member State, for example where it is prohibited as being misleading the consumers.[13]

- When there exists on a market, or on a substantial part of it, a *strong resistance from* a significant proportion of *consumers to relabelled pharmaceutical products.*[14]

When is a change in the packaging *not necessary*?

- When the importer is able to achieve packaging which may be marketed by, for example, affixing to the original external or inner packaging new labels in the language of the Member State of importation, or by adding new user instructions or information in the language of the Member State of importation[15] or by replacing an additional article not capable of gaining approval in the Member State of importation with a similar article that has obtained such approval.[16]

- When the change in the packaging is explicable *solely* by the parallel importer's attempt to secure a *commercial advantage.*[17]

3.2 Second Requirement: no Adverse Effect to the Original Condition of the Product

The ECJ made clear that the original condition of the *product inside the*

---

[12] *Bristol-Myers Squibb*, para. 53; *Eurim-Pharm*, para. 43; *MPA Pharma*, para. 25. This is always to be seen in relation to the specific market for the product, thus if different target groups in the Member State of importation require different package sizes, repackaging into all the respective sizes would be necessary – see *Bristol-Myers Squibb*, para. 54; *Eurim-Pharm*, para. 44; *MPA Pharma*, para. 26.

[13] *Pharmacia & Upjohn*, para. 43; for an early case of relabelling see ECJ, 10 October 1978, Case C-3/78 – *Centrafarm*.

[14] ECJ April 23, 2002, Case C-443/99, para. 31 – *Merck, Sharp & Dohme*; *Boehringer Ingelheim*, para. 52.

[15] *Bristol-Myers Squibb*, para. 55; *Eurim-Pharm*, para. 45; *MPA Pharma*, para. 27.

[16] *Bristol-Myers Squibb*, para. 55.

[17] *Pharmacia & Upjohn*, para. 44.

packaging is decisive. If the repackaging is carried out under conditions which cannot affect the original condition of the product inside the packaging, the essential function of the trade mark as a guarantee of origin is safeguarded. In such a case the consumer or end user actually receives products manufactured under the sole supervision of the trade mark owner.[18]

The trade mark owner may therefore oppose any repackaging involving a risk of the product inside the package being exposed to tampering or to influences affecting its original condition.[19] This risk must be assessed in the light of the nature of the product and the method of repackaging.[20]

The following are circumstances which are *not* capable of affecting the original condition of a pharmaceutical product:

- the trade mark owner has placed the product on the market in *double packaging* and the repackaging affects only the external layer, leaving the inner packaging intact[21] (for example the mere removal of blister packs, flasks, phials, ampoules or inhalers and their replacement in new external packaging).[22]
- the repackaging is carried out under the supervision of a public authority in order to ensure that the product remains intact.[23]
- in principle (but see below), only self-adhesive labels are applied to original external or inner packaging, or new user instructions or information in the language of the Member State of importation or an extra article, such as a spray, are added from a source other than the trade mark owner.[24]
- it is impossible for any isolated error (for example the misgrouping of blister packs with different use-by dates, overtime storage, damage of light-sensitive products by light during repackaging) to confer on the trade mark owner the right to oppose any repackaging of pharmaceutical products in new external packaging.[25]

---

[18]   *Bristol-Myers Squibb*, para. 67.
[19]   *Bristol-Myers Squibb*, para. 59; *Eurim-Pharm*, paras 48–49; *MPA Pharma*, paras 30–31.
[20]   *Hoffmann-La Roche*, para. 10.
[21]   Ibid.
[22]   *Bristol-Myers Squibb*, para. 61; see also   *Eurim-Pharm*, para. 51; *MPA Pharma*, para. 33.
[23]   *Bristol-Myers Squibb*, para. 60; *Eurim-Pharm*, para 50; *MPA Pharma*, para. 32; *Hoffmann-La Roche*, para. 10.
[24]   *Bristol-Myers Squibb*, para. 64; *Eurim-Pharm*, para. 55; *MPA Pharma*, para. 36.
[25]   *Bristol-Myers Squibb*, para. 63; see also *Eurim-Pharm*, paras 52–53; *MPA Pharma*, paras 34–35.

However, the original condition of a product inside a packaging might for example be *indirectly affected* in the following situations:

- the external or inner packaging of the repackaged product, or a new set of user instructions or information, omits certain important information or gives *inaccurate information* concerning the nature, composition, effect, use or storage of the product.[26]
- an extra article inserted into the packaging by the importer and designed for the ingestion and dosage of the product does not comply with the method of use and the doses envisaged by the manufacturer.[27]
- the packaging of the repackaged product is not such as to give the product adequate protection.[28]

3.3 Third Requirement: Identification of Repacking and the Person Responsible for Repackaging

As the main issue is to protect the identification of origin by the trade mark of the manufacturer, the ECJ has always required that the importer states on the packaging that the product has been repackaged by him.[29] In particular, where the parallel importer has added an extra article from a source other than the trade mark owner, he must ensure that it is correctly indicated in such a way as to dispel any impression that the trade mark owner is responsible for it.[30]

The indication of repackaging must be

- clearly shown on the external packaging of the repackaged product;
- printed in such a way as to be understood by a person with normal eyesight, exercising a normal degree of attentiveness;[31]
- with a clear indication as to who manufactured the product.[32]

---

[26]   *Bristol-Myers Squibb*, para. 65; *Eurim-Pharm*, para. 56; *MPA Pharma*, para. 37.

[27]   *Bristol-Myers Squibb*, para. 65.

[28]   *Eurim-Pharm*, para. 56.

[29]   *Hoffmann-La Roche*, para. 12.

[30]   *Bristol-Myers Squibb*, para. 73.

[31]   *Bristol-Myers Squibb*, para. 71; *Eurim-Pharm*, para. 62; *MPA Pharma*, para. 43.

[32]   To further avoid that the end user would be led to believe that the importer would be the owner of the trade mark and that the product was manufactured under his supervision; *Bristol-Myers Squibb*, para. 74; *Eurim-Pharm*, para. 64; *MPA Pharma*, para. 45.

In the *Loendersloot* whisky case, in which the parallel importer only removed
the identification numbers and the name of the approved importer, the court
expressly did not require the identification of relabelling and the person
responsible for it. The ECJ indicated that this followed from the fact that the
trade was outside the area of pharmaceutical products, also having regard to
the nature of the action of the importer.[33]

3.4   Fourth Requirement: No Damage to the Reputation of the Trade Mark

The interest of the trade mark owner must be safeguarded to the extent that the
reputation of his trade mark, and consequently his reputation, will not suffer
from inappropriate presentation of the repackaged product, since the product
originates from him and bears his trade mark. Even though the fact that the
product has been repackaged must be stated on the package, it is likely that
consumers will associate the presentation of the product with the original trade
mark owner. ·

Thus the ECJ acknowledges a legitimate interest of the trade mark owner
in being able to oppose the marketing of a repackaged product, if the reputation of the trade mark and thus its owner may suffer from

- an inappropriate presentation of the repackaged product. In assessing
  whether the presentation is liable to damage the reputation of the trade
  mark, account must be taken of the nature of the product and the market
  for which it is intended,[34] since pharmaceutical products are in a sensitive area in which the public is particularly demanding as to the quality
  and integrity of the product;
- a defective, poor quality or untidy packaging has been held to have the
  potential to damage the trade mark's reputation.[35] This will, however,
  depend on whether the product is sold to hospitals or to consumers.
  Even though, in the case of prescription drugs, the prescription by a
  doctor may itself give consumers some degree of confidence in the quality of the product, the presentation of the product is of greater importance to the consumer, who purchases the product in a pharmacy. On the
  other hand, according to the ECJ, the presentation of the product will be
  of little importance to professionals who administer the products sold to
  hospitals and to patients;[36]

---

[33]   *Loendersloot*, paras 47–49.
[34]   *Bristol-Myers Squibb*, para. 75; *Eurim-Pharm*, para. 65; *MPA Pharma*, para. 46.
[35]   *Bristol-Myers Squibb*, para. 76; *Eurim-Pharm*, para. 66; *MPA Pharma*, para. 47.
[36]   *Bristol-Myers Squibb*, para. 77; *Eurim-Pharm*, para. 67; *MPA Pharma*, para. 48.

- a use of distinctive design features of the original packaging on a new packaging, which could also form a 'legitimate reason' for the trade mark owner to oppose sale of the imported product, if there would be a risk of confusion as to a connection between the parties (affiliation or special relationship).[37]

3.5 Additional Requirement: Notice and Provision of a Sample to the Trade Mark Owner

As long ago as in *Hoffmann-La Roche* the ECJ required that the importer give the proprietor of the trade mark prior notice of the sale of the repackaged product.[38] The owner may also require the importer to supply him with a specimen of the repackaged product before it goes on sale. The trade mark owner is thus enabled to check that the repackaging meets the requirements set out above. According to the ECJ, this requirement also affords the trade mark owner a better possibility of protecting himself against counterfeiting.[39]

In the fairly recent *Boehringer Ingelheim* ruling, the requirements for prior notice were developed further:

- the parallel importer itself must give notice to the trade mark owner;[40]
- a reasonable time must be allowed for the trade mark owner to react to the intended packaging, considering also the parallel importer's interest in proceeding to the market as soon as possible.[41]

However, in *Loendersloot,* a case concerning relabelling of whisky, the ECJ stated that the trade being outside the area of pharmaceutical products, and having regard to the nature of the action of the importer, the interests of the trade mark owner (in particular his need to combat counterfeiting) would have been given sufficient weight as long as he receives notice even without a specimen.[42]

---

[37] See EFTA Court July 8, 2003, E-3/02, para. 53 – *Paranova.*

[38] *Hoffmann-La Roche,* para. 12.

[39] *Bristol-Myers Squibb,* para. 78; *Eurim-Pharm,* para. 69; *MPA Pharma,* para. 49.

[40] Notice by other sources, such as the authority which issues a parallel import license to the importer, is not sufficient; *Boehringer Ingelheim,* para. 64.

[41] *Boehringer Ingelheim,* para. 66; in the following paragraph the ECJ found a period of 15 working days reasonable under the specific circumstances and when the parallel importer simultaneously supplied a sample of the repackaged product.

[42] *Loendersloot,* paras 47–49.

4. OPEN ISSUES

In June 2004 the Court of Appeals (England and Wales) made reference to the
ECJ for a preliminary ruling on a number of issues, in particular:

- who bears the burden of proving that the new packaging complies with
  each of the conditions set out in the ECJ case-law?
- does the necessity requirement have to be shown not only as regards the
  repackaging in itself, but also as regards the presentation of the new
  packaging?[43]
- does 'de-branding' (where the original trade mark is not affixed to the
  new exterior packaging) or 'co-branding' (where the importer applies
  his own logo or get-up to the new exterior packaging) damage the reputation of the trade mark of the manufacturer?
- do the five requirements also apply for overstickered products?
- issues concerning certain effects of a failure to comply with the notice
  requirement.

This case is currently pending before the ECJ.[44]

---

[43] See also the pending reference to the ECJ of May 2005 by the Austrian
Supreme Court, Case C-276/05.
[44] Case C-348/04.

7. Controlling third party use at the border

Luca Giove

1. INTRODUCTION

Multinational companies seek to protect their business by preventing the parallel importation of their goods from countries where the goods are released in the market at lower prices (sometimes being of lower quality). Such protection is sought through trade mark law and in particular through infringement actions against parallel importers. Within the European Economic Area (EEA) this right is removed, as a result of the combination of the two principles of exhaustion and the single market. However, trade mark holders can block at the borders of the EEA the parallel importation of goods from countries elsewhere in the world by virtue of trade mark protection.[1]

Parallel importation, a concept well known to IP lawyers, is subject to a number of decisions both at European Court of Justice (ECJ) and national level, as well as to academic debate. However there are grey areas which still require further exploration. In particular there are commercial activities carried out by third parties, which are similar to but do not fall within the scope of the traditional definition of parallel importation and the lawfulness of which is uncertain. These areas include the mere transit of, or transit trade (that is transactions in non-Community goods which have not completed import formalities and have not therefore been formally imported into the Community) in genuine branded non-Community goods in the EEA, as well as collateral activities such as warehousing, when their final destination lies outside the EEA.

---

[1]   Applicability of the so-called 'international exhaustion' principle was held inadmissible under the Trade Marks Directive in *Silhouette International Schmied GmbH & Co. KG v Hartlauer Handelsgessellschaft mbH* Case C-355/96 [1998] ECR I-4799, [1998] ETMR 539. A leading Italian case is Corte Cassazione, 18 November 1998, no. 11603 *Jolka-Colgate Palmolive* published in *Giurisprudenza Annotata di Diritto Industriale* 1998, no. 3740.

This chapter addresses this issue at Community level,[2] taking into account in particular the recent case of *Class International BV v Unilever NV and Others*,[3] for which an opinion of Advocate General Jacobs was delivered on 26 May 2005 and the ruling of the ECJ was issued on 18 October 2005.

2. THE TRADE MARKS DIRECTIVE

From a legal standpoint, assessment of the lawfulness of the transit of trade mark protected through the EEA involves identifying the scope of the rights granted to trade mark owners under the Trade Marks Directive.[4] This assessment also requires identifying the exact meaning of 'transit activities', a term employed by EU customs legislation.

The content of the exclusive rights granted to trade mark proprietors is identified by Article 5 of the Trade Marks Directive:

> The proprietor shall be entitled to prevent all third parties not having his consent from using in the course of trade: (a) any sign which is identical with the trade mark in relation to goods or services which are identical with those for which the trade mark is registered; [. . .].

Article 5 also sets out a non-exhaustive list of activities that amount to use in the course of trade and that third parties may not perform. Among these activities, the following are particularly relevant to this chapter: (i) 'offering the goods, or putting them on the market or stocking them for these purposes under that sign [. . .]' and (ii) 'importing or exporting the goods under the sign'.

Decontextualising these rules and reading them independently of the entire corpus of rules applicable to trade marks, one might think that their construction did not raise any issue. At first glance, Article 5 provides for an absolute and exclusive right of the trade mark proprietor to use a trade mark 'in the course of trade' for goods or services identical with those for which the trade mark is registered, specifying certain activities. This is not, however, the case: the legislature has created a list of activities from which

---

    [2]   Although the questions referred to the ECJ were raised in reference to the EEA, the Court ruled only in respect of the Community arguing that Regulation 40/94 and the Customs Code were not applicable to the EEA (paras 23–27).

    [3]   [2006] ETMR 11.

    [4]   First Council Directive 89/104 of 21 December 1988. Article 9 of Council Regulation 40/94 of 20 December 1993 on the Community trade mark confers the same protection on proprietors of a Community trade mark.

third parties are excluded for the sake of avoiding misunderstandings as to the contents of trade mark proprietors' rights. The meaning of 'using in the course of trade' is unclear and Article 5, like any other rule of law, both raises doubts and requires interpretation.

3. A DEFINITION OF EXTERNAL ACTIVITIES

External transit is a procedure under which goods are 'imported from a non-member country and pass through one or more Member States before being exported to another non-member country',[5] those goods being exempted from import duties and other charges. The most relevant activity relating to external transit is customs warehousing, which enables importers to store imported goods temporarily, when the final manner of disposal of the goods remains unknown at the time of importation (in other words it is not known whether they will be re-exported outside the Community or released into it, in which latter case import duties will be payable). Further, while maintaining their status of non-Community goods and therefore being 'in transit', such goods may be traded between different dealers, regardless of whether those traders are established in Member States).

4. DOUBTS ABOUT THE INTERPRETATION OF ARTICLE 5 OF THE TRADE MARKS DIRECTIVE

Activities that do not involve the entry of goods into the Community are not 'relevant' under customs legislation. However, if one considers trade mark law and the terminology of Article 5 of the Trade Marks Directive of 'using in the course of trade', one might be led to think that external transit, customs warehousing and external trade are 'relevant' in that they may not be performed by third parties. Indeed, as mentioned, the meaning of 'using in the course of trade' could be construed very broadly by considering it to be inclusive of all commercial and professional use of a trade mark occurring within the territory of the Community.

---

[5]   ECJ decision in *Polo/Lauren Company* Case C-383/98 [2000] ECR I-2519, [2000] ETMR 535, para. 34.

5.   CLASS INTERNATIONAL BV V UNILEVER NV AND OTHERS[6]

A broad interpretation of Article 5(1) was given by two companies of the leading multinational group GSK SmithKline, Beecham plc (SKB) and Beecham
Group plc (Beecham), in a recent case referred to the ECJ from a Dutch court
and decided by the ECJ on 18 October 2005. SKB and Beecham owned registered Community and Benelux figurative trade marks for the word
AQUAFRESH, depicting in red, white and blue a stylised strip of toothpaste.
Class International BV (Class), a Dutch company, sourced containers of
AQUAFRESH toothpaste from South Africa and shipped them to Rotterdam
in the Netherlands, where the containers were stored in a warehouse.

In March 2002 those containers were detained by the Dutch customs
authorities on the application of SKB and Beecham on suspicion of their being
counterfeit, but it later became clear that the goods were genuine (having been
manufactured under licence in South Africa). However, Class failed to obtain
their release by the President of the Rechtbank of Rotterdam and an issue arose
as to whether storing non-EEA sourced genuine branded goods in the territory
of a Member State under EU customs procedure amounted to use of a trade
mark in the course of trade which third parties were not able to perform under
Article 5.

6.   THE QUESTIONS REFERRED TO THE ECJ

The Regional Court of Appeal of the Hague sought guidance on this issue
from the ECJ. That court asked (a) whether bringing into the EEA, in the
context of external transit procedures, non-Community goods bearing a
genuine trade mark, storing such goods in a Member State's warehouse or
offering for sale or selling the goods so stored (in all cases without the
consent of the trade mark proprietor and therefore without the possibility of
applying the exhaustion doctrine) should be regarded as falling within the
scope of Article 5(1) and (b) upon which of the parties the burden of proof
rests as regards trade mark infringement proceedings arising out of such
activities.

---

[6]   According to the available information, Colgate-Palmolive Company and
Unilever NV were not part of the proceedings before the ECJ because Class discontin-
ued the Dutch proceedings *vis-à-vis* those defendants.

7. THE INTERESTS OF TRADE MARK PROPRIETORS AND AN ASSESSMENT OF ENFORCEABILITY

A possible starting point for an answer may be found in the reasons why trade mark proprietors would seek to assert their rights in relation to the trade activities involving non-Community goods when they occur within the Community. The reasons may be in principle twofold. First, trade mark proprietors may seek to prevent such activities simply because they want to block trade in non-Community goods destined for countries outside the Community, by means of trade mark protection. Secondly, trade mark proprietors may wish to prevent such activities because they are worried that non-Community goods will be eventually released into the Community market where, as we have seen, applicable laws allow them to prevent such release.

With regard to the interest of trade mark owners in blocking trade directed towards non-Member States, it is necessary to assess whether, under the Trade Mark Directive, such interest is granted protection at all and whether there are other interests that are capable of being affected by transit procedures.

With regard to the interest of trade mark proprietors in preventing unauthorised release of the goods in the Community market, it is certain that the Trade Mark Directive grants protection. However, since external transit activities do not *per se* amount to a release in the Community market,[7] those activities may only be prohibited to the extent that they *always* carry with them a risk that the branded goods are put into free circulation in the Community.

8. BLOCKING TRADE DIRECTED TOWARDS NON-MEMBER STATES: THE ADVOCATE GENERAL'S OPINION

In the absence of specific provisions on transit activities, one must examine whether there are functions of the trade mark, protected under the Trade Mark Directive, which reflect this concern of trade mark proprietors and are therefore capable of being affected by transit procedures (thus justifying limitations upon free trade).

That approach was followed by Advocate General Jacobs in rendering his opinion. As to the first question, he reasoned as follows. Article 5(1) is actionable by the trade mark proprietor when the use of the mark by a third party affects, or is liable to affect, the functions of the trade mark and in particular the essential function of guaranteeing to consumers the origin of goods, as was

---

7   As was pointed out also by the ECJ in *Class* (paras 42 and 43).

held in *Arsenal.*[8] Consequently the proprietor is entitled to prohibit the use of the trade mark when the use affects his own interests as proprietor of the trade mark, having regard to its functions. The essential function cannot be compromised solely by the fact that goods genuinely bearing that mark are subject to the external transit procedure and/or stored in a warehouse and/or are offered for sale or sold (as long as such goods retain their status as non-Community goods), because in all such cases the goods are not in free circulation within the Community. In this context, the Advocate General did not regard as crucial the specific mention of 'importing', 'stocking' and 'offering for sale' within the non-exhaustive list of activities which may be prohibited to third parties under Article 5(3)(b) and (c), this being consistent with the interpretative focus on the function(s) of trade marks.

The ECJ, on the other hand, did not adopt this approach but – consistently with it – noted: 'The putting on the market in the Community of goods coming from a third country is subject to their release for free circulation within the meaning of Article 24 EC'.[9]

9. AN ASSESSMENT OF THE TRADE MARK FUNCTIONS AND THE ACTIVITIES LISTED IN ARTICLE 5(3)

The Advocate General's Opinion and the ECJ ruling on this issue can be assessed from different perspectives. If one considers the negative impact on the market and on free trade, which might make it possible to prevent external transit activities of genuine branded goods, the Opinion (and the ECJ decision, which stayed true to it) should be welcomed. If one assesses the Opinion according to ECJ case law, one finds that the Opinion is consistent with it and is well grounded. The function of trade marks has been constantly identified by the ECJ in guaranteeing to consumers the origin of goods and, when it has been necessary to determine the lawfulness of third parties' use of a trade mark, ECJ decisions often resort to the impact of such use on the distinctive function of trade marks.[10]

---

[8]   See the ECJ decision in *Arsenal Football Club plc v Reed* Case C-206/01 [2002] ECR I-10273, [2003] ETMR 19, paras 15 and 54.

[9]   *Class*, para. 35.

[10]   Apart from *Arsenal*, see also *Farmitalia Carlo Erba-Eurim Pharm* (Cases C-71-94 and C-73-94); *Audi Quattro* (Case C-317/91); *Hag II* (Case C-317/91). As noted by the Advocate General, the decision is also consistent with the ruling of the ECJ in *Rioglass* Case C-115/02 [2004] ETMR 38 where it was held that a procedure which consists in transporting goods lawfully manufactured in a Member State to a non-member country by passing through one or more Member States, does not involve any

Nor may the Opinion or the ruling be criticised by considering the other functions of trade marks, which from time to time scholars or national case law argue to be protectable. Guaranteeing a constant quality of the products or services associated with a trade mark and protecting the attractive force of the trade mark in similar manner to the distinctive function relate to the impact of the trade mark on the consumers' public and are not therefore likely to be affected by external transit activities. External transit activities exclude the free circulation of the goods, which arguably is the prerequisite for any impact on the consumers' public.

However, further legal arguments may lead one to oppose to the conclusions of the Advocate General (and indirectly to the holdings of the ECJ). Indeed, some activities are specifically barred to third parties according to Article 5(3) of the Trade Marks Directive even though they do not affect always the typical trade mark functions. In particular:

(i)   affixing the trade mark to goods or to their packaging when the goods are not put into the market in the relevant territory but are exported abroad; or
(ii) temporarily importing the goods without releasing them into the market (in view of their subsequent export) or
(iii) manufacturing them for exportation outside the relevant territories.

These are all activities which, as such, do not affect the typical trade mark functions[11] and express a trend in trade mark legislation to grant extra-territorial

---

marketing of the goods in question and is therefore not liable to infringe the specific subject-matter of the trade mark. That decision did not however concern the Trade Marks Directive. In this regard the analogy argument raised by GSK and SB in connection with *Polo-Lauren* Case C-383/98 [2000] ETMR 535 where the statement that 'there is a risk that counterfeit goods placed under the external transit procedure may be fraudulently brought on to the Community market' was considered inapplicable by the Advocate General because it was made 'in examining the validity of a regulation which seeks to empower customs authorities to take action when such goods are found in the course of checks on goods in external transit'. This argument is not completely convincing because, in that case too, the external transit did not affect the distinctive function of the trade mark. However, one may agree with Advocate General Jacobs that *Polo-Lauren* was different in that the goods were counterfeit while, in *Class*, the external transit procedures concerned genuine branded goods, this distinction possibly justifying different treatment.

[11]   Before the implementation of Article 5(5) of the Trade Marks Directive in Italy, Italian case law and scholars were divided about the lawfulness of such activities. See Vanzetti, *La Nuova Legge Marchi*, Giuffré 1998, pp. 27–28 and C. Galli, 'Attuazione della Direttiva n. 89/104/CEE' in *Le Nuove Leggi Civili Commentate*, CEDAM 1995, pp. 1148 and 1149 and the case law and scholars cited there.

protection.[12] However, such activities are mentioned by Article 5(3), which also refers to 'offering the goods, *or* putting them on the market or stocking them for these purposes under that sign, or offering or supplying services thereunder'. Thus, at least 'offering the goods' and 'stocking them for the purpose of offering them' should be treated in the same way as (i) 'affixing' the trade marks or (ii) temporarily 'importing' or (iii) 'exporting' them. Indeed, none of these activities involve the release of goods into the relevant market and they therefore have no direct impact on the function of guaranteeing consumers (or on any of the other functions mentioned above). In other words, either (i) in the same way, all activities mentioned in Article 5(3) should be barred to third parties *only* when the goods are eventually released in to the market or (ii) in the same manner, all such activities (including offering for sale/selling and stocking with a view to selling/offering for sale) should *always* be prevented to third parties, including in the context of external transit.

Since the first solution is extremely limitative of the protection granted to trade mark proprietors and is contrary to the practice of European courts, Article 5(3) may suggest that the above activities are also barred to third parties in the context of external transit activities.

In the light of the above, doubts may be raised as to whether the Opinion of the Advocate General and the ECJ ruling are consistent with the Trade Marks Directive, even if it must be stressed again that a different solution would prevent 'traders established and working in the Community [. . .] to be involved in trade in trade marked goods, which cannot have been the objective of the legislature'.[13]

A possible justification for the application of different treatment to the various activities mentioned under Article 5(3) may be found in the higher risk of release into the relevant market resulting from activities such as 'affixing' the trade marks or (ii) temporarily 'importing' or (iii) 'exporting', when compared to activities carried out on goods which preserve their status of 'non-Community goods'.

---

[12]   The fact that Art. 5(3) reflects this trend was noted by Italian commentators of the statutory provisions of Italian Law which implemented the Trade Marks Directive. See Olivieri in Marasà, Masi, Olivieri, Spada, Spolidoro, Stella Richter, *Commento tematico alla legge marchi*, Milano, Giappichelli 1998, 43.

[13]   See para. 56 of the Advocate General's Opinion.

10. THE INTEREST IN PREVENTING THE UNAUTHORISED RELEASE OF GOODS IN THE COMMUNITY MARKET

Trade mark proprietors may also wish to block goods at the borders of the EEA because they are worried that those goods are then released into the Community, this concern being reflected in the protection granted under Community legislation against parallel imports from non-Member States.

As held by the ECJ,[14] it cannot be reasonably argued that such activities carry *per se* the risk of unauthorised parallel import into the Community (although this was claimed by SKB and Beecham[15]). Rather, it is appropriate to assess whether further circumstances (such as those stated before the referring court in *Class* posed its questions) may indirectly render external transit activities unlawful because they always reveal an actual risk that the goods will be fraudulently released within the Community or, if the narrower approach of the ECJ is adopted, because the offering or the sale *necessarily* entails putting them on the market in the Community.[16] Such assessment leads to a review of which elements of fact can reveal such intention or necessarily entails such result.

Advocate General Jacobs carried out this kind of review in his Opinion, when he envisaged additional circumstances as requested by the referring court. First, he examined whether the answer with regard to external transit procedures and the storing activities would be different (i) if the final destination of the goods were specified or (ii) if no purchase agreement of those goods had been executed with a customer in a third country. Consistently with his approach (based on the functions of a trade mark) the answer of the Advocate General was negative – unless, obviously, the final specified destination lay within the Community.

Secondly, the Advocate General assessed the relevance of further circumstances:

(i) the place of establishment of the trader;
(ii) the possibility that the goods were being offered for sale or sold by the trader established in a Member State, from that Member State, to another trader established in a Member State, while the place of delivery was not yet specified; or
(iii) the place of delivery was specified but the final destination was not;

---

14 See para. 43 of the ECJ decision.
15 See para. 24 of the Advocate General's Opinion
16 See para. 59 of the ECJ decision.

(iv)   the goods were offered for sale or sold by the trader established in a
       Member State, from that Member State, to another trader established
       outside the Community, when the place of delivery and/or final destina-
       tion was not, or not yet, specified;
(v)   the goods were offered for sale or sold by the trader established in a
       Member State, from that Member State, to another trader established
       outside the Community, who the parallel trader knew, or supposed,
       would eventually resell or supply to ultimate consumers within the
       Community.

Advocate General Jacobs held that (i) the place of establishment was irrelevant; the circumstances mentioned in (ii) and (iii) were not capable of rendering unlawful the trading activities until the final destination of the goods was
determined and turned out to be a place within the Community. Similarly the
Advocate General held the same view with regard to the circumstance
mentioned in (iv), with the (again obvious) qualification that, when the final
specified destination of the goods is within the Community, the trade mark
proprietor is entitled to prevent release or delivery within the Community.
Finally, as regards (v), the Advocate General expressed the view that the trade
mark proprietor was entitled to prevent release or delivery.
      The ECJ's starting point – that only the offer or the sale that *necessarily*
entails putting the branded goods on the market in the Community can be
prevented – led to even harsher conclusions for trade mark proprietors.
According to the ECJ not only can the trade mark proprietor not assert his right
if 'the owner of the goods, the addressee of the offer or the purchaser engage
in parallel trade' but he cannot do so even if 'a trader who offers or sells those
goods to another trader on the sole ground that that trader is likely then to put
them on the market in the Community', the latter circumstance being considered differently, as we have seen, by Advocate General Jacobs.
      It is difficult not to share the very reasonable (and in the authors' opinion,
more balanced) view of Advocate General Jacobs on the additional circumstances envisaged by the Dutch Court. However, an assessment of such
elements by national courts (which appears to the authors to be the most
appropriate *locus* for this kind of evaluation) on a case-by-case basis could
lead to different results.

11.   THE ADVOCATE GENERAL AND THE ECJ RULING
ON BURDEN OF PROOF

Such harsh conclusions for trade mark proprietors wishing to enforce their
rights efficiently against parallel imported goods *before* their release into the

market could be in principle 'softened' by having the burden of proof resting with the trader. In this regard the Advocate General advised that national law would determine which party should bear the burden of proof, this clearly resulting from the preamble of the Trade Marks Directive,[17] unless the issue at stake is whether the goods were put on the market in the Community under the trade mark with the proprietor's consent. In such a case, the burden of proof will rest on the owner of the goods as was ruled by the ECJ in *Zino Davidoff*[18] and further confirmed in more general terms for all conditions required to establish exhaustion in another decision not mentioned by the Advocate General (*Van Doren*[19]).

The conclusions of Advocate General Jacobs constituted a departure from the submissions of the Commission, which considered as applicable by analogy the rulings of ECJ case law in *Sebago* and *Zino Davidoff*.[20] According to the Commission that case-law, establishing that the owner of the goods must furnish evidence that the trade mark proprietor consented to their being put in the free circulation, is applicable also with regard to the circumstance that the goods were introduced in the Community with a view not to marketing them in such territory but to transporting them to a third country.

The ECJ decision did not follow the Opinion of the Advocate General, but this did not lead to the adoption of the Commission's view. According to the Court (i) the burden of proof is not a matter of national laws of Member States and (ii) it is for the trade mark proprietor to prove the facts which would give grounds for asserting his rights, by proving either the release for free circulation of the non-Community goods bearing his mark or an offer or sale of the goods which necessarily entails their being put on the market in the Community.

---

[17]　The 8th and the 10th recitals.

[18]　Joined Cases C-414/99 to C-416/99. Para. 54.

[19]　*Van Doren v Lifestyle* Case C-244/00 [2003] ETMR 75. However, in *Van Doren* it was held that where the trader succeeds in establishing that there is a real risk of partitioning of national markets (such as in case goods are marketed in the EEA under exclusive distribution systems), 'it is for the proprietor of the trade mark to establish that the products were initially placed on the market outside the EEA by him or with his consent. If such evidence is adduced, it is for the third party to prove the consent of the trade mark proprietor to subsequent marketing of the products in the EEA' (see para. 41).

[20]　See footnote 13 and *Sebago and Maison Dubois* Case C-173/98 [1999] ETMR 681.

12.   THE *ZINO DAVIDOFF* RULING AND THE ECJ DECISION

In the Opinion of the Advocate General, the ruling of *Zino Davidoff*[21] could not be applied, by analogy, to the destination of goods subject to external transit activities (as proposed by the Commission), because that ruling was rendered in a different context. According to the Advocate General, while in *Zino Davidoff* the circumstance to be proved (that is the consent of the trade mark proprietor) had the serious effect of extinguishing the exclusive rights of the trade mark proprietor, in the case at stake 'the trade mark proprietor is seeking to prevent a trader from using his mark in the course of trade'. Such reasoning is highly unclear. It is possible that the Advocate General meant that the case before him was different because, if the goods subject to external transit activities are released, the trade mark proprietor will not be in principle prevented from subsequently enforcing his exclusive rights. It could however be argued that, in a case where release has occurred, enforcement of the exclusive rights of trade mark proprietors may in practice become extremely difficult.

As regards the ECJ's view on the onus of proof, it is difficult to provide a general comment given the very concise reasoning which grounded it. It is however arguable that the position of the ECJ, that the ninth recital in the preamble of the Directive (which states the objective of the same protection for trade mark proprietors) requires uniformity in the Member States in a matter such as the onus of proof. This is however contradicted by other recitals (the Commission mentioned the eighth and tenth recital in this regard) and, more generally, by the provisions set forth by the Directive and that are aimed at obtaining a certain degree of uniformity for the substantive rules on trade marks as opposed to procedural rules.

13.   CONCLUSIONS

Class International BV v Unilever NV and Others provides a clear picture where free trade interests prevail over the interests of trade mark proprietors, without any possibility for them to assert their rights before goods are released on the market in the Community even where, for example, the goods are sold to a trader who is likely to put the goods on such market.

Such a position seems in fact particularly burdensome for trade mark

---

[21]   As noted by the Advocate General, reference by the Commission to *Sebago* is not easily understandable since in *Sebago* the ECJ did not rule on the burden of proof.

proprietors. It is likely, however, that the conflicting interests of manufacturers/trade mark owners on the one side, and parallel importers and traders on the other, will grant to the ECJ further occasions to clarify these kinds of issues and to find the best balance between trade mark protection and free trade.[22]

---

[22]   Indeed, reference on very similar questions has been made to the ECJ by order of the Bundesgerichtshof (Germany) of 2 June 2005 in *Montex Holdings Ltd. v Diesel S.p.A.* The questions referred were the following:
'(a) Does a registered trade mark grant its proprietor the right to prohibit the transit of goods with the sign?
(b) If the answer is in the affirmative: may a particular assessment be based on the fact that the sign enjoys no protection in the country of destination?
(c) If the answer to (a) is in the affirmative and irrespective of the answer to (b), is a distinction to be drawn according to whether the article whose destination is a Member State comes from a Member State, an associated State or a third country? Is it relevant in this regard whether the article has been produced in the country of origin lawfully or in infringement of a right to a sign existing there held by the trade-mark proprietor?'

8. Compatibility of products: the ECJ's *Gillette* Ruling

Rainer Hilli

CONTEXT OF THE RULING

The European Court of Justice (ECJ) decision in *Gillette*[1] followed a reference for a preliminary ruling by the Finnish Supreme Court (Korkein oikeus) on the interpretation of Article 6(1)(c) of Council Directive 89/104 (the Trade Mark Directive). In summary the Finnish Supreme Court asked the ECJ to determine the circumstances in which the use of a third party's trade mark is to be considered lawful in terms of that Directive.

The case concerns trade mark use in a situation where a competitor refers to the proprietor's trade mark when marketing a product, in this case razor cartridges. The legal question is twofold: (i) how are the limitations upon the effect of a trade mark with regard to spare parts or accessories to be interpreted and (ii) if referral to a trade mark is permissible, how may such a referral to another's trade mark be made in order to comply, in both cases with Section 4(2) of the Trade Mark Act, when interpreted in accordance with Article 6(1)(c) of the Trade Mark Directive.

THE FACTS

The Gillette Company is the proprietor of the trade marks GILLETTE and SENSOR in Finland. Gillette Group Finland Oy markets, *inter alias*, products for wet shaving in Finland. LA-Laboratories Ltd Oy, a limited liability company domiciled in Helsinki, Finland undertakes production activities relating to techno-chemistry, pharmaceuticals, natural products and nonfood products and trades in those products both domestically and abroad.

LA-Laboratories sells razor handles and, in separate packages, razor cartridges for its own handles under the brand name PARASON FLEXOR,

---

[1]   *Gillette Co., Gillette Finland Co. Oy v LA-Laboratories Ltd Oy* Case C-228/03 [2005] ECR I-0000; [2005] ETMR 67.

both of which are manufactured by a manufacturer in the US without commercial connection to Gillette. These PARASON FLEXOR razor cartridges are
sold in packages with red stickers containing the words 'SUITABLE FOR
ALL GILLETTE SENSOR RAZORS'. Gillette asked LA-Laboratories to
remove the stickers or the packaging bearing the references in question from
the market and to confirm that it would not in the future use Gillette's trade
marks on the packaging of the products it sells. When LA-Laboratories did not
comply with this request, Gillette initiated legal proceedings before the
District Court of Helsinki.

During the District Court proceedings, it was not disputed that the razor
cartridge was the principal product and not a spare part for the shaving system.
The District Court concluded that both the cartridge and handle were separate
principal parts of the shaving system, not spare parts; in consequence, the
marketing of the razor cartridge did not fall under the limitation upon the
exclusive trade mark right under Section 4(2) of the Finnish Trade Mark Act.
According to the District Court, since that provision referred essentially to
spare parts and accessories, the limitations to exclusive right of the trade mark
proprietor to which it referred were not applicable to the principal part of the
goods. The Court held further that a possible extended interpretation of the
limitation was likely to dilute the exclusivity conferred through trade mark
registration and would be neither acceptable nor reasonable in trade mark law.

According to the District Court, even if the razor cartridges had fallen
within the scope of the limitation in Section 4(2) of the Act, it would not have
been necessary to demonstrate the purpose of the PARASON FLEXOR razor
cartridges by using Gillette's trade marks without Gillette's consent.
Moreover, LA-Laboratories' use of Gillette's trade marks evidently did not
comply with acceptable business practice, nor was it reasonable in relation to
Gillette's rights. Consequently, the District Court ruled that LA-Laboratories
was prohibited from continuing or repeating the infringement of Gillette's
exclusive right pertaining to the Finnish trade marks GILLETTE and
SENSOR.

The Court of Appeals, in contrast, determined that the razor cartridge was
comparable to a spare part. That gave no weight to the fact that it was undisputed before the District Court that the razor cartridge was the principal part
of the shaving system. According to the Court of Appeals, the shaving system
was a combination of a shaft and a razor cartridge: when a razor cartridge is
replaced, that which is replaced is part of the shaving system. Consequently
razor cartridges sold separately were comparable with spare parts.

Although LA-Laboratories sold its own PARASON FLEXOR razor
handles, the Court of Appeals considered that LA-Laboratories had a justified
need for referring to Gillette's trade marks when marketing the PARASON
FLEXOR razor cartridges, and that its reference had not been made in such a

way as to create the impression that the cartridges originated from the trade mark proprietor. As a consequence, the Court of Appeals annulled the judgment by the District Court and dismissed Gillette's claims. The ruling was appealed by Gillette and the Supreme Court granted leave to appeal.

NORMATIVE BACKGROUND IN FINLAND

The Trade Mark Act was harmonized with the Trade Mark Directive in Finland with effect from 1 February 1993. To the extent that a disputed issue is covered by the Trade Mark Directive, the Finnish court must now rely on the text of the Trade Mark Directive and any applicable decisions of the ECJ.

Under the Trade Mark Act, Section 4(2)

> the unauthorized use referred to in paragraph 1 above is deemed to mean, inter alia, that someone, when releasing spare parts, accessories or other such (parts) that are suitable for another (manufacturer's) goods, refers to the latter's distinctive mark in a manner that will serve to create the impression that the goods that have been released originate from the holder of the distinctive mark or that the holder has consented to the use of the distinctive mark.

Paragraph 2 limits the general rule concerning the exclusive right in the trade mark in paragraph 1 with regard to the use of another's mark for spare parts, accessories and other such (parts) that are suitable for another (manufacturer's) goods. However, in that case, according to the section of the law, no reference may be made to the other's distinctive mark in the manner deemed unsuitable in paragraph 2. The Finnish legislature considered the provision to be in compliance with Article 6(1)(c) of the Trade Mark Directive.

In accordance with Article 6(1)(c), of the Trade Mark Directive,

> the holder of a trade mark must not prohibit someone else from using the trade mark in business activity whenever its use is necessary to indicate the intended purpose of a product or service, in particular as accessories or spare parts, provided he uses them in accordance with honest practices in industrial or commercial matters.

The Trade Mark Act has to be interpreted in the light of the Directive and in particular with that Article.

SPARE PARTS AND ACCESSORIES

The first relevant question that the Supreme Court had to consider was the definition of a spare part when interpreting the above provisions. The second relevant question was what type of reference to another's trade marks was permissible when marketing spare parts and accessories.

It was undisputed in the matter that a razor cartridge is not an accessory or a spare part but, rather, the principal product. A narrow interpretation of the Directive, concerning the spare parts and accessories alone, would thus mean that the limitation referred to in the Trade Mark Act, Section 4(2) would automatically not apply to the razor cartridges in this case because they were not a spare part, accessory or other such part.

Judgments have been given in similar cases, with Gillette or its affiliates (and the purchasers of razor cartridges from ASR in packaging marked 'Fits SENSOR') as claimants in other European Union Member States and, while the reasoning of the different national courts and legal scholars varies, most of the court judgments have been in Gillette's favour, concluding that such use should not be permitted.

As the spare part limitation should be uniformly interpreted under the harmonized EU trade mark law, there should also be a uniform legal practice within national Finnish courts as well as within the European Union. The Supreme Court at Gillette's request therefore referred the case to the ECJ. Accordingly, by order of 23 May 2003, the Supreme Court decided to stay the proceedings and to refer the following questions to the Court:

When applying Article 6(1)(c) of the Trade Mark Directive:
(1) What are the criteria
(a) on the basis of which the question of regarding a product as a spare part or accessory is to be decided, and
(b) on the basis of which those products to be regarded as other than spare parts and accessories which can also fall within the scope of the said subparagraph are to be determined?

(2) Is the permissibility of the use of a third party's trade mark to be assessed differently, depending on whether the product is like a spare part or accessory or whether it is a product which can fall within the scope of the said subparagraph on another basis?
(3) How should the requirement that the use must be 'necessary' to indicate the intended purpose of a product be interpreted? Can the criterion of necessity be satisfied even though it would in itself be possible to state the intended purpose without an express reference to the third party's trade mark, by merely mentioning only for instance the technical principle of functioning of the product? What significance does it have in that case that the statement may be more difficult for consumers to understand if there is no express reference to the third party's trade mark?
(4) What factors should be taken into account when assessing accordance with honest commercial practice? Does the mentioning of a third party's trade mark in connection with the marketing of one's own product constitute a reference to the fact that the marketer's own product corresponds, in quality and technically or as

regards its other properties, to the product designated by the third party's trade mark?

(5)   Does it affect the permissibility of the use of a third party's trade mark that the economic operator who refers to the third party's trade mark also markets, in addition to a spare part or accessory, a product of his own which that spare part or accessory is intended to be used with?

THE FIRST, SECOND AND THIRD QUESTIONS

With regard to the first, second and third questions the ECJ observed that trade mark rights are an essential element in the system of undistorted competition which the EC Treaty seeks to establish and maintain. Under such a system, an undertaking must be in a position to keep its customers by virtue of the quality of its products and services, something which is possible only if there are distinctive marks which enable customers to identify them. In that context, the essential function of a trade mark is to guarantee the identity of origin of the marked goods or services to the consumer or end user by enabling him, without any possibility of confusion, to distinguish the goods or services from others which have another origin. For the trade mark to be able to fulfill its essential role in the system of undistorted competition which the Treaty seeks to establish and maintain, it must offer a guarantee that all the goods or services bearing it have been manufactured or supplied under the control of a single undertaking which is responsible for their quality.[2]

According to Article 6(1)(c) of the Trade Mark Directive the trade mark owner may not prohibit a third party from using the mark in trade where it is necessary to indicate the intended purpose of a product or service, in particular as accessories or spare parts. That provision does not lay down criteria for determining whether a given intended purpose of a product falls within its scope, but merely requires that use of the trade mark be necessary in order to indicate such a purpose.

Moreover, since the intended purpose of the products as accessories or spare parts is cited only by way of example, those doubtless being the usual situations in which it is necessary to use a trade mark in order to indicate the intended purpose of a product, the application of Article 6(1)(c) of Directive 89/104 is, as the United Kingdom Government and the Commission of the European Communities pointed out in their observations, not limited to those situations. Therefore, in the circumstances of the main proceedings, it is not necessary to determine whether a product must be regarded as an accessory or

---

[2]   *Gillette*, n.1, at paras 25, 26.

a spare part. The ECJ has already in previous cases held that use of a trade mark to inform the public that the advertiser specializes in the sale, or that he carries out the repair and maintenance, of products bearing that trade mark which have been marketed under that mark by its owner or with his consent, constitutes a use indicating the intended purpose of a product. That information is necessary in order to preserve the system of undistorted competition in the market for that product or service.[3] The same applies to the case in the main proceedings, where LA-Laboratories was using Gillette's marks in order to provide the public with comprehensible and complete information as to the intended purpose of the product which it markets, that is as to its compatibility with the product which bears those trade marks. In addition, such use of a trade mark is necessary that information cannot in practice be communicated to the public by a third party without use being made of the trade mark of which the latter is not the owner. This was pointed out by the Advocate General in his Opinion 'use must in practice be the only means of providing such information'.[4]

Thus, to determine whether other means of providing such information may be used, the ECJ considered it is necessary to take into consideration, for example, the possible existence of technical standards or norms generally used for the type of product marketed by a third party and which are known to the public for which that type of product is intended. Those norms, or other characteristics, must be capable of providing that public with comprehensible and full information on the intended purpose of the product marketed by that third party in order to preserve the system of undistorted competition on the market for that product.

The ECJ left it for the national court to determine whether, in the circumstances of the referred case, LA-Laboratories; use of Gillette's trade marks was necessary, taking account of the requirements enunciated here and of the nature of the public for which the product marketed by LA-Laboratories was intended. The ECJ concluded that the answer to the first, second and third questions was therefore that the legitimacy of the use of a trade mark under Article 6(1)(c) of the Trade Mark Directive depends on whether that use is necessary to indicate the intended purpose of a product.

THE FOURTH QUESTION

The ECJ has consistently held that the condition of 'honest use' within the

---

[3]   Ibid., paras 32, 33.
[4]   Ibid., Opinion, paras 64, 71.

meaning of Article 6(1) of Directive 89/104 constitutes in substance the
expression of a duty to act fairly in relation to the legitimate interests of the
trade mark owner. Such an obligation is similar to that imposed on the reseller
where he uses another's trade mark to advertise the resale of products covered
by that mark. In that regard, use of the trade mark will not comply with honest
practices in industrial or commercial matters where it is done in such a way as
to give the impression that there is a commercial connection between the
reseller and the trade mark proprietor. Nor may such use affect the value of the
trade mark by taking unfair advantage of its distinctive character or repute.
Where a third party presents its product as an imitation or replica of the product bearing the trade mark of which it is not the owner, such use of that mark
does, as a rule, not comply with honest practices.[5]

The ECJ acknowledged that it was for the national court to determine
whether LA-Laboratories' use of Gillette's trade marks was in accordance
with honest practices, taking into account the conditions to which it referred,[6]
in particular the overall presentation of LA-Laboratories' product, the circumstances in which the LA-Laboratories' own marks are displayed in that presentation, the circumstances in which a distinction is made between
LA-Laboratories' mark and the allegedly infringed mark, as well as the effort
made by LA-Laboratories to ensure that consumers can distinguish its products from those of which it is not the trade mark owner.

The ECJ firmly endorsed the United Kingdom's observation that the fact
that a third party uses another's trade mark in order to indicate the intended
purpose of its product does not necessarily mean that it is presenting that
product as being of the same quality as, or having equivalent properties to,
those of the product bearing the trade mark.[7] Whether there has been such a
presentation depends on the facts: it is for the national court to determine
whether it has taken place by reference to the circumstances. Moreover,
whether the product marketed by the third party has been represented as
being of the same quality as, or having equivalent properties to, the product
whose trade mark is being used is a factor which a trial court must take into
consideration when it considers whether such use is in accordance with
honest practices in industrial or commercial matters. The ECJ then
concluded that

> use of the trade mark will not be in accordance with honest practices in industrial
> and commercial matters if, for example:

5   Ibid., paras 40 to 42.
6   Ibid., para. 46.
7   Ibid., para. 47.

- it is done in such a manner as to give the impression that there is a commercial connection between the third party and the trade mark owner;
- it affects the value of the trade mark by taking unfair advantage of its distinctive character or repute;
- it entails the discrediting or denigration of that mark;
- or where the third party presents its product as an imitation or replica of the product bearing the trade mark of which it is not the owner.[8]

THE FIFTH QUESTION

The ECJ agreed with the Finnish and British submissions that there was nothing in the Trade Mark Directive to prevent a third party from relying on Article 6(1)(c) where it is marketing a product itself.[9] However, a third party's use of another's trade mark must then be necessary to indicate the intended purpose of the product which it markets. Again, that use must be in accordance with honest practices in industrial and commercial matters, as assessed by the trial court.[10]

WHEN IS TRADE MARK USE ALLOWED FOR COMPATIBLE PRODUCTS?

The Finnish Supreme Court was left with several open issues to be determined based upon the facts of the case, when construing its own Act in the light of the ECJ's interpretation of the Directive.

The ECJ requires that the question of trade mark use be dealt with in two steps:

Step 1 Is use of third party trade marks necessary to indicate the intended purpose of the compatible products? The ECJ clarifies the requirement of necessity by stating that use is necessary if the use of another's trade mark is the only means of providing the public with comprehensible and complete information as to the intended use of the razor blades and there are no other means of describing the intended use, e.g. by using a generic reference.

Step 2 If the use of another's trade marks is considered necessary, consider whether that use of the trade marks is made in accordance with honest commercial practices, as defined by the ECJ.

The requirements in both step 1 and step 2 have to be met if the use of the third party trade marks to be permissible.

---

8 Ibid., para. 49.
9 Ibid., para. 51.
10 Ibid., para. 53.

The ECJ found that the lawfulness of the use of the trade mark under Article 6(1)(c) of the Trade Mark Directive depends on whether that use is necessary to indicate the intended purpose of a product. It said:

> Use of the trade mark by a third party who is not its owner is necessary in order to indicate the intended purpose of a product marketed by that third party where such use in practice constitutes the only means of providing the public with comprehensible and complete information on that intended purpose in order to preserve the undistorted system of competition in the market for that product.[11]

In the view of the ECJ, national courts must determine 'whether other means of providing such information may be used' for example by 'norms generally used'. According to the ECJ, such norms (or other characteristics) must be capable of providing the public with comprehensible and full information on the intended purpose of the product. The ECJ further observed that the fulfilment of the necessity criteria must be assessed by the national court and that, in conducting its assessment, the national court must take into account the nature of the public for which the product is intended.

The principle of legal security provides that the law should primarily be interpreted in accordance with its wording and that any exceptions to this principle should be interpreted narrowly. Article 5 of the Trade Mark Directive is the main rule and Article 6(1)(c) merely an exception. Use of another party's registered trade mark is, as a rule, prohibited and the necessity test in accordance with the exception in Article 6(1)(c) must therefore be strict. Article 6(1)(c) should not be interpreted in a way which would make it possible arbitrarily to circumvent the protection of registered trade marks. If it were possible to deviate from the wording of a statutory provision in a broad sense, the predictability and legal security conferred by the law would be diminished.

SOME THOUGHTS ON THE DECISION STILL TO COME

The relevant question to be assessed by the Finnish Supreme Court will be whether the use of the GILLETTE and SENSOR trade marks on the PARASON FLEXOR packages is the 'only means' of providing consumers with information regarding the intended purpose of LA-Laboratories' products or whether this can be indicated without the use of Gillette's trade marks, for example, by using a generic reference.

The Finnish Supreme Court will probably look at competing products on

---

[11]   Ibid., para. 39.

the Finnish market and consider if they bear reference to other products by using trade marks or generic terms.

The ECJ does not address the question as to whose responsibility it is to consider the availability of potential suitable generic references, should it be necessary to do so. It would seem that such an obligation would lie upon the party referring to another's trade mark.

The Dutch Supreme Court[12] held that it was possible to indicate the intended use of razor blade cartridges by describing the shaving system, thus avoiding mention of Gillette's trade marks. According to the Dutch Supreme Court, mention of the words 'Gillette' and 'Sensor' was not necessary ('no need whatsoever') to enable consumers to use the marketed blades and served the sole purpose of profiting from the well-known GILLETTE trade mark.

In *Gillette v LA-Laboratories* the ECJ referred to its earlier decision in *BMW*[13] and held that the information is necessary for the preservation of the system of undistorted competition in the market for that product or service.[14] Although the ECJ held that this principle still applies, it added that the use must in practice be the only means of providing such information. The necessity to refer to the third party mark resulted from the fact that the specialized service of repairing BMW motor cars could not be offered or provided without using the BMW brand name. The establishment of efficient competition among providers of repair services and of adequate information to consumers justified the necessity of referring to the third party brand name. It is questionable if such a situation exists within the market for razor blade systems. However, irrespective of whether the supplier of a blade system additionally offers a razor handle of its own, it may be assumed that the use of a trade mark naming indication is not necessary for establishing efficient competition for razor blade systems in the marketplace since the production and offering of a razor holder fitting the razor blade system of a competitor is easy to achieve and is of only negligible economic significance.

The ECJ as well as the Advocate General have observed that the purpose of Article 6(1)(c) is to reconcile the fundamental interests of trade mark protection with those of the free movement of goods and freedom to provide services. Accordingly the object of those provisions is to ensure the balance between the trade mark holder's interest in having the trade mark fully carry out its essential function of guaranteeing the origin and quality of the products

---

[12]   *Hermans Grope BV v The Gillette Company Inc. and The Gillette Company Netherlands BV*, 6 October 2000 [2002] ETMR 12.

[13]   *Bayerische Motorenwerke AG (BMW) and BMW Nederland BV v Ronald Karel Deenik*, Case C-63/97, [1999] ETMR 339.

[14]   *Gillette*, para. 29.

on the one hand and the other operator's interest in having full access to the market on the other.

The Finnish Supreme Court is likely to consider whether LA-Laboratories could operate in the market without any use of or reference to Gillette's trade marks. It may consider that the primary intended purpose of LA-Laboratories' razor blades is to function together with its own handles. The secondary intended purpose of use of LA-Laboratories' razor blades would thus be that its blades could be used together with other manufacturers' (and not only Gillette's) handles. In the matter before the Finnish Supreme Court, the primary intended purpose is evident to the consumers without reference to the trade marks of others. The secondary intended purpose, that is that the razor blades fit other manufacturers' handles, is also obvious according to the prevailing practice but can, when necessary, be conveyed by using generic references indicating that purpose to the consumers. It is consequently unnecessary to use third party's trade marks in order to establish undistorted competition on the market.

The Finnish Supreme Court may consider whether the PARASON FLEXOR twin blades are sold in packages with red stickers bearing the words 'This razor is SUITABLE for all Gillette SENSOR HANDLES' is regarded as 'taking unfair advantage of the distinctive character or repute of a trade mark'. The Court may also consider whether the intended purpose of LA-Laboratories' products could have been communicated to consumers, for example by textual small-print on the back of the product package. Every potential consumer would be able to understand the intended purpose of the product by reading such a text.

The guarantee function of the trade mark may also be relevant. This is also because consumers, by virtue of the trade mark SENSOR, identify a particular Gillette technology (moving twin blade technology) among razor blade cartridges possessing some other technology, for example Mach3 technology. The Court may further consider whether, by referring to the SENSOR trade mark, LA-Laboratories may create among consumers the impression that PARASON FLEXOR razor blade cartridges possess the more sophisticated SENSOR technology.

As mentioned previously, the use of another's trade mark does not necessarily mean that it is presented as being of the same quality as (or having equivalent properties to) the product bearing the trade mark. However, the ECJ held that this question is a factor which the Supreme Court shall take into consideration when assessing use in accordance with honest business practices.

Finally, reference to another's trade mark may easily be understood by the consumers as a statement that there exists a commercial connection or an implied licence between the owner of the trade marks and the company using those trade marks. It is common for consumer products (such as razor blades) to be manufactured by the same manufacturer for different businesses. A brand manufacturer may also produce goods for third parties that are sold under other brand names. The Finnish Supreme Court may consider whether consumers receive the impression that the manufacturer of PARASON FLEXOR blades is the same entity as the manufacturer of GILLETTE SENSOR blades.

SUMMARY

The Finnish Supreme Court has not yet resolved how the facts fit within the guidance given by the ECJ. That Court's *Gillette* ruling seems to widen the 'spare part' exemption so as to permit the use of another's trade mark on a wider variety of compatible products. However, the Advocate General stated in his Opinion that the use of a third party's trade mark to indicate intended purpose will arise more often for accessories and spare parts. Therefore the question of whether the product bearing reference to another's trade mark is a main part or a spare part should be given prominence in the overall assessment of the case. The words 'in particular' in Article 6(1)(c) support the interpretation that the threshold for the fulfillment of the necessity criterion should be higher for main parts than for accessories and spare parts.

The Finnish Supreme Court handed down its decision in *Gillette v LA-Laboratories* on 22 February 2006. That court dismissed Gillette's trade mark infringement action, basing its decision on the ruling of the European Court of Justice. The court accepted that the reference to Gillette's trade marks was the only way to inform consumers about the intended purpose of LA's razor blades. Such information was useful to the consumer only when it was presented in a form that was easily understood and perceived by him. LA's packaging featured the brand name PARASON FLEXOR sufficiently clearly to indicate that it was not a Gillette product; the text of the sticker only clarified that those blades could be used with Gillette's products. This being so, LA's use did not create the impression that there existed a commercial link between the respective undertakings.

Three of the court's five judges held that the text on the sticker was a neutral announcement as to product compatibility and could not be said to have imitated Gillette's product. The other two judges thought that the portrayal of the parties' respective trade marks together in a similar type size might create some superficial confusion among relevant customers. However, the risk of confusion was small. LA had not acted contrary to honest business practices. In the circumstances there was no need to require the use of a disclaimer so as to clarify that there was no link between the two manufacturers.

9. Repairs and other specialist services in the light of the ECJ'S *BMW* ruling

Montiano Monteagudo and Núria Porxas

1. INTRODUCTION

The trade mark right, or, more specifically, the *ius prohibendi* ('right to prohibit') that constitutes its negative content, is not absolute. Apart from the doctrine of exhaustion of rights, there are additional reasons for the existence of other permitted uses of third party trade marks. These reasons are based on the need to protect certain interests that coexist with, but simultaneously oppose, the interests of the trade mark owner and that are essentially linked to the proper function of the market to ensure transparency through the provision of complete and adequate information. Thus it has become necessary to adopt measures that make it possible for these opposing interests to coexist. To this end, trade mark law has established certain limitations on the trade mark owner's right to prohibit or exclude conduct that *a priori* infringes the exclusive scope of the trade mark.

In this regard Article 17 of the TRIPs Agreement[1] allows the establishment of limited exceptions to the rights conferred by a trade mark, such as the fair use of descriptive terms, provided that such exceptions take account of the legitimate interests of the owner of the trade mark and of third parties. More specifically, Article 6(1) of the Council Directive 89/104[2] (the 'Directive') states that the trade mark shall not entitle the proprietor to prohibit a third party from making certain references, in the course of trade, provided he does so in accordance with honest practices in industrial or commercial matters. Paragraphs (a), (b) and (c) of Article 6(1) set out the exempted references. These relate to the use of

---

[1]   Trade-Related Aspects of Intellectual Property Rights, Annex 1C of the Marrakech Agreement establishing the World Trade Organization, signed in Marrakech, Morocco, on 15 April 1994.
[2]   First Council Directive 89/104 of 21 December 1988 to approximate the laws of the Member States relating to trade marks.

- one's own name and address;[3]
- indications concerning the kind, quality, quantity, intended purpose, value, geographical origin, the time of production of goods or of rendering of the service, or other characteristics of goods or services;[4]
- most importantly in this context, the use of the trade mark where it is necessary to indicate the intended purpose of a product or service, in particular as accessories or spare parts.[5]

This provision is repeated in practically identical terms in the national regulations that have implemented the Directive in the European Union Member States,[6] and in Article 12 of the Community Trade Mark Regulation.[7]

Without prejudice to the specific elements of the application of the three atypical trade mark uses referred to in Article 6(1), the single objective premise which they have in common is that the use of the trade mark complies 'with honest practices in industrial or commercial matters'. An understanding of the meaning of this vague legal term is essential.

The well-known ruling in 1999 of the European Court of Justice (ECJ) in *BMW*[8] (hereafter 'the Ruling') remains the principal point of reference for the interpretation of the application of Article 6(1) of the Directive and, in particular, of the third instance listed in it. The ECJ, in response to a request for a preliminary ruling from a national court, analysed whether the owner of the BMW trade mark (registered only for vehicles but not for automotive-related services) was entitled to prohibit a third party who was not an 'official' or authorized distributor of BMW from using its trade mark to advertise to consumers (i) the sale of second-hand vehicles of this mark and (ii) the rendering of specialized services for BMW vehicles.

In analysing the first situation the ECJ referred to the principle of exhaustion of the trade mark right, provided under Article 7 of the Directive[9] and

---

3   Ibid., Article 6(1)(a).

4   Ibid., Article 6(1)(b).

5   Ibid., Article 6(1)(c).

6   By way of example, please refer to Article 37 of the Spanish Trade Mark Law 17/2001 of 17 December 2001.

7   Council Regulation 40/94 of 20 December 1993 on the Community trade mark.

8   *Bayerische Motorenwerke AG (BMW) and BMW Nederland BV v Deenik* Case C-63/97 [1999] ETMR 339, [1999] ECR I-905.

9   By Article 7 of the Directive, 'The trade mark shall not entitle the proprietor to prohibit its use in relation to goods which have been put on the market in the Community under that trade mark by the proprietor or with his consent'. In the current version of the Directive as amended by the Agreement on the European Economic Area (Article 65(2), in relation with Annex XVII, number 4), the term 'in the Community' in Article 7(1) of the Directive should be replaced by 'in a Contracting Party' for the purposes of such Agreement.

stating that the use of a third party's trade mark in the resale or the advertising of the resale of goods does not constitute an infringement of the trade mark as long as it relates to specific goods that have previously been put on the market under that trade mark with the consent of its proprietor for example second-hand BMW cars. Since the objective of this chapter is not to discuss the concept of exhaustion, we will make no further reference to the Ruling from the perspective of the resale of branded articles. We will instead focus on the rendering of specialized services for trade marked goods, since it is in relation to these services that the Ruling applied Article 6(1)(c).[10] Specifically, the Ruling analyses whether use of the BMW trade mark, without the authorization of its owner to advertise repair and maintenance services for vehicles of the same make, infringes the trade mark[11] or whether it is a permitted use under Article 6(1)(c) (being *necessary* to indicate the intended *purpose* of a . . . service'). In summary the Ruling, following the Opinion of Advocate General Jacobs,[12] holds that a party who repairs BMW vehicles may indicate this in his shop window (use by reference or collateral use), provided that he does not create the impression that he is an authorized repairer/garage of the trade mark owner and thereby, through such association, harms the trade mark's reputation.

The principles established by the Ruling for the analysis of the use for information purposes of a third party's trade mark have been upheld consistently since the Ruling was made. It therefore now represents a fundamental piece of consolidated case law. Thus the Ruling is crucial for the correct interpretation of Article 6(1) of the Directive and for establishing the limits on the atypical use of third party trade marks and, in particular, when a trade mark is used to indicate the purpose of specialized services.

This being the case, the Ruling is of practical interest to both the suppliers of repair services and other specialized services (in addition to, obviously, manufacturers of accessories and spare parts) on the one hand, and to the manufacturers of the goods that are the subject of such services (again, in addition to the manufacturers of the products for which the accessories

---

[10]   According to the Ruling, because the rule regarding exhaustion (that is, Article 7 of the Directive) is not applicable to the supply of services.

[11]   In relation to the infringement, in *BMW* the trade mark was not registered for services, but only for products. This is an issue which we will not examine and that the Ruling does not consider either, since, even though no identity is given, the similarity may suffice for an infringement to exist and, in this context, the determination of whether the services referring to the repair or maintenance of a specific product are 'similar' to that product lies within the responsibility of the national courts. We would argue that such similarity is undeniable.

[12]   Opinion of Advocate General Francis Jacobs, delivered on 2 April 1998 in Case C-63/97 *Bayerische Motorenwerke AG (BMW)*.

and spare parts are intended) on the other. Purely on the basis of the analysis of these conditions on the application of the exception, the former will be able to determine if their use of the trade mark is permitted.

Our purpose is not to discuss the Ruling, which is now established case law. Rather our purpose is to reflect, in the light of the Ruling, on the limits of the atypical or permitted uses of a third party's trade mark consisting of indicating the purpose of specialized services, with the ultimate aim of giving practical guidelines to both groups of interested parties referred to above.

2. APPLICATION OF THE EXCEPTION

2.1 Introduction

Although a proper justification of our contention would require doctrinal analysis, something which goes beyond the scope of this chapter, we must emphasize that, in our opinion, the circumstances regulated in Article 6(1) of the Directive are true *exceptions* to the trade mark right. That is, they do not concern situations in which the requirements for the *ius prohibendi* to be exercised are not met, but rather situations that are a priori trade mark infringements but that are tolerated by the law if they comply with certain *specific conditions* that seek to achieve the coexistence of the parties' respective interests. In other words, the conduct referred to in Article 6(1) *prima facie* infringes the exclusive right of the trade mark owner under Article 5 of the Directive but it is exempted owing to its specific nature, that also deserves protection (under Article 6(1) of the Directive, this conduct is excluded from the scope of the *ius prohibendi*). Accordingly Article 6(1) does not limit the right of exclusion, but rather introduces exceptions to this right. The Ruling clearly supports this classification as an 'exception' in its response to questions two and three of the national court,[13] in which it establishes that the use

---

[13]   The second question to the Court for a preliminary ruling was: 'If someone, without the authorisation of the trade mark proprietor, makes use of that proprietor's trade mark, registered exclusively for specified goods, for the purpose of announcing to the public that he (a) carries out repair and maintenance work on the goods which have been placed on the market under that trade mark by the proprietor or with his consent, or that he (b) is a specialist or is specialized with regard to such goods, does this, under the scheme of Article 5 of the Directive, involve: (i) use of the trade mark in relation to goods which are identical to those for which it was registered, as referred to in Article 5(1)(a); (ii) use of that trade mark in relation to services which must be deemed to constitute use of the trade mark within the meaning of Article 5(1)(a) or use of the trade mark as referred to in Article 5(1)(b), on the assumption that it can be stated

of the BMW trade mark without its owner's authorization in advertisements
such as 'repairs and maintenance of BMWs', 'BMW specialist' and 'specialized in BMWs' is a use of the trade mark that falls within the scope of its
exclusivity, that is, a use of the trade mark as this is defined in Article 5(1)(a)
of the Directive.[14]

Even though it may seem so, this consideration is not without importance,
as the limitations on the trade mark right are *exceptions* to a trade mark
infringement under Article 5. Thus, the application of Article 6(1) involves
solely and exclusively determining whether the specific conditions referred
to above are fulfilled, as their fulfilment determines, as a matter of law, an
exception to the infringement. This explains the enormous practical importance of correctly interpreting the scope of these exceptions.

In relation to the three circumstances indicated above, Article 6(1)
contains a single *common* requisite to the three limitations on the trade mark
right: that the unauthorized use be in compliance 'with honest practices in
industrial or commercial matters'. In addition, the specific requisites of each
of the three atypical uses must obviously be fulfilled. For the sake of
simplicity, we will first examine the specific requisites and will then
consider the more complex issue of whether the facts that satisfy those
conditions comply with 'honest practices in industrial or commercial
matters'.

2.2   Specific Applicability of Article 6(1)(c)

As indicated, Article 6(1)(c) of the Directive bars the trade mark proprietor
from preventing certain use of the trade mark by third parties, in the course
of trade, if that use is necessary to indicate the purpose of a product or
service, particularly as an accessory or spare part. That is, the law regards
as licit the use of another's trade mark to indicate the purpose of a product
or service as far as this use is necessary. Such a need exists in the accessory
and spare part business, as mentioned in Article 6, and also in such businesses as the rendering of services that are bound in with certain branded
products, as was the case of the repair and maintenance services analysed
by the Ruling and which it expressly placed within the sphere of this

---

that there is an identity between those services and the goods for which the trade mark
was registered; (iii) use of the trade mark as referred to in Article 5(2); or (iv) use of
the trade mark as referred to in Article 5(5)?'

The third question to the Court for a preliminary ruling was: 'For the purpose of
answering Question 2, does it make any difference whether announcement (a) or
announcement (b) is involved?'

[14]   In particular, paras 38 to 42 of the Ruling.

provision.[15] This expansion of the applicability of this rule to cover those cases of the rendering of specialized services was possible since, in these categories of activity, the use of the trade mark is necessary in order to be able to identify the products that are subject to the rendered service.

The provision under discussion thus leads us to consider a significant range of products (which, logically, grows incrementally in proportion to the technology evolution) which, for their complex nature, require or might require

- the substitution of their component parts;
- their being complemented and improved by the use of accessory articles; and/or, also according to the Ruling,
- their maintenance or repair by expert services, adapted to their specific complexity.

The markets for these products are governed and guarded by the principle of free enterprise. That is, where there is no intangible right to impede their manufacture, whether it be a right in a product itself or over its accessories or spare parts, such as an industrial design right, such spare parts, accessories or specialized services may be manufactured or supplied by third parties with no connection to the trade mark proprietor, without the need for his consent. This situation makes it necessary for these third parties, on entering into their respective markets, to be able to inform prospective consumers about the purpose or utility of their services and, for this purpose, they must be permitted to mention the principal product's trade mark. Traditionally those economic activities linked to the automotive sector have been described as composing the principal market in which the permitted mention of another's trade mark is fundamental for expressing the purpose or function of an accessory product or component or of a specialized repair or maintenance service. Many product or service markets other than those of the automotive industry are in the same situation.

We are thus faced with an exception that is essential to protect the general interest of achieving and preserving market transparency. The Ruling establishes explicitly that the exception seeks to reconcile the fundamental interests of trade mark protection with those of the free movement of goods and the freedom to provide services in the common market.[16] In this sense, the

---

15   '[T]he use of the trade mark to inform the public that the advertiser repairs and maintains trade-marked goods must be held to constitute use indicating the intended purpose of the service within the meaning of Article 6(1)(c). Like the use of a trade mark intended to identify the vehicles which a non-original spare part will fit, the use in question is intended to identify the goods in respect of which the service is provided' (para. 59 of the Ruling).

16   Para. 62 of the Ruling.

indication of the principal product's trade mark is not only fundamental for
the manufacturer of the secondary products mentioned by the law, and for
the suppliers of such specialized services comparable to those analysed in
the Ruling who would have practically no access to their relevant market if
they could not refer to the purpose of their products or services, but also for
the obtaining by the consumers of adequate and sufficiently complete information to enable them to choose between different offers competing with
one another in the market. Recognition of these two interests, which are in
contrast with the trade mark proprietor's interest, is the result of a lengthy
and complex process at the heart of European trade mark law.

Not every conceivable use of another person's trade mark is legitimate,
even if through this use the purpose of a product or service is effectively
indicated. Only when such indication is *necessary* do we see before us a
legitimate use. The ECJ established that, on the facts upon which it had been
asked to rule, no doubt arose about the requirement or need of the analysed
use, since in its own words,

> if an independent trader carries out the maintenance and repair of BMW cars or is
> in fact a specialist in that field, that fact cannot in practice be communicated to
> his customers without using the BMW mark.[17]

Therefore the quality of 'necessary' is also related to the provision of information to the market. As a consequence, the use of the sign is necessary to
maintain an undistorted system of competition in the market for the relevant
product or service.

All in all, the conduct that seeks to attain the protection of Article 6(1)(c)
must thus consist in a trade mark use by a third party with the intention of
merely informing the relevant consumers of the purpose of the offered product or service and, even then, it is lawful only if the mention of the trade mark
is necessary.

2.3 Accordance with Honest Practices in Industrial or Commercial Matters

The fact that conduct that objectively appears to fit within the category of

---

[17] Para. 60 of the Ruling. The proprietor of the trade mark opposed the existence
of such need, alleging that Deenik could offer his maintenance and repair services without mentioning a specific automobile brand. In para. 54 of his Opinion, Advocate
General Jacobs describes this suggestion as unrealistic since, if a repair shop is specialized in the maintenance and repair of BMW cars, it will scarcely be able to communicate such circumstance effectively to its customers without making use of the sign
BMW.

permitted use under Article 6(1)(c) of the Directive is not, in any case, sufficient to trigger the exception. It is also necessary to make a subsequent determination and evaluation of *how* the use in question comes into play, as it is necessary that the use be 'in accordance with honest practices in industrial or commercial matters'. This indeterminate legal term has been considered as the equivalent of other legal concepts in the law system that have a greater pedigree, such as the general principle of good faith that must govern the exercise of any right. In our opinion, and as we seek to demonstrate from an objective point of view, the 'honest practice' condition should be the equivalent to not perpetrating an act of unfair competition. To come to this conclusion it is necessary to consider the basis of the exception, as the same causes that justify the tolerance of the trade mark infringement, essentially those coexistent interests that are also worthy of protection and require the possibility of descriptive and informative, not distinctive, use of a third party's trade mark, evolve into real conditions and limit the application of the exception.

As has been stated, the exceptions contained in Article 6(1) are motivated by the protection of certain interests which are concurrent with the interest of the trade mark proprietor and require the making of a descriptive use of a trade mark. Taking into account that the trade mark right is not of an absolute nature but is linked to a purpose and that, therefore, the right of exclusion is only an instrument to fulfil the trade mark's functions, when the *necessary* use of someone else's trade mark for the protection of concurrent interests does not affect the trade mark's functions (or does not affect them in a more than strictly indispensable manner), the exclusive right is made to yield.

In our opinion, the ultimate purpose of protection and stimulation of economic competition and the prevention of unjustified invasions of the trade mark's functions are the essential basis for giving content to the only objective premise included in Article 6(1), that of 'accordance with honest practices in industrial or commercial matters'. The Ruling was innovative in its time because it considered this scenario from a new perspective, determining that the functions of the trade mark are not restricted to the essential and traditional trade mark function (the distinctive or merely indicative origin of the products and services of an enterprise). Instead, those functions were shown to include the related guarantee function and the currently ubiquitous advertising function concerning the assemblage and communication of a certain image (goodwill, branding).[18] The Ruling provides the criteria

---

[18]   As regards the marketing function of the trade mark, see Advocate General Ruiz-Jarabo Colomer's Opinion in *Arsenal Football Club plc v Reed* Case C-206/01 [2002] ETMR 82 and the Ruling of the ECJ in *Peak Holding AB v Axolin Elinor AB* Case C-16/2003 [2005] ETMR 28.

for establishing an appropriate balance of interests, taking into consideration the advertising or marketing function of the trade mark, denying that the trade mark can be made increasingly powerful until it turns into an absolute monopoly but conferring upon it, nevertheless, a certain and proportionate protection.

Thus, logically, such classic cases in which another person's distinctive sign is used as a trade mark are not admitted,[19] but neither are other cases permitted in which the reference made to someone else's trade mark can be interpreted by the consumers as a(n) (erroneous) reference to the manufacturer of the spare parts and accessories or to the provider of the specialized services, or, which is the same, as a(n) (erroneous) reference to the circumstance that the affected products are original ones or products with the endorsement of the trade mark proprietor by virtue of a licence agreement.

It is in this context that the Ruling, when considering the situations in which the use of a third party's trade mark makes it possible to take advantage of the repute associated to it, damaging it in some way (or at least causing its dilution), also acknowledges that a certain degree of protection must be accorded to the advertising function of the trade mark, even though it does so neither in an absolute nor unconditional way. The mere fact that the provider of specialized services gains an advantage from the use of the trade mark is not sufficient to prevent its use. In other words, the fact that the advertising of his services in relation to the products of such trade mark, being correct and honest, confers upon his own activity a certain aura of quality does not provide sufficient justification to prohibit such a trade mark use.[20] Detriment to the reputation of the trade mark or, on the other side of the coin, the taking advantage of such reputation or prestige by the provider of services, will only prevent the application of the exception when the use of the mark exceeds that which is necessary and justified. Thus it is inevitable that a certain advantage will be derived from the positive associations linked to a third party's trade mark; this is inherent in those cases considered by the exception. This inevitable exploitation must be tolerated if the ultimate aim of Article 6(1)(c)

---

[19]   Very clearly, in the context of Paragraph (b): see *Windsurfing Chiemsee* Joined Cases C-108/97 and C-109/97 [1999] ECR I-2779, [1999] ETMR 585, para. 28): 'Article 6(1)(b), which aims, inter alia, to resolve the problems posed by registration of a mark consisting wholly or partly of a geographical name, does not confer on third parties the right to use the name as a trade mark but merely guarantees their right to use it descriptively, that is to say, as an indication of geographical origin, provided that it is used in accordance with honest practices in industrial and commercial matters'.

[20]   Paras 53 and 63 of the Ruling.

is to be effective, which is to reconcile the fundamental interests of the protection of the trade mark right and of the free movement of goods within the Common Market.[21]

Consequently, according to the Ruling, infringement in these cases can only be assumed when the trade mark is used in such a way as to cause the impression that there exists a commercial connection between the service provider and the trade mark proprietor (as could have been the case, in BMW, if the defendant had created the implication that he was affiliated to BMW's official distribution network). Thus there is no need to assess whether an advertiser profits unjustifiably from the reputation of a competitor's distinctive signs, when the reference made to those signs is a necessary condition for the existence of effective competition in the affected market.[22] If, however, the trade mark proprietor were entitled to prohibit the use of his trade mark on the sole ground that the user would inevitably take some sort of advantage from it, we would be, in the words of Advocate General Francis Jacobs, imposing an undue restriction on the trader's freedom, an unjustified impediment to trade or fair competition.[23]

This consideration leads to the conclusion that the requirement of conformity of the conduct with the parameters of loyalty and competitive fairness supported by our legal system seeks to avoid the misuse or abuse of the exception so as to conceal dishonest acts: this suggests that there is an equivalence between the requirements laid down for lawful use under Article 6(1) and the suppression of unfair competition. As established by the Ruling,[24] and as has been corroborated repeatedly in the jurisprudence of the ECJ,[25] the condition requiring use of the trade mark to be made in accordance with honest practices in industrial or commercial matters must be regarded as constituting in substance the expression of a duty to act fairly in relation to the legitimate interests of the trade mark owner.

The principal objective premises for these atypical uses may now be identified as follows: (i) given that they may not invade the distinctive function of the trade mark, they must be descriptive uses – without the function of distinguishing goods – and they must not entail any risk of confusion or association; and (ii) given that they may not gratuitously invade the advertising function of the trade mark, they must be neutral uses that do not constitute an unjustified

---

21   Para. 62 of the Ruling.
22   *Toshiba Europe* Case C-112/99 [2001] ECR I-7945, [2002] ETMR 26, para. 54.
23   Paras 55 and 56 of Advocate General Jacobs' Opinion.
24   Para. 61 of the Ruling.
25   *Gerolsteiner & Brunnen GmbH & Co. v Putsch GmbH* [2004] ETMR 40, para. 24; *Gillette Co., Gillette Finland Co OY v LA-Laboratories Ltd OY*, Case C-228/03 [2005] ETMR 67, para. 41.

or disproportionate exploitation of the repute associated with the third party's sign. This excludes, evidently, any use made as if it were a trade mark. Only once we have recognized this can we find the point of balance which the system seeks between the patrimonial value of the trade mark, necessarily linked to its functions (most particularly to the publicity function), and the protection of the other interests that coexist with it, particularly the interest in transparency of information in the market which is an essential requisite for the free and proper development of trade of goods and services.

In any case, following our opinion, the requisite does not intend to prohibit one specific act of unfair competition, but rather all such acts. Thus, an act of passing-off or an act constituting the enjoyment of an undue advantage of someone else's reputation, such as those we have just mentioned, would be prohibited. Furthermore, the right to prohibit should not give way to any conduct to be classified as acts of unfair competition, such as fraud, unfair imitation or denigration.[26] Therefore, in these cases the conduct should, in our opinion, also be classed as a trade mark infringement.

2.4 Practical Considerations

In summary, the use of the trade mark by a person who is not its owner must be, according to Article 6(1)(a), a *necessary* use and also a *neutrally descriptive* use – it must not have advertising purposes or by other means freely and unjustifiably invade the role of the trade mark.

As regards necessary use, the 'need' referred to must always be a matter of fact that is assessed according to the particular circumstances of each case and after consideration of the different interests in question. In all events, the following guidelines may be of assistance in assessing whether the use of another's trade mark is necessary:

- The use is only necessary if it is the only means to furnish the public with understandable and complete information as to the purpose of the product or service. As a consequence:
  - the need to use another's trade mark will not permit, for instance, the citation of a given trade mark if the services provided by the user are not strictly specialized with regard to products bearing that trade mark but relate instead to the category of products within

---

[26]   In *Gillette Co.* the ECJ added to the ruling in *BMW* that the use of the trade mark will not be in accordance with Article 6(1)(c) either if it discredits or denigrates that mark (para. 44), or where the third party presents its product as an imitation or replica of the product bearing the trade mark of which it is not the owner (para. 45).

which such products belong. In this sense, the ECJ has stated that it is necessary to take into account, for instance, the potential existence of technical criteria or of generally used rules for the kind of product commercialized by the third party and which are known by the public to whom this kind of product is addressed.[27]

– notwithstanding the above, as the ECJ has also stated, the existence of these rules or technical criteria may not be enough in order to exclude the need to refer to another's mark, given that it is necessary for these rules and criteria to furnish to the public, according to the specific sector of the public, comprehensive information as to the purpose of the product or service.

As regards the second requirement, the descriptive use, the establishment of the parameters of lawful competition, is also a factual matter that must always be assessed on a case-by-case basis according to the specific circumstances and always from the global perspective of the advertisement or of any other relevant use of the trade mark in question.[28] The consumer's perception may be of crucial importance. In any case, logically, those cases in which a third party's sign is used as a trade mark are not permitted. Nor, as we have seen, are those uses allowed where, for other reasons, a reference to another's trade mark may be mistakenly interpreted by the consumer as a mistaken reference to the party that manufactures spare parts or the accessories or provides the specialized services, or similarly where the consumer mistakenly refers to products as being original or as having a guarantee or endorsement by virtue of a licence agreement.

Even though a case-by-case analysis is always required, it is possible to put forward a series of rules, principles or factors the presence of which may be helpful in order to assess whether the use by a third party of another's trade mark is a permitted descriptive use or an infringement of the trade mark.

The basic guidelines for the use of another's trade mark under Article 6(1)(c) are as follows:

• One should avoid any use of another's trade mark that suggests or causes the impression of the existence of a commercial link with its owner. Manufacturers or suppliers of accessories or spare parts and those people providing specialized services should avoid, therefore, suggesting to the consumer that there exist organizational links (for

---

[27]   *Gillette Co.,* paras 36 and 37.
[28]   *Toshiba Europe,* para. 58.

instance, membership of the same group) or legal links (for instance, a licence agreement) with the trade mark's owner.

- In order to avoid such suggestion, it is recommended for the person providing the service to attach one of his own trade marks, used as a trade mark, in addition to the descriptive use of the third party mark that might in theory entail a risk of confusion.
- The manner of use of the third party's trade mark should not create the impression that the third party's trade mark is a trade mark of the user's product or service. To this end, the third party's trade mark should not be featured in a position of prominence in the advertisement, packaging or other medium. Descriptive indications which include a third party trade mark should appear typographically in the background, thus reflecting their merely informative meaning or purpose.
- One should avoid any other use of another's trade mark that implies an undue benefit, if it is unjustified, of the reputation associated to someone else's trade mark.
- One should avoid any use of another's trade mark that, in any other way, suggests that the user is engaging in behaviour that constitutes unfair competition, avoiding in particular the denigration or discrediting of the third party's trade mark or representing that one's products are imitations or replicas of the product identified by such trade mark.

In this context a third party using another's trade mark in order to specify the purpose of the products and services which it provides does not necessarily imply that he is offering them as being of the same quality or as possessing equivalent features. Whether a representation of this nature has been made will always depend on the specific facts.[29]

This guidance may not be sufficient in all cases, given that the mention of another's trade mark, even by itself, may implicitly entail a risk of confusion. Accordingly the user of another's trade mark is not only bound by the restrictions described above but also by a positive duty to adopt preventive measures by furnishing additional information in order to avoid misrepresenting the truth to the consumer[30].

Accordingly, manufacturers and suppliers of accessories or spare parts and businesses that provide specialized services must clearly and visibly

---

[29] *Gillette Co.,* end of para. 49.
[30] 'The effort made by that third party to ensure that consumers distinguish its products from those of which it is not the trade mark owner' is one of the factors to take into account when assessing the accordance of such use with fair practices. Also *Gillette Co.,* para. 46.

specify the origin of their products and services, avoiding the use of expressions such as 'original' or 'official' products or services or of similar classifications and leaving out any deliberated obscurity. It may even be more appropriate for them to declare that their products or services do not originate from the owner of the trade mark and that there exist no other organizational or juridical links with him.[31]

---

[31]   In *Toshiba Europe* the ECJ considered necessary, in order to make a comparative advertisement, even the use of the reference numbers for the spare parts manufactured by the trade mark owner in order to indicate the function of the third party's spare parts. When assessing the specific use it took into account the fact that in the third party's materials the identity of Katun was clearly distinguishable from that of Toshiba Europe.

10. Refills, recharged batteries and recycled products[1]

Wolfgang Kellenter

1. INTRODUCTION

Many producers of trade marked goods do not confine themselves simply to putting their products on the market. Rather, they build up a system that allows them to benefit from the product even after it is no longer capable of fulfilling its originally intended purpose. For instance, the producer of SodaStream drink-makers offers to take back empty carbon dioxide cylinders in order to refill them and then redistribute them. It is in the interests of such undertakings to maintain exclusive control over these secondary markets. The question is, can SodaStream invoke trade mark law to prevent third parties from refilling and redistributing its cylinders?

Even if an undertaking is not itself engaged in refilling or recycling its own products, it may have a genuine interest in preventing third parties from doing so. Every refilled or recycled product sold may take the place of a new product, especially as reworked products are normally cheaper than the originals. Some second-hand car dealers, for example, specialise in repairing and reselling cars which have been involved in accidents. If such a dealer were to repair a damaged MERCEDES car, could Mercedes rely on trade mark law to prevent the sale of that car? Would the situation be any different if all the spare parts used to repair the car had been supplied by Mercedes itself?

1.1 The Acts under Consideration

The acts of refilling, recharging or recycling pertain to products that have been put on the market but which, after they have been in use for a certain period of time, require special treatment in order to be usable again.

---

[1] The author would like to thank his colleague Daniel Kurth for his valuable contribution to this chapter.

1.1.1 Refills

Products which consist of a container with a particular content may eventually be emptied as a result of use. The container – a gas cylinder, for instance, or an ink cartridge – may then be refilled by third parties, whether with contents made by the original producer or with similar contents provided by a different producer. Such products might also be refilled with a totally different content – a COCA-COLA bottle with apple juice, for example.

1.1.2 Recharged batteries

A special case of refilling is the recharging of batteries. In their original condition they are, in a non-technical sense, filled with electric power. When the battery is used, this power is eventually exhausted and the battery has to be 'refilled' in order to be used again.[2]

1.1.3 Recycled products

The term 'recycled products' relates to products which, in the course of their use, have in some way become impaired – for example the paintwork or varnish may be in a poor condition, or they may have been damaged as a result of an accident. 'Recycling' covers two different ways of treating these products. The first is repairing the product, restoring it to its original condition. The second involves working on the product, not in order to restore its original condition but to create a different product which, as such, can be put on the market again. It would probably not be very profitable to restore used jeans to their original condition as new jeans. But if there is a market for used jeans in loud colours, why not dye them and resell them as used dyed jeans?

1.1.4 Summary

All these acts are treatments of *used products* which need to be *reworked* in some way in order to be *put on the market again*.[3] From an economic point of view, such treatments can be regarded as beneficial because products are brought back into the economic cycle rather than being discarded. If, however, the product bears a trade mark and is redistributed under that mark after it has been reworked, such behaviour may come into conflict with the trade mark rights of the original distributor.

---

[2]   The recharging of rechargeable batteries by parties who want to redistribute them is not a major business. Normally, batteries – rechargeable or not – are *recycled* by resolving them into their different metallic constituents. Typically, only consumers or end-users recharge batteries. On this see below, Section 3.2.

[3]   This chapter is concerned with the issue of redistributing reworked trade mark products. The separate issue of using a trade mark to *promote the services* of reworking trade marked products is covered in Chapter 9.

1.2 The Approach Taken

The German courts have been trying to solve this conflict for over a century. As yet, however, the European Court of Justice (ECJ) has not had to address the issue directly. Nevertheless, it is crucial that we analyse current ECJ case law in analogous or related cases in order to determine how the ECJ might evaluate conflicting interests and on which grounds it would base its decision. The experience of the German courts in dealing with this issue provides valuable additional insight.

2. ANALYSIS OF THE ECJ CASE LAW

2.1 Relevance of Current ECJ Case Law

ECJ case law in this area is concerned mainly with parallel importation where new goods – often pharmaceutical products – are purchased in one country, repackaged and then imported into a second country where they can be profitably resold. A major postulate for the legitimacy of this is, according to the ECJ, that the repackaging cannot affect the original condition of the product.[4]

While this 'original condition' test may be appropriate in relation to new products, the products discussed in this chapter have already lost their original condition over the course of time; when they are reworked their condition is altered. It is therefore evident that a direct application of the tests set out by the ECJ in its parallel importation cases is impossible.

Nevertheless, the ECJ rulings contain a detailed discussion of the various interests at stake in those cases. Those interests constitute the framework within which questions relating to refilled or recycled products must be answered.

2.2 Interests of the Persons Concerned

2.2.1 Holder of the trade mark

According to the ECJ, part of the specific subject matter of the trade mark right is the proprietor's right to oppose any use of the trade mark which is liable to impair the *guarantee of origin*.[5] The guarantee of origin means that

---

[4]   ECJ, *Frits Loendersloot trading as F. Loendersloot Internationale Expeditie v George Ballantine & Son Ltd and others* Case C-349/95 [1998] E.T.M.R. 10 ('*Loendersloot*'), para. 29; cf. Chapter 7.

[5]   *Loendersloot*, para. 24; ECJ, *Bristol-Myers Squibb v Paranova* A/S Case C-427/93 [1996] ETMR 1 ('*Bristol-Myers Squibb*'), para. 48; ECJ, *Hoffmann-La Roche v Centrafarm* Case 102/77 [1978] ('*Hoffmann-La Roche*'), para. 7.

the consumer or end-user can be certain that a trade marked product offered to him has not been subject at a previous stage of marketing to interference by a third party, without the authorisation of the trade mark owner, so as to affect the original condition of the product.[6] The proprietor can thus legitimately oppose the further marketing of a product bearing a trade mark if that product has been subject to interference by a third party without his authorisation.[7]

Moreover, the ECJ considers that, in a system of undistorted competition, undertakings must be able to attract and retain customers on the basis of the quality of their products, which is made possible only where distinctive signs let them be identified. The trade mark, therefore, must constitute a guarantee that all products which bear it have been manufactured under the control of a single undertaking to which responsibility for their quality may be attributed.[8]

What the ECJ does not mention specifically is the fact that the proprietor normally invests time, effort and money in establishing goodwill in his trade mark and in maintaining the quality of products sold under the mark. This investment also has to be protected.

2.2.2   Competitors

Competitors, on the other hand, are interested in competing with the original producer by rendering their own services, namely by reworking and distributing used products. In many of its decisions (mainly concerning cross-border cases), the ECJ has stressed the importance of the fundamental interest in the free movement of goods within the common market. The ECJ has held that the owner of a trade mark is not permitted to oppose the use of the mark where such opposition would contribute to the artificial partitioning of the markets between Member States.[9]

This principle applies at a lower level too: the trade mark owner cannot be allowed to use the mark simply to keep competitors out of the market for reworked goods. A trade mark is a medium for identifying a product and thus guaranteeing its origin. It does not serve as a means of controlling the further distribution and disposition of a product, for instance by building up an exclusive distribution system.

2.2.3   Customers

The interests of potential customers are ambivalent. A customer might benefit

---

[6]   *Loendersloot*, para. 24; *Bristol-Myers Squibb*, para. 47; *Hoffmann-La Roche*, para. 7.

[7]   *Loendersloot*, para. 25.

[8]   ECJ, *CNL-Sucal NV v Hag GF AG* Case C-10/89 [1990] ('HAG II'), para. 13; *Loendersloot*, para. 22; *Bristol-Myers Squibb*, para. 43.

[9]   *Hoffmann-La Roche*, para. 10; *Loendersloot*, para. 28.

from better terms – especially a lower price – from a competitor who has reworked a trade marked product. In contrast, he might prefer to have the guarantee of quality which only the original distributor can provide. In particular, a brand-conscious customer who pays a premium in order to obtain a trade marked product will expect that there are no goods marketed under the same brand which would devalue the reputation of, or the image associated with, that product. For instance, a person who buys expensive new Levi's jeans, intending to show the world that he wears only high quality jeans, would not like to come across someone wearing used yellow denim shorts bearing the same mark. At this point we are brought back to a consideration of the interests of the trade mark owner: a customer who feels that the prestige of the trade mark with which he has chosen to identify himself is beginning to wane will eventually look for a different product to fulfil his needs.

2.2.4 Conclusion
An examination of the problems of refilled or recycled products must reconcile the interests of the different market participants, in particular the trade mark owner's interest in labelling his product and thereby guaranteeing its origin and quality and his competitors' interest in freedom of competition. These interests influence the application of the relevant provisions governing trade mark infringement in relation to refilling, recharging or recycling trade marked products.

3. FIRST STEP: INFRINGEMENT OF THE TRADE MARK

Before we even reach the stage of trying to balance conflicting interests, we must assess whether a particular act falls within existing provisions governing trade mark infringement. European law governs trade mark infringement in Art.5 of the Trade Mark Directive[10] and Art.9 of the Community Trade Mark Regulation.[11] Both (nearly identically) stipulate:

> The proprietor shall be entitled to prevent all third parties not having his consent from using in the course of trade: (a) any sign which is identical with the trade mark in relation to goods or services which are identical with those for which the trade mark is registered.

---

[10] First Council Directive 89/104 of 21 December 1988 to approximate the laws of the Member States relating to trade marks.
[11] Council Regulation 40/94 of 20 December 1993 on the Community trade mark.

3.1 Identical Trade Mark – Identical Goods

The requirement that there be an identical trade mark and goods identical with those for which the trade mark is registered does not usually present a significant obstacle to a finding of infringement. Very often the original trade mark remains on the product during and after the reworking process or, if it is removed, it will normally be reaffixed subsequently. Similarly, the reworking will usually not be so significant that the reworked product is no longer the same as the type of product for which the trade mark is registered.

3.2 Use in the Course of Trade

Additionally, it is required that the trade mark be used in the course of trade, thus excluding acts within the purely private sphere, or wholly internal acts within a company or other organisation, from the scope of trade mark protection. If the use of the mark remains a personal matter, the guarantee of origin is not affected, there being no third person who could wrongly associate the altered product with the original producer.

There is thus no trade mark infringement if a private person reworks a used product or refills an empty container which bears a trade mark. Equally, someone taking the batteries from his MP3 player and recharging them by means of a recharging device, for re-use in his MP3 player, is not acting illegally.

The same principle applies to an entrepreneur recycling or refilling goods *on behalf of* a private person. An exception would be where the entrepreneur reworking the product gives the impression that he has permission from the original distributor to do so; in this case he is acting not only on behalf of the private person but also, ostensibly, on behalf of the original distributor whose labelling right he is arrogating. This constitutes use of the trade mark in the course of trade, which may be prohibited by the proprietor if done without his consent.

To be legitimate, use of a trade mark must remain internal. In a decision on towel dispensers, the German Federal Supreme Court reasoned that, if an indefinite number of people would have access to the goods, it would no longer be an internal use but use in the course of trade.[12]

3.3 Without the Consent of the Proprietor

Another requirement is that the trade mark be used without the proprietor's consent. If the proprietor waives his right to prohibit the use of the trade mark, the use is not illegal.

---

[12]   German Federal Supreme Court Case KZR 43/85 [1987], GRUR 1987, 438.

The consent need not be declared explicitly; implied consent will suffice. However, finding implied consent can sometimes be difficult. According to the German Federal Supreme Court, even the delivery by the original manufacturer of spare parts for automobiles cannot be presumed to be implied consent to any reworking of cars under its trade mark because typically the supplier expects a lawful use of the spare parts, for example repairing a private person's car. Clearly, if the proprietor explicitly prohibits the use of his trade mark on a recycled or refilled product it will not be possible to find implied consent. In such a case, the trade mark is only used legitimately if one of the exceptions discussed below applies.

3.4 Use of the Trade Mark as Such

Besides these requirements, derived from the wording of Art.5 of the Trade Mark Directive,[13] the ECJ will only find an infringement if the trade mark is used as such:[14] It must be used for the purpose of distinguishing the goods in question as originating from a particular undertaking.[15] Merely informative use of the trade mark, in contrast, does not affect the guarantee of origin.[16]

The question is, under which circumstances can the trade mark – although still affixed to the product – lose its function as a trade mark? In principle, a customer who sees a product bearing a trade mark has no cause to doubt the normal function of the trade mark as a guarantee of the product's origin. Accordingly only explicit and manifest circumstances will suffice to deprive a trade mark of its normal function.[17]

3.4.1 Additional reference
In German case law, a trade mark was held to have lost its branding function when an additional sign was affixed to the product – a rebuilt gambling machine – explicitly stating that the machine, originally distributed by the original trade mark holder under its trade mark, had been rebuilt by another party and redistributed under a different mark.[18] In such a case, the mention of the original trade mark is only an informative reference to the original

---

[13] Art.9 of the Community Trade Mark Regulation.
[14] This requirement is sometimes understood as part of the 'use in the course of trade' requirement.
[15] ECJ, *Bayerische Motorenwerke AG (BMW) and BMW Nederland BV v Deenik* Case C-63/97 [1999] ETMR 339 (*'BMW'*), para. 38.
[16] Cf. *BMW*, para. 54.
[17] Reichsgericht Case II 161/38 [1939], RGZ 161, 29.
[18] German Federal Supreme Court Case 1 ZR 259/95 [1998], GRUR 1998, 697.

product; it is no longer an indicator associating the product in its current condition with its original manufacturer.

Such additional reference must be *affixed to the product*. It is not sufficient to put a note on the packaging, as this does not remain on the product permanently. Similarly, it would not suffice to display a sign in the saleroom. In both cases a person faced with the product after it has been unpacked or removed from the saleroom would naturally understand the original trade mark as associating the product in its current condition with the original producer.[19]

Even if the sign is affixed to the product itself, the method of attaching it should be sufficiently permanent. Attaching a paper label to a glass bottle is insufficient if that label is likely to come loose due to contact with the liquid content of the bottle.[20] Such a paper label would likewise be inadequate on a clutch system, as it would wear off in a short time due to the operating conditions of the clutch.[21] Whether a simple paper label can be regarded as sufficiently permanent will depend on the circumstances of the individual case.

The note or additional reference must show clearly that the original trade mark holder no longer guarantees the quality of the product. It has been held insufficient simply to attach an adhesive label to a LEXMARK ink cartridge stating 'Green Cartridge',[22] to paint the word 'remanufactured' on to a clutch system[23] or to add the term 'Pianova based on' to the original trade mark STEINWAY on grand pianos.[24] The main issue in these cases was that it was not made clear to the purchaser what the additional reference was supposed to indicate. The word 'remanufactured' in the clutch case could also have been understood as relating only to a wearing part and not the entire clutch system. Similarly, the term 'Pianova based on Steinway' did not clearly indicate that an old product had been totally reworked. Instead, the remaining trade mark could still give the impression to a consumer that the product had been refurnished by the original distributor or at least with his permission. Thus in all these cases the additional labels did not serve to deprive the original trade marks of their normal function of associating the product with the trade mark holder.

Only in the recent *SodaStream* case[25] has the German Supreme Court considered the strict requirements to be fulfilled. A SodaStream gas cylinder,

[19]   Similarly ECJ, *Arsenal Football Club plc v Matthew Reed Case* C-206/01 [2002] ETMR 19 (*'Arsenal'*), para. 57.
[20]   German Federal Supreme Court 1 ZR 165/54 [1956], GRUR 1957, 84.
[21]   Hamburg Court of Appeals Case 3 U 176/96 [1997], GRUR 1997, 855; Munich Court of Appeals Case 6 U 6251/90 [1992], WRP 1993, 47.
[22]   Frankfurt Court of Appeals Case 6 U 93/99 [1999], GRUR 2000, 1062.
[23]   Hamburg Court of Appeals Case 3 U 176/96 [1997], GRUR 1997, 855; Munich Court of Appeals Case 6 U 6251/90 [1992], WRP 1993, 47.
[24]   Hamburg Court of Appeals Case 3 U 58/00 [2001], GRUR 2001, 749.
[25]   German Federal Supreme Court Case 1 ZR 44/02 [2004], GRUR 2005, 162.

bearing the trade mark 'SodaStream' engraved on the valve and an additional label featuring the mark on the body of the cylinder, was refilled by a third person. Before putting it back on the market, the refiller replaced the label with his own label. The engraving on the valve, however, remained. The court explained that, when put on the market for the first time, the engraving as well as the label associated both the cylinder and its content with the trade mark owner. After the label had been exchanged, and another label affixed bearing the refiller's mark and clearly indicating that the cylinder had been refilled by him, the engraving was deprived of its function of associating the content of the cylinder with the trade mark holder. Once the new label had been applied, the function of the engraving was limited to associating the container itself with the trade mark owner.[26]

The *SodaStream* court based its judgment mainly on the perception of consumers purchasing such a refilled gas cylinder. In this particular case the court assumed that a typical consumer would normally recognise that the trade mark on the valve no longer served to indicate the proprietor, because the new label showed a different person as refiller. It conceded, however, that under different circumstances the decision could have been different. For instance, if the consumer had previously been used to having the cylinders refilled only by the original producer, he might understand the new label as indicating that the refilling was done by a company with a formal business relationship with the original distributor. If that perception could be proved, the trade mark would retain its function of associating the product with the proprietor.

3.4.2 Second brand
The perception of consumers also becomes relevant if there is no real additional reference but the refiller or recycler has simply added his mark as a second brand. In a very limited number of cases such a second brand may be sufficient to destroy the connection between the original mark and its owner. For instance the brand BRABUS for the company which modifies Mercedes cars will usually be understood as indicating that the automobile in its current condition originates from the Brabus company, and no longer from Mercedes. Nevertheless, these exceptions rarely appear.

3.4.3 Total removal of the original mark
Given the difficulties in formulating and affixing a suitable additional clarificatory reference to a trade marked product, the simplest solution – in terms of trade mark law – would seem to be the total removal of the mark. In such a

---

[26] With regard to the container, however, the proprietor's rights were exhausted, cf. below Section 4.4.1.

case there is unlikely to be a danger of the product being associated with the trade mark owner. However, a redistributor will not normally favour this option as he wishes to profit from the fact that the product which he has reworked originates from the trade mark owner. Moreover, the removal of a trade mark might bring him into conflict with the law of unfair competition which protects, for instance, against the obstruction of the proprietor's advertising.

3.4.4 No additional reference

Austrian case law apparently considers that in some cases the condition of the reworked product may be sufficient in itself to deprive the trade mark of its normal function, so that no additional reference on the product is required. The Austrian Supreme Court had to decide, on the basis of the implemented Trade Mark Directive, a case where parts of a cleaning machine for conveyor belts were reworked and redistributed.[27] These parts did not – apart from their original trade mark – bear any clarificatory reference or second brand. However, they had been reworked in a way that clearly indicated – even for a person that did not know the original product – that they were no longer new.[28] According to the Supreme Court, that should be sufficient to avoid a trade mark infringement. This, however, goes too far. Although an end-user might clearly recognize that the product has been reworked, he cannot reliably conclude that it has lost its relation to the trade mark holder. He can just as well expect that it has been reworked by the trade mark owner himself or at least by a company related to the trade mark owner.[29] The product, although clearly recognizable as having been reworked, does not of itself unequivocally indicate that the trade mark owner no longer guarantees its quality.

3.4.5 Additional reference necessary even if use is permitted for other reasons

At the other extreme is the approach taken by the ECJ in its decisions on the repackaging of pharmaceutical goods that, even if use of the trade mark is already permitted for other reasons,[30] an additional reference is always necessary in order to legitimise use of the mark.[31] In *Hoffmann-LaRoche* the ECJ held that it was correct in principle to allow the trader to sell a repackaged

---

[27] Austrian Supreme Court Case 4 Ob 133/94 [1994], GRUR Int. 1995, 810.
[28] There were traces showing that the parts were abraded; a new layer was applied in a colour different from the product's original colour.
[29] Similarly *BMW*, para. 51.
[30] Cf. ECJ, *Eurim-Pharm Arzneimittel GmbH v Beiersdorf* AG Case C-71/94 [1996] (*'Eurim-Pharm'*), para. 58.
[31] *Hoffmann-La Roche*, para. 12; *Eurim-Pharm*, paras 59 et seq.

product on condition that he states on the new packaging that the product has been repacked by him, the application of this principle not being limited to medicinal products. Subsequently, however, in *Loendersloot* the ECJ conceded that, in formulating those conditions, account had been taken of the legitimate interests of the trade mark owner with regard to the particular nature of pharmaceutical products.[32] Consequently in *Loendersloot*, which was about the repackaging of whisky, the condition of affixing an additional reference to the product was not mentioned. Given that this aspect of *Hoffmann-La Roche* has been distinguished as relating to the particular nature of pharmaceutical products, there is no obvious reason why the ECJ should apply it in a refilling or recycling case.

It is possible to conclude from this discussion that use of a trade mark on a refilled or recycled product, where that use is not otherwise permitted for other reasons, can be legitimised by affixing a clear reference to the product which explicitly deprives the original trade mark of its normal function of associating the product with the trade mark owner.

3.5 Bagatelles

In some cases, the act of reworking a trade marked product is so minimal that one cannot speak in terms of 'infringement' at all, for example if the redistributor only sews on a button that has dropped off a branded garment.[33] Trade mark law does not give the proprietor the right to prevent such bagatelles.

4.   SECOND STEP: EXHAUSTION OF RIGHTS DOCTRINE

4.1 Overview

Apart from the conditions for trade mark infringement listed above, we must consider an additional provision when dealing with the issue of refilled or recycled products. Art.7(1) of the Trade Mark Directive[34] stipulates: 'The trade mark shall not entitle the proprietor to prohibit its use in relation to goods which have been put on the market in the Community under that trade mark by the proprietor or with his consent'. Art.7(2) disapplies this 'where there

---

32   *Loendersloot*, para. 48.
33   One may also presume that this is regularly done with the proprietor's implied consent.
34   Art.13(1) of the Community Trade Mark Regulation.

exist legitimate reasons for the proprietor to oppose further commercialisation of the goods, especially where the condition of the goods is changed or impaired after they have been put on the market'.

Art.7 of the Trade Mark Directive reflects the terms used by the ECJ in judgments which, in interpreting Articles 30 and 36 of the EC Treaty, recognise in Community law the principle of exhaustion of the rights conferred by a trade mark.[35]

4.2 Exhaustion

Art.7 is the starting point for reconciling the conflicting interests of the trade mark holder and the refiller or recycler.[36] Without the exhaustion of rights doctrine, a trade mark holder can control possession, distribution and marketing of his products throughout their entire lifespan. Such boundless trade mark protection would unacceptably impair the freedom of the market. For this reason the rights of a trade mark owner in his product are explicitly extinguished when the product is put on the market for the first time by him or with his consent.

A typical feature of products which need to be reworked is that they are placed on the market by the proprietor beforehand – the need to rework products rarely arises before goods have left the proprietor's warehouse. Consequently, paragraph 1 extinguishes the rights of the trade mark holder in those goods.

Exhaustion covers all the rights of the trade mark owner in the goods which have been put on the market, such as the right to prohibit the use of the trade mark in relation to the resale,[37] the right to make use of the trade mark for advertising[38] and the right to affix the trade mark to a product.[39]

4.3 Exceptions

As Art.7(2) shows, exhaustion of the trade mark owner's rights is not without exceptions. If there are legitimate reasons to oppose further commercialisation, the rights are reconstituted. But as this conflicts with the principle of free movement of goods, the exceptions can only apply as far as is justified in order

---

[35]   *Bristol-Myers Squibb*, para. 31; ECJ, *Pharmacia & Upjohn SA v Paranova A/S* Case C-379/97 [1999] ETMR 937 (*'Pharmacia & Upjohn'*), para. 13.

[36]   Cf. above, Section 2.2.

[37]   ECJ, *Parfums Christian Dior SA and Parfums Christian Dior BV v Evora* BV Case C-337/95 [1997] ETMR 26 ('Dior'), paras 36 and 38.

[38]   *Dior*, paras 36 and 38.

[39]   *Bristol-Myers Squibb*, paras 32 et seq.

to safeguard the rights which constitute the specific subject matter of trade mark law, that is the guarantee of origin.[40] This must be considered when examining whether there exist legitimate reasons as required by Art.7(2), especially if the condition of the goods is changed or impaired.

In Germany the courts have, from the outset, proceeded on a similar basis. An overview of the developments in Germany therefore provides a basis for a clearer understanding of Art.7(2).

4.4   Legitimate Reason 1: Change in the Nature of the Product

One approach to deciding whether there is a legitimate reason is to examine whether the refilling or recycling of the product changes its *particular nature*.[41] The nature of any product is made up of the specific characteristics which the end-user or consumer attributes to it. These, in turn, derive from the quality of the product which the end-user expects as a result of his experience with the product and from the image of the product created by the trade mark owner in the consumer's mind by means of advertising. Ultimately, the trade mark owner himself defines the particular nature of his product through the product's quality and his marketing efforts.

In deciding whether the particular nature of the product has been changed, we must take into account the interests of the opposing parties mentioned above. On the one hand, if the product is changed and that change was beyond the control of the trade mark holder, he can no longer guarantee the quality of the product. In particular:

- Refills: after refilling an original container which bears a trade mark – or which itself is protected by trade mark law as a three-dimensional shape – the mark relates to a content that is different from the particular content which was originally put on the market.
- Recharged batteries: if a battery is recharged by a third party, the proprietor cannot ensure that it complies with the technical requirements he guarantees for batteries that originate from his own business. However, the recharging of batteries is a mere private business that normally does not affect rights of a trade mark owner.[42]
- Recycled products: when a product is recycled, it goes through a process of alteration which can be more or less intensive. The end-product is different from the product that left the business of the trade

---

40   *Loendersloot*, para. 21 et seq.
41   This aspect also appears in the ECJ jurisdiction, cf. *Eurim-Pharm*, para. 49.
42   See above, Section 3.2.

mark owner, although it still bears his trade mark and thus gives the impression that it derives – as it is – from his business.

On the other hand, we must consider the legitimate interest of competitors in undistorted competition. Thus not every treatment of the product can be understood as a change in its nature as this would close the market in favour of the trade mark owner.

These aspects must be balanced when examining whether there has been a change in the particular nature of the product. Case law provides us with the following illuminating decisions:

4.4.1   Refills

As mentioned, in *SodaStream*[43] the mark on the valve of the SodaStream gas cylinder lost, according to the German Federal Court, its function of guaranteeing the origin of the contents because of a newly affixed paper label. Nevertheless, it retained its function of guaranteeing the origin of the cylinder itself. The trade mark rights relating to the cylinder, however, where exhausted because the cylinder had been put on the market. The court further explained that the refilling of the container did not change its particular nature and was not therefore an exception to the exhaustion, as the refilling with carbon dioxide gas was the intended use of the gas cylinder.

In another case concerning the refilling of glass bottles[44] the circumstances were slightly, but significantly, different. The bottle, which was designed to be filled with mineral water, had been refilled with table water. Since this was not the use intended for the bottle, it was held contrary to the particular nature of the bottle and the trade mark owner could oppose the refilling. A similar decision resulted where ink cartridges were refilled with ink of a different origin[45] and also where an undertaking producing paper towels offered its own products to refill towel dispensers which were supplied by a different undertaking.[46] In these cases the interest which the trade mark holder had in not being associated with a content that differed from the content distributed by himself was judged to be more important than the refiller's interests. Only a clear additional reference on the product, which would have destroyed such a connection,[47] or the consent of the proprietor, could have prevented the use of the trade mark on the refilled product constituting an infringement.

---

43   German Federal Supreme Court Case 1 ZR 44/02 [2004], GRUR 2005, 162.
44   Zweibrücken Court of Appeals Case 2 U 21/98 [1999], GRUR 2000, 511.
45   Frankfurt Court of Appeals Case 6 U 93/99 [1999], GRUR 2000, 1062.
46   German Federal Supreme Court Case KZR 43/85 [1987], GRUR 1987, 438.
47   In *Lexmark* the hint, however, was not sufficient, cf. above, Section 3.4.1.

4.4.2 Recycled products

In a case concerning grand pianos bearing the famous trade marks STEINWAY and STEINWAY & SONS[48] it was ruled that the particular nature of the pianos was changed as the 'soul of the instrument',[49] meaning the sounding board and the sounding posts, had been replaced. A similar decision was reached where the passenger compartment of a MERCEDES car had been replaced after the car was involved in an accident.[50] Since the replacement parts had themselves been supplied by Mercedes, it seems somewhat strange that Mercedes was nevertheless permitted to oppose the redistribution of the repaired automobile. However, when we consider the function of the trade mark as guaranteeing the origin and thus a certain quality of the product, this decision is understandable. A modern automobile is not just the sum of its parts; it is also the result of an assembly process. The trade mark consequently guarantees not only the quality of the constituent parts of the car, but also the quality of the assembly process. This aspect, however, could no longer be guaranteed by Mercedes after the car had been fully reassembled by the recycler.

A case decided by the Reichsgericht[51] dealt with a reworked kilowatt-hour meter.[52] The court decided that, with such delicate devices, the interest of the trade mark holder in controlling their functionality was especially high and that no other person was entitled to redistribute recycled devices under the original trade mark without the proprietor's consent. This point also arose in a case concerning clutches[53] which were disassembled and reassembled after some parts had been exchanged. The court explained that, in relation to a product containing a complex operating unit, the tuning of the different parts is a major element of the trade mark's quality guarantee.

Another, more recent decision on the particular nature of a product was the 'Dyed Jeans' case of the German Federal Supreme Court.[54] Used Levi's jeans were dyed in colours different from the original colours (very loud colours, in contrast to the quiet original colours) in order to supply a specific consumer group. The court considered that an aspect of the particular nature of the Levi's jeans was their quiet colour; thus the new loud colour made them different products.

---

[48] Hamburg Court of Appeals Case 3 U 58/00 [2001], GRUR 2001, 749.
[49] The expression used by the court.
[50] German Federal Supreme Court Case 1 ZR 198/88 [1990], GRUR 1990, 678.
[51] The Reichsgericht had to decide several famous cases in this sector, such as *'Singer'* and *'Linotype'*.
[52] Reichsgericht Case II 161/38 [1939], RGZ 161, 29.
[53] Hamburg Court of Appeals Case 3 U 176/96 [1997], GRUR 1997, 855; Munich Court of Appeals Case 6 U 6251/90 [1992], WRP 1993, 47.
[54] German Federal Supreme Court Case 1 ZR 210/93 [1995], GRUR 1996, 271 = IIC 1997, 131.

4.4.3 Conclusion

Case law shows that the question whether the particular nature of a product is changed depends on its character. One normally expects that products consisting of complex elements, which are especially precious or in respect of which safety is a prime concern, have not been subject to interference by a third party. On the other hand one expects that durable goods like automobiles, which are regularly maintained, repaired and redistributed, have been subjected to a certain degree of alteration. Therefore, simply repairing wear or damage deriving from normal usage does not affect the guarantee of origin and quality represented by the trade mark and cannot be understood as a change in the product's particular nature. In such cases more extensive interference with the goods is required in order to constitute an exception to the exhaustion rule.

4.5 Legitimate Reason 2: Damage to the Reputation of the Trade Mark

Even if all these requirements are fulfilled, the person reworking a trade marked product must consider one final condition. The use of the trade mark on the reworked product must not be such as to be liable to damage the reputation of the trade mark and its owner.[55] However, the ECJ's formulation of this rule is narrow; it must be *established* that, given the specific circumstances of the case, the use of the trade mark *seriously damages* the reputation of the mark.[56]

5. FINAL REMARKS

The above discussion shows that whether refilling or recycling constitute trade mark infringement depends very much on the particular circumstances of the case. To be on the safe side, a person refilling or recycling a trade marked product should seek the consent of the proprietor. Failing this, he would be well advised to affix a clear additional reference to the product to clarify that it has been reworked by him.

In most cases the doctrine of exhaustion of rights will not assist a person reworking a product. As stated above, the owner of the trade mark has some influence in determining the particular nature of his product. This gives him some control in relation to the question whether the particular nature has changed and thus whether an exception to the exhaustion of rights rule

---

[55] *Loendersloot*, para. 28; *Dior*, para. 45.
[56] *Dior*, para. 46.

should be allowed. It is only where the product has originally been filled with a standard content and is subsequently refilled with such content, or where the extent of recycling does not extend beyond eliminating damage arising from normal usage, that the claim that the trade mark holder's rights are exhausted might prove successful.

11. Honest commercial use in light of the ECJ's *Gerolsteiner* Ruling

Grace Smith

... Article 6 [of Directive 89/104/EEC] seeks to reconcile the fundamental interests of trade-mark protection with those of free movement of goods and freedom to provide services in the common market in such a way that trade mark rights are able to fulfil their essential role in the system of undistorted competition which the Treaty seeks to establish and maintain ... (*Gerolsteiner Brunnen GmbH & Co. v Putsch GmbH*)[1]

A BALANCING ACT: THE CONTEXT

In a number of decisions over the past two years, the European Court of Justice (ECJ) has had to consider the balance struck by Council Directive 89/104 between the restrictive rights granted to trade mark owners and the overall policies of market freedom and unrestricted competition. Fundamental to this balance is the idea of 'honest practices in industrial and commercial matters' in Article 6 of the Directive. However, the ECJ's freedom in approaching Article 6 has been constrained by a number of earlier decisions in relation to Article 5. The result has been the decision in *Gerolsteiner*, a case the conclusions of which are at once difficult to reconcile with the scheme and purpose of the Directive, yet eminently predictable in light of the Court's earlier decisions.

Articles 5 to 7 of the Directive provide the logical structure in which any question of trade mark infringement is to be considered. Article 5 provides the *prima facie* test for infringement. Since Article 5 creates a general prohibition, the scope of which is cut down by the exclusions in Articles 6 and 7, if a sign infringes within the meaning of Article 5 it then becomes necessary to consider whether a particular use of the sign is excluded from the ambit of Article 5 by Articles 6 or 7.

It is not the purpose of this article to examine in depth the case law on

---

[1]   Case C-100/02 [2004] ETMR 40.

Article 5. It is sufficient to note the conclusion of the Court in *Arsenal Football Club plc v Matthew Reed*[2] that

> the exclusive right under Article 5(1)(a) of the Directive was conferred in order to enable the trade mark proprietor to protect his specific interests as proprietor, that is, to ensure that the trade mark can fulfil its functions. The exercise of that right must therefore be reserved to cases in which a third party's use of the sign affects or is liable to affect the functions of the trade mark, in particular its essential function of guaranteeing to consumers the origin of the goods.[3]

The ECJ reached this conclusion by reference to Article 5, and specifically the reference in that article to use 'in the course of trade'. By concluding that a use is not 'in the course of trade', a court preempts any consideration of the specific exclusions in Article 6. The danger of this approach is twofold. First, that court is forced to deal with questions of the balance between trade mark restriction and free competition without the benefit of the specific provisions for this purpose in Article 6. In addition, as is seen in *Gerolsteiner*, when the ECJ does come to consider Article 6, it is constrained by its Article 5 jurisprudence to reach conclusions which are at odds with the policies underlying the Directive.

GEROLSTEINER: THE FACTS

Gerolsteiner came to the ECJ by way of preliminary reference from the German Bundesgerichtshof for a preliminary ruling on the meaning of Article 6 of the Directive. The claimant, Gerolsteiner Brunnen GmbH & Co., was the owner of the word mark GERRI for mineral water, non-alcoholic beverages, fruit-juice based drinks and lemonades. The defendant, Putsch GmbH, marketed soft drinks under the brand name 'Kerry Spring', which were manufactured in County Kerry, Ireland, by an Irish company, Kerry Spring Water, using water from a spring called Kerry Spring.

Gerolsteiner sued, claiming that the defendant's use of the word 'Kerry' infringed its rights in the GERRI trade mark. The Bundesgerichtshof having found that there was sufficient likelihood of aural confusion between the marks to satisfy the requirement of Article 5(1)(b) of the Directive, the defendant sought to rely on Article 6 on the basis that the word 'Kerry' was an indication of the geographical origin of the goods. Article 6(1) provides that:

> The trade mark shall not entitle the proprietor to prohibit a third party from using, in the course of trade,

---

2   Case C-206/01 [2002] ECR I-10273, [2003] ETMR 19.
3   Para. 51.

(a) his own name or address;

(b) indications concerning the kind, quality, quantity, intended purpose, value, geographical origin, the time of production of goods or of rendering of the service, or other characteristics of goods or services;

(c) the trade mark where it is necessary to indicate the intended purpose of a product or service, in particular as accessories or spare parts;

provided he uses them in accordance with honest practices in industrial or commercial matters.

The Bundesgerichtshof referred two questions to the ECJ for a preliminary ruling, essentially asking (i) whether Article 6 could be relied on where the defendant uses the mark as a trade mark and (ii) if so, whether the fact that the mark was used as a trade mark must be taken into account in considering whether the use is 'in accordance with honest practices in industrial or commercial matters'.

THE FIRST QUESTION: TRADE MARK USE

The Court dealt with the two questions together, but effectively dispensed with the first question in three paragraphs, simply noting the Commission's submission that, in the course of the drafting of the Directive, the proviso to Article 6(1), which in earlier drafts had read 'provided he does not use them as a trade mark', was replaced by the current requirement that the use be 'in accordance with honest practices'.[4] In these circumstances, the Court held, an expression such as 'as a trade mark' cannot be regarded as appropriate for placing a limitation upon the scope of Article 6.[5]

The Court provided no basis for its conclusion other than its reference to the drafting history. While this provides some indication that the concept of use in accordance with honest practices is not coterminous with the concept of use other than as a trade mark, it does not necessarily mean that use as a trade mark is permissible. Indeed, there are strong arguments for the view that use as a trade mark should always be considered to be use other than in accordance with Article 6(1).

The Court failed to consider the underlying purpose of Article 6(1)(b). Examination of the various items included in Article 6(1)(b) suggests that the reason for imposing specific limits on the scope of the trade mark owner's exercise of his right is to ensure that a trader is free to describe his goods to prospective purchasers. There are strong policy arguments for ensuring that

---

4   Para. 14.
5   Para. 15.

traders are free to provide as much information as possible about their product, and to display that information on the product packaging. To allow a trader to use his registered mark to limit the information another trader may provide is obviously both contrary to this policy and unnecessary to protect the trade mark owner's brand. The argument that Article 6(1)(b) was intended to permit descriptive use is reinforced by the catch-all reference to 'other characteristics of goods or services'. This policy of providing information to consumers about the characteristics of goods or services does not, however, require that traders be free to use those characteristics as the trade names of their goods or services.

The Court also failed to address the anomalous practical results of allowing the use of a geographical indication as a trade mark to come within the provisions of Article 6(1). The Irish manufacturers of Kerry Spring presumably adopted the name Kerry Spring for the same reason that most traders adopt names for their products, that is in the hope that they will appeal to customers and assist in developing a successful brand and a successful business. Some traders adopt names that include indications of geographical origin, while some do not.

The value which a name and an associated brand has is, in general, derived not from the fact that the name is an indication of geographical origin but rather from the association which is built up in the public mind between the name and the product in question. When a trader enters a new market, as in this case when an Irish brand is launched in the German market, the value of this connection between the name and the product is minimal. However, the trader has a continued interest in using the same name in order to take advantage of economies of scale in packaging and marketing and in order to develop a single, coherent brand across the wider market. The value of such uniform international brands can be seen in a number of high profile re-brandings, such as the re-branding of JIF as CIF on the UK and Irish markets, to bring it into line with the mark used in continental Europe. The result of the decision in *Gerolsteiner* is that a trader is more likely to be able to maintain a uniform brand across the market if the name which he adopts is an indication of the type mentioned in Article 6(1)(b). For example, the hypothetical manufacturer of BIG pens would have a defence to a suit from the manufacturers of BIC pens, whereas the manufacturer of SIC pens would not. On the assumption that both names were adopted, and are maintained, for similar commercial reasons, it is difficult to see the logic in this conclusion.

The Court, in its decision in *Windsurfing Chiemsee*[6] less than five years earlier, stated unequivocally that Article 6(1)(b)

---

[6] *Windsurfing Chiemsee* Joined Cases C-108/97 and C-109/97 [1999] ECR I-2779, [1999] ETMR 585.

does not confer on third parties the right to use the name as a trade mark but merely guarantees their right to use it descriptively, that is to say, as an indication of geographical origin, provided that it is used in accordance with honest practices in industrial and commercial matters.[7]

What, then, inspired the ECJ's sudden change of heart, particularly in light of strong policy arguments in favour of the view set out in *Windsurfing Chiemsee*. Although it is not referred to, the Court's conclusion on the question of use 'as a trade mark' is the logical and unavoidable consequence of the conclusions cited from *Arsenal,* cited above. The Court in *Arsenal,* and in its earlier decision in *Hölterhoff,*[8] took the view that where a trade mark was used other than for 'its essential function of guaranteeing to consumers the origin of the good', such use was not use 'in the course of trade' for the purpose of Article 5. In effect, the Court restricted the scope of infringement in Article 5 to use of the registered mark as a trade mark. Article 6, as already mentioned, operates as a limit on the scope of Article 5. Thus, if Article 5 can only operate where a mark is used as a trade mark, it follows as a logical and necessary consequence that Article 6, if it is to have any meaning, must also apply where a mark is used as a trade mark. This point, raised by the defendants before the Court,[9] was extensively canvassed by the Advocate General in his opinion[10] but is notably absent from the reasoning of the ECJ itself.

THE SECOND QUESTION: HONEST USE

The Court devotes the last four paragraphs of its opinion to considering the meaning of the proviso to Article 6(1), 'provided he uses them in accordance with honest practices in industrial or commercial matters'. The Court reiterates the view, originally expressed in *BMW,*[11] that the proviso is 'in substance the expression of a duty to act fairly in relation to the legitimate interests of the trade mark owner'. The Court then states that

the mere fact that there exists a likelihood of aural confusion between a word mark registered in one Member State and an indication of geographical origin from another Member State is therefore insufficient to conclude that the use of that indication in the course of trade is not in accordance with honest practices.[12]

---

[7]   Para. 28.
[8]   *Hölterhoff v Freiesleben* Case C-2/00 [2002] ETMR 917, [2002] ECR I-4187.
[9]   See para. 25 of the Opinion of Advocate General Stix-Hackl.
[10]   Paras 42–46.
[11]   *Bayerische Motorenwerke AG (BMW) and BMW Nederland BV v Deenik* Case C-63/97 [1999] ETMR 339, [1999] ECR I-905.
[12]   Para. 25.

According to the Court,

> the circumstances to be taken into account by [the national Court] would include in
> particular the shape and labelling of the bottle in order to assess, more particularly,
> whether the producer of the drink bearing the indication of geographical origin
> might be regarded as unfairly competing with the proprietor of the trade mark.[13]

The underlying rationale of this aspect of the decision is difficult to extract.
The reference to the 'shape and labelling of the bottle' seems to suggest an
analysis of the extent to which the use of the mark causes confusion. However,
the use of the word 'therefore' in reference to aural confusion suggests a
different conclusion. The Court clearly takes the view that the fact that mere
aural confusion is insufficient to find dishonesty is a consequence of the equation of honesty and fairness in *BMW*. This only makes sense if the duty to act
fairly is assessed subjectively, as a duty not to damage the reputation of the
mark intentionally to or seek to take advantage of it. Bearing this in mind, the
reference to 'shape and labelling' takes on a different emphasis. It requires an
analysis of the extent to which the defendant is intentionally taking advantage
of the claimant's mark and reputation by copying the get-up of his product.
This is similar to the analysis of honesty required under the 'own name'
defence in the common-law tort of passing off.[14]

By shifting the analysis to a subjective test, the ECJ explicitly accepts that
the mere fact of confusion in the market will not be enough, in and of itself, to
render the use of a mark not in accordance with honest practices. It is hard to
fault this conclusion, given the position of Article 6 in the logical scheme of
the Directive, as discussed above. Where a mark is not identical to the registered mark, or is used on goods which are not identical, Article 5 requires that
there be a 'likelihood of confusion'. A similar mark, or an identical mark on
similar goods, will only fall to be considered under Article 6 if there exists a
likelihood of confusion sufficient to satisfy Article 5. Thus, for Article 6 to
have any application in respect of such marks, it must be capable of application despite the existence of confusion in the market. The decision in
Gerolsteiner can, however, be criticised for failing to make this point explicit.

The subsequent decision in *Anheuser Busch Inc. v Budejovický Budvar,
narodni podnik*[15] goes some way to clarifying this position. However, it also
appears to highlight the danger of the Court's acceptance of Article 6(1) as a
defence where a sign is used as a trade mark.

---

[13] Para. 26.
[14] *Rodgers v Rodgers* (1924) 41 RPC 277; *Asprey and Garrard Ltd v WRA
(Guns) Ltd* [2002] ETMR 47; [2002] FSR 31; *Scandecor Development AB v Scandecor
Marketing AB* [1999] FSR 26 (CA); [2001] 2 C.M.L.R. 30; [2002] F.S.R. 7 (HL).
[15] Case C-245/02 [2004] ECR I-0000, [2005] ETMR 27.

AFTER *GEROLSTEINER: ANHEUSER BUSCH INC. V BUDEJOVICKÝ BUDVAR*

This decision arises from the long-running dispute between the American and Czech breweries over the use of BUDWEISER and other marks for beer. The Finnish Courts referred a number of questions in relation to the TRIPs agreement to the ECJ. As well as responding to the questions raised, the ECJ also discussed the possibility that Article 6(1)(a) of the Directive might be relevant.

A number of significant points arise from the Court's analysis of Article 6(1).

First, the ECJ accepts that a company can invoke the defence in Article 6(1)(a) in respect of a trade or company name, despite the non-binding joint declaration of the Commission and Council made at the time the Directive was adopted, to the effect that the defence should only be open to natural persons, which it chooses not to follow.[16] In so doing, the Court has shown a willingness to widen the scope of the defence provided by Article 6(1).

The Court also analyses in detail the condition of honest practice in Article 6. After echoing the statement in *BMW* and *Gerolsteiner* to the effect that honest practice can be equated with a duty to act fairly, the Court identifies three factors of which account should be taken. These are

> first . . . the extent to which the use of the third party's trade name is understood by the relevant public, or at least a significant section of that public, as indicating a link between the third party's goods and the trade-mark proprietor or a person authorised to use the trade mark, and secondly . . . the extent to which the third party ought to have been aware of that. Another factor to be taken into account when making the assessment is whether the trade mark concerned enjoys a certain reputation in the Member State in which it is registered and its protection is sought, from which the third party might profit in selling his goods.[17]

These three factors merit some detailed consideration. The first factor can be equated with confusion on the part of the public. Given the acceptance by the *Gerolsteiner* court that use can be in accordance with honest practice despite causing confusion, it is unclear how a court is meant to take it into account. As mentioned earlier, confusion is a question which goes more to the analysis of Article 5 than Article 6, and it seems unlikely to be the sole determinative factor in most Article 6 cases.

The second, more significant factor requires an analysis of 'the extent to which the third party ought to have been aware' of the confusion caused by his

---

16   Para. 80.
17   Para. 83.

use of the mark. This does not ask whether the defendant causes confusion but to what extent that confusion is excusable. What the ECJ does not indicate is when this assessment should be made. Presumably if a defendant knew (or should have known) at the time he adopted a particular trade name that it was likely to cause confusion with the claimant's business, that would be relevant here. Consider, however, the example in *Gerolsteiner*. It is unlikely that the Irish manufacturers of Kerry Spring water considered the possibility of confusion with the claimant's mark when that product was first launched. However, it may have been considered by the defendant when it launched the product on the German market. Certainly, by the time the case reached the ECJ, the defendants were eminently aware of the confusion. At which of these times should the second factor in *Anheuser Busch* be considered?

Strictly speaking, the third factor requires objective analysis of the reputation of the registered trade mark. The reference to the possibility of the third party profiting does not necessarily require a consideration of whether the third party seeks to profit from the reputation. However, in considering whether the claimant's mark enjoyed a reputation of which the defendant could have taken advantage, a court will find it hard to avoid considering whether the defendant sought to take advantage of it.

Anheuser-Busch is important for its results, as well as for the analysis which the Court offers. It seems clear that, in appropriate circumstances, the defendants would be permitted to market beer under the title 'Budweiser Budvar', that being one of their trade names. Applying *Gerolsteiner*, they could use this name as a mark under which to market goods: the fact that it caused confusion with the claimant's product would not prevent the defendants relying on the defence in Article 6. Thus the claimants, the registered owners of the mark BUDWEISER, could not prevent the defendants marketing beer under a similar or identical mark. This surely cannot be the correct balance between the various 'fundamental interests' referred to by the Court in *Gerolsteiner*.

ANOTHER PERSPECTIVE: *GILLETTE*[18]

The recent *Gillette* decision[19] provides further analysis of the condition of honest use. This case deals with the use of a trade mark 'where it is necessary to indicate the intended purpose of goods'. The defendant is using the claimant's trade mark itself, referring to the claimant's goods in order to

---

[18]   *The Gillette Company and Gillette Group Finland Oy v LA-Laboratories Ltd Oy* Case C-228/03 [2005] ETMR 67.
[19]   Discussed in detail in chapter 8 above.

describe his own. In these circumstances the ECJ's comments may not be of general application to the other two heads of Article 6(1), but they are still noteworthy.

First, the Court notes that the requirement of honest practice is 'similar to that imposed on the reseller where he uses another's trade mark to advertise the resale of products covered by that mark'.[20] On the basis of this conclusion, national courts may make use of the extensive caselaw on parallel imports to inform their decisions on Article 6(1).

The Court then states a number of conditions which will prevent use being in accordance with honest practices.

First, the Court states that use of a trade mark will not comply with honest practices if it is done 'in such a manner that it may give the impression that there is a commercial connection between the reseller and the trade mark proprietor'.[21] This is difficult to reconcile with *Gerolsteiner* and *Anheuser Busch*. Whereas both earlier decisions refer to confusion, they view it as one factor among many and accept that it is not incompatible with honest practice. Indeed, as suggested above, confusion is in most cases a prerequisite for the application of Article 6(1). However, the Court in *Gillette* addresses a specific instance where the marks used are identical and it is possible this absolute prohibition should be restricted to that case.

Secondly and thirdly, use may not 'affect the value of the mark by taking unfair advantage of its distinctive character or repute'[22] and will not be in accordance with honest practices if it 'discredits or denigrates the mark'.[23] These conditions require an analysis both of the intentions of the defendant and of the objective results of the defendant's use of the mark.

Fourthly, the Court expressly states that the manufacture or marketing of replica goods will not be in accordance with honest practices.[24]

The Court then offers a more generalised test, taking account of

> the overall presentation of the product marketed by the third party, particularly the circumstances in which the mark of which the third party is not the owner is displayed in that presentation, the circumstances in which a distinction is made between that mark and the mark or sign of the third party, and the effort made by that third party to ensure that consumers distinguish its products from those of which it is not the trade mark owner.[25]

---

20 Para. 41.
21 Para. 42.
22 Para. 43.
23 Para. 44.
24 Para. 45.
25 Para. 46.

Of particular interest here is the final point: a trade mark owner can expect a third party who uses his mark for one of the purposes set out in Article 6(1) to make reasonable efforts to minimise confusion between their respective products. This will be particularly relevant where, as in *Gillette*, the defendant refers to the claimant's goods, but is also of more general application. It is reasonable to ask, where a claimant is restrained from protecting his mark by virtue of one of the interests protected by Article 6, that the person relying on that Article should have some responsibility to ensure that confusion is avoided, or at least minimised.

CONCLUSION

There are difficulties with the ECJ's jurisprudence on Article 6. In particular, the view of the scope of Article 5 outlined in *Arsenal* has forced the Court down a dangerous path in recognising that Article 6 can be relied on where a mark is used for trade mark purposes. However, given the repeated confirmation of the *Arsenal* view, it seems unlikely that this point will be reconsidered in the short term.

Bearing that in mind, a number of conclusions can be drawn from the Court's approach to honest use. First, whereas confusion is a relevant factor in assessing honest use, it will not be determinative, except possibly in cases under Article 6(1)(c).[26] Second, regard will be had to the overall get-up of a product or service in considering whether a mark is used honestly. Third, the focus on fairness necessitates a close consideration of a defendant's apparent motives in using a potentially infringing sign. This will include considering the extent to which the defendant should have foreseen any confusion which subsequently arises, and the extent to which the claimant's mark has a reputation of which the defendant appears to be taking advantage. It will also be important to consider the affect which a defendant's actions have on the value of the mark. Finally, the Court appears to have recognised an obligation on a party relying on Article 6 to take such steps as are reasonable to minimise the confusion caused by his use of a sign or mark which is similar or identical to the claimants.

---

[26] That is, where use of the trade mark is necessary to indicate the intended purpose of a product or service, in particular as accessories or spare parts.

12. 'Descriptiveness' in American trade mark law

David W. Quinto and Anthony P. Alden

1. DEFINITION OF 'DESCRIPTIVE'

The centrality of 'descriptiveness' in United States trade mark law cannot be exaggerated. A term that is judicially considered too descriptive of a product or service may simply not be granted trade mark protection or, if subject to protection, may encounter formidable defences to infringement claims. Yet no aspect of American trade mark law is as dependent on the eye of the beholder as the determination of whether a term is descriptive.[1] As the Second Circuit Court of Appeals has observed, 'where most of the trade mark battles are fought are [where] the terms which are primarily descriptive'.[2]

Descriptive terms are distinguished within the spectrum of trade mark distinctiveness from 'generic' and 'suggestive' terms. A generic term 'refer[s] to the genus of which the particular product is a species',[3] such as SHREDDED WHEAT (baked wheat biscuit)[4] or FIRST AID (bandages and other medical items).[5] These terms lack any distinctiveness and naturally cannot serve as a trade mark under any circumstances.[6] In contrast, a suggestive term

---

[1]   The Second Circuit has conceded that making such a determination is 'tricky business at best', *Banff, Ltd. v Federated Department Stores, Inc.*, 841 F.2d 486, 489 (2d Cir. 1988), and the Fifth Circuit has admitted that the classification is frequently difficult to make: *Soweco, Inc. v Shell Oil Co.*, 617 F.2d 1178, 1183 (5th Cir. 1980).

[2]   *West & Co. v Arica Inst., Inc.*, 557 F.2d 338, 342 (2d Cir. 1977).

[3]   *Two Pesos, Inc. v Taco Cabana, Inc.*, 505 U.S. 763, 768 (1992).

[4]   *Kellogg Co. v Nat'l Biscuit Co.*, 305 U.S. 111 (1938).

[5]   *In re Nat'l Patent Dev. Corp.*, 1 USPQ 2d 1921 (TTAB 1986).

[6]   The test for genericness has two elements. The first is to identify the genus or class of goods at issue and the second is to determine whether the relevant purchasing public understands the designation sought to be registered primarily as referring to that genus or class of products. See *H. Marvin Ginn Corp. v Int'l Ass'n of Fire Chiefs, Inc.*, 782 F.2d 987 (Fed. Cir. 1986) (holding that FIRE CHIEF was not generic for a magazine about firefighting because the relevant purchasing public did not refer to the class of firefighting publications as 'fire chief').

'stands for an idea which requires some operation of the imagination to connect it with the goods'.[7] The inherently distinctive nature of a suggestive term, such as FRIENDLY as used for shoes,[8] entitles it to trade mark protection without the need for further analysis.

Descriptive terms fall between generic terms and suggestive terms. A mark is descriptive if it describes the intended purpose, function or use of the goods; the size of the goods; the provider of the goods; the class of users of the goods; a desirable characteristic of the goods; the nature of the goods or the end effect upon the user.[9] In contrast to generic terms, descriptive terms can gain trade mark protection if they acquire distinctiveness over time. But, unlike suggestive terms, descriptive terms are insufficiently distinctive to warrant automatic trade mark protection.

A term is classified as 'descriptive' only if a substantial portion of prospective purchasers recognizes it as descriptive.[10] Thus it does not matter how the non-purchasing segment of the population uses the term.[11] In evaluating descriptiveness, courts examine how the 'reasonably informed shopper' views the term.[12] In making that determination, courts may consider dictionary definitions as evidence of the ordinary significance of words, and the testimony of lexicographers as evidence of the probable descriptive meaning attached to a mark by the public.[13]

Prior decisions are of little use in gauging whether a given mark will be classified as descriptive. However, the following examples of marks that have been held to be descriptive may serve to shed some practical light on the concept: AFTER TAN (after-sunning lotion)[14]; FASHIONKNIT (sweaters)[15]; IMPERIAL (whiskey)[16]; LITTER BASKET (trash receptacles)[17]; PAPER

---

[7]   *Platinum Home Mortgage Corp. v Platinum Fin. Group, Inc.*, 149 F.3d 722, 727 (7th Cir. 1998).
[8]   *General Shoe Corp. v Rosen*, 111 F.2d 95 (4th Cir. 1940).
[9]   2 J.T. McCarthy, *McCarthy on Trademarks and Unfair Competition* §11:16 (4th ed. & Supp. 2005).
[10]   *Bada Co. v Montgomery Ward & Co.*, 426 F.2d 8, 11 (9th Cir. 1970).
[11]   *Blisscraft of Hollywood v United Plastics Co.*, 294 F.2d 694, 699 (2d Cir. 1961).
[12]   *G. Heileman Brewing Co. v Anheuser-Busch, Inc.*, 873 F.2d 985, 995 (7th Cir. 1989).
[13]   *Hancock v Am. Steel & Wire Co.*, 203 F.2d 737, 740 (CCPA 1953); *Stix Prods., Inc. v United Merchants & Mfrs., Inc.*, 295 F. Supp. 479, 488–89 (SDNY 1968).
[14]   *Aloe Creme Labs., Inc. v Estee Lauder, Inc.*, 533 F.2d 256 (5th Cir. 1976).
[15]   *Franklin Knitting Mills, Inc. v Fashionit Sweater Mills, Inc.*, 297 F. 247 (SDNY 1923).
[16]   *Hiram Walker & Sons, Inc. v Penn-Maryland Corp.*, 79 F.2d 836 (2d Cir. 1935).
[17]   *Sterling Prods. Co. v Crest Mfg. Co.*, 314 F. Supp. 204 (E.D. Mich. 1970).

CUTTER (paper ornaments)[18]; SHOPPERS FAIR (grocery store)[19] and WORLD BOOK (encyclopedia).[20]

1.1 'Merely Descriptive Terms' v 'Common Descriptive Terms'

Courts sometimes distinguish between 'common descriptive terms' and 'merely descriptive terms'.[21] A common descriptive term is one that is 'commonly used as [a] . . . description of a kind of goods'.[22] Unlike merely descriptive terms, common descriptive terms are never accorded protection. Were the rule otherwise, later entrants into a market would be foreclosed from accurately describing their products. One can imagine the difficulty that competitors would have if the first producer of a decaffeinated coffee were granted protection in DECAFFEINATED, or if the first manufacturer of a beer containing reduced available carbohydrates were exclusively entitled to the use of LIGHT.[23] For that reason, courts may strain to find that a term is already in common use if they believe that it will be used frequently in the future.

Self-laudatory terms are especially likely to be found to be commonly descriptive. For example, the Trademark Trial and Appeal Board found that the slogan THE BEST BEER IN AMERICA, used to sell Samuel Adams beer, was descriptive and incapable of acquiring distinctiveness as a trade mark.[24] Significantly, the applicant showed that it had promoted its slogan extensively to popularize its beer, which had become a commercial success nationally. Further, a competitor had advertised its beer as 'Better than "The Best Beer in America" ' without identifying Samuel Adams by name, thus implicitly recognizing that the slogan had earned distinctiveness by becoming a source identifier. Nevertheless, the court's decision reflected the view that self-laudatory claims 'should be freely available to all competitors in any given field to refer

---

[18]   *Papercutter, Inc. v Fay's Drug Co.*, 900 F.2d 558 (2d Cir. 1990).
[19]   *Shoppers Fair of Arkansas, Inc. v Sanders Co.*, 328 F.2d 496 (8th Cir. 1964).
[20]   *Field Enter. Educ. Corp. v Cove Indus., Inc.*, 297 F. Supp. 989 (EDNY 1969).
[21]   See *G. Heileman Brewing Co.*, 873 F.2d at 991–92; *Miller Brewing Co. v G. Heileman Brewing Co.*, 561 F.2d 75, 79 (7th Cir. 1977).
[22]   *G. Heileman Brewing Co.*, 873 F.2d at 991–92.
[23]   In *Miller Brewing*, 561 F.2d at 75, Miller was denied protection in LITE, the 'phonetic equivalent of "light" '. The court was dismissive of Miller's attempts to show that the public associated LITE with its beer. However, the Internal Revenue Service had asked brewers not to describe any of their products as 'low-calorie'. Thus, the court may have been influenced by the absence of any practicable alternative to the use of 'light' to describe a less-fattening beer.
[24]   *In re Boston Beer Co.*, 47 USPQ 2d 1914 (TTAB 1998), *aff'd*, 198 F.3d 1370 (Fed. Cir. 1999).

to their products or services'.[25] Other self-laudatory terms that have been held
to be unprotectable as common descriptive terms include 'We Treat You
Right',[26] 'We'll Take Good Care of You',[27] 'Best' and 'Premier'.[28]

1.2   Special Categories of Terms that may be 'Descriptive'

As American trade mark jurisprudence developed, the law concerning descriptiveness evolved from general judicial guidelines to rules concerning specific
categories of terms. Some of the more common categories that trade mark law
practitioners encounter are

- *Foreign terms.* Because the focus is on whether a term is *perceived* as
  descriptive, courts will not usually view obscure terms and words from
  ancient languages as descriptive.[29] However, the 'doctrine of foreign
  equivalents' applies to words taken from languages in use today.
  Accordingly, words from modern languages will be tested for descriptiveness by determining what they mean to the segment of the purchasing public familiar with that language.[30] For example, GASA as the
  name of a toilet paper was held descriptive because 'gasa' means
  'gauze' in Spanish.[31]
- *Personal names.* Personal names, whether given names or surnames, are
  not technically descriptive. Nonetheless, they are treated as merely
  descriptive terms that gain protection only when the public comes to
  identify them as marks, rather than as personal names.[32]
- *Geographic terms.* Geographically descriptive terms are placed in the
  same category as terms that describe a quality or feature of goods.[33]
  Thus a geographic term is not protectable as a trade mark until it
  acquires distinctiveness, with the qualification that geographic terms
  that describe where a product is made (for example, 'Scotch' whisky

---

[25]   Ibid. at 1920–21.
[26]   *Am. Dairy Corp. v RTO, Inc.*, 16 USPQ 2d 1077 (N.D. Ill. 1990).
[27]   *Genovese Drugstores, Inc. v TGC Stores, Inc.*, 939 F. Supp. 340 (DNJ 1996)
(suggesting, however, that the result might have differed had plaintiff shown distinctiveness).
[28]   *In re Best Software, Inc.*, 58 USPQ 2d 1314 (TTAB 2001).
[29]   *Pac. Telesis Group v Int'l Telesis Communications*, 994 F.2d 1364, 1368–69
(9th Cir. 1993); *Telechron, Inc. v Telicon Corp.*, 198 F.2d 903, 905–06 (3d Cir. 1952);
Stix Prods., 295 F. Supp. 479.
[30]   *In re Hag Aktiengesellschaft*, 155 USPQ 598, 599–600 (TTAB 1967).
[31]   *In re Northern Paper Mills*, 64 F.2d 998 (CCPA 1933).
[32]   *Lane Capital Mgmt., Inc. v Lane Capital Mgmt., Inc.*, 192 F.3d 337 (2d Cir. 1999).
[33]   *In re Nantucket, Inc.*, 677 F.2d 95, 99 (CCPA 1982).

and 'Wisconsin' cheese) are treated as common descriptive terms and are never protectable as trade marks.[34]

- *Style or grade terms.* Designations of style or grade, by definition, describe a characteristic of a product. For that reason, they are considered descriptive.[35] That rule applies even when the style or grade designations are arbitrary and unique to a manufacturer[36] although a style or grade designation that gains distinctiveness over time will become protectable.[37] Some size and style designators have acquired a very distinctive meaning, such as '501' for a style of Levi Strauss denim jeans and '747' for certain Boeing aircraft. Any rule that did not allow the protection of style and size designators in such circumstances would engender confusion.

1.3 The Blurry Line Between 'Descriptive' and 'Suggestive' Terms

Although reasonable minds may differ as to whether a distinctive mark has become generic (for example, do Americans really call small cigars 'Whiffs'[38] and all manned spacecraft 'Space Shuttles'[39]?), generic terms are, as a rule, easily distinguished from descriptive terms. However, it is often extremely difficult to distinguish descriptive terms from suggestive terms. This difficulty is compounded by the fact that marks that are a composite of descriptive terms, or that have descriptive as well as suggestive significance, will often be classified as suggestive.[40]

---

[34] See *World Carpets, Inc. v Dick Littrell's New World Carpets*, 438 F.2d 482, 484–85 (5th Cir. 1971); *Restatement (Third) of Unfair Competition* §14 comment d (1995).

[35] See *In re Union Oil Co.*, 88 F.2d 492 (CCPA 1937) ('76' gasoline refused registration as descriptive of grade or quality).

[36] *Arrow Fastener Co. v Stanley Works*, 59 F.3d 384 (2d Cir. 1995) ('T-50' held unprotectable because customers perceived it as referring to a particular staple gun); see also *In re Armco Steel Corp.*, 127 USPQ 135 (TTAB 1960). However, the Federal Circuit has held that numeric designations may not be considered descriptive in the absence of evidence of how the numbers are actually used. See *Eastman Kodak Co. v Bell & Howell Document Mgmt. Prods. Co.*, 994 F.2d 1569 (Fed. Cir. 1993). Because such evidence cannot be presented until a mark is used, a competitor cannot challenge an intent-to-use application for a numerical descriptor on the basis that it is merely descriptive. Ibid.

[37] *Dayton Progress Corp. v Lane Punch Corp.*, 12 USPQ 2d 1695, 1707 (WDNC 1989), *aff'd*, 917 F.2d 386 (4th Cir. 1990).

[38] *In re Consol. Cigar Corp.*, 13 USPQ 2d 1481 (TTAB 1989).

[39] *Nat'l Aeronautics & Space Admin. v Bully Hill Vineyards, Inc.*, 3 USPQ 2d 1674 (TTAB 1487).

[40] See *In re Colonial Stores, Inc.*, 394 F.2d 549 (CCPA 1968) (SUGAR & SPICE, used for bakery products, was suggestive because it did more than simply describe two ingredients).

The line between descriptive and suggestive terms is drawn on a case-by-case basis.[41] As a consequence, courts not infrequently reach unexpected conclusions. For example, the following marks that seem suggestive have all been held descriptive: CONSUMER PROTECTION PLAN (auto repair insurance)[42]; COZY WARM ENERGY SAVERS (flannel pyjamas)[43]; CREME DE MENTHE (chocolate mint candies)[44]; ESCAPE FROM THE ORDINARY (clothing)[45]; HERITAGE (life insurance plans)[46]; IVY LEAGUE (clothing)[47]; JOY (perfume)[48]; JOY (detergent)[49]; MUSTANG (trailers)[50]; PIZZAZZ (pizza)[51]; and PLATINUM (home mortgages).[52]

Examples of marks that seem descriptive but that have been held to be suggestive include ACTION SLACKS (pants)[53]; ARTYPE (cut-out letters for artists)[54]; AUDIO FIDELITY (phonograph records)[55]; CHEW 'N CLEAN (dentifrice)[56]; COPPERTONE (suntan lotion)[57]; FLORIDA TAN (suntan

---

[41]   A few courts have held that whether a mark is distinctive, suggestive, or something else is a question of law. See *United States Gold & Silver Invest., Inc. v Director, United States Mint*, 682 F. Supp. 44 (D. Or. 1987), *aff'd*, 885 F.2d 620 (9th Cir. 1989); *Jeno's, Inc. v Comm'r of Patents & Trademarks*, 227 USPQ 227 (D. Minn. 1985). However, most courts have held that the categorization of the term on the spectrum of distinctiveness is a factual issue. See *Equine Techs., Inc. v Equitechnology, Inc.*, 68 F.3d 542 (1st Cir. 1995); *Lane Capital Mgmt., Inc.*, 192 F.3d 337 (2d. Cir. 1989); *Ford Motor Co. v Summit Motor Prods., Inc.*, 930 F.2d 277 (3d Cir. 1991); *Dayton Progress Corp.*, 917 F.2d 836; *Security Ctr. Ltd. v First Nat'l Security Ctrs.*, 750 F.2d 1295 (5th Cir. 1985); *Platinum Home Mortgage Corp.*; *WSM, Inc. v Hilton*, 724 F.2d 1320 (8th Cir. 1984); *In re Nett Designs, Inc.*, 236 F.3d 1339 (Fed. Cir. 2001).
[42]   *CPP Ins. Agency, Inc. v Gen. Motors Corp.*, 212 USPQ 257 (S.D. Cal. 1980) (acronym 'CPP' held descriptive).
[43]   *20th Century Ware, Inc. v Sanmark-Stardust, Inc.*, 747 F.2d 81 (2d Cir. 1984).
[44]   *In re Andes Candies, Inc.*, 478 F.2d 1264 (CCPA 1973).
[45]   *Norm Thompson Outfitters, Inc. v Gen. Motors Corp.*, 448 F.2d 1293 (9th Cir. 1971).
[46]   *American Heritage Life Ins. Co. v Heritage Life Ins. Co.*, 494 F.2d 3 (5th Cir. 1974).
[47]   *House of Worsted-Tex, Inc. v Superba Cravats, Inc.*, 284 F.2d 528 (CCPA 1960).
[48]   *Jean Patou, Inc. v Jacqueline Cochran, Inc.*, 201 F. Supp. 861 (SDNY 1962), *aff'd*, 312 F.2d 125 (2d Cir. 1963).
[49]   *Clinton Detergent Co. v Procter & Gamble Co.*, 302 F.2d 745 (CCPA 1962).
[50]   *Westward Coach Mfg. Co. v Ford Motor Co.*, 258 F. Supp. 67 (SD Ind 1966), *aff'd*, 388 F.2d 627 (7th Cir. 1968).
[51]   *Pizzazz Pizza & Restaurant v Taco Bell Corp.*, 642 F. Supp. 88 (ND Ohio 1986).
[52]   *Platinum Home Mortgage Corp.*
[53]   *Levi Strauss & Co. v R. Josephs Sportswear*, 28 USPQ 2d 1464 (TTAB 1993).
[54]   *Artype, Inc. v Zappulla*, 228 F.2d 695 (2d Cir. 1956).
[55]   *Audio Fidelity, Inc. v London Records, Inc.*, 332 F.2d 577 (CCPA 1964).
[56]   *In re Colgate-Palmolive Co.*, 406 F.2d 1385 (CCPA 1969).
[57]   *Douglas Labs. Corp. v Copper Tan, Inc.*, 210 F.2d 453 (2d Cir. 1954).

lotion)[58]; HANDI-WIPES (dust cloths)[59]; LOC-TOP (bottle closure caps)[60]; MOVIEBUFF (database of movie information)[61]; POLY PITCHER (pitcher made of polyethylene)[62] and RAPID-SHAVE (shaving cream).[63]

2. IMPORTANCE OF THE DESCRIPTIVENESS DETERMINATION

If a merely descriptive term acquires distinctiveness, also referred to as 'secondary meaning', it will become protectable as a common law mark and will be eligible for registration on the Principal Register of the United States.[64] As the United States Supreme Court has explained:

> Marks which are merely descriptive of a product are not inherently distinctive. When used to describe a product, they do not inherently identify a particular source, and hence cannot be protected. However, descriptive marks may acquire the distinctiveness which will allow them to be protected under the [Federal Trademark] Act. ... This acquired distinctiveness is generally called 'secondary meaning'.[65]

A mark acquires distinctiveness or secondary meaning when consumers begin to believe that goods or services commercialized with the mark have a common source or origin.[66] However, there is no bright line test for determining what percentage of consumers must achieve that level of consciousness before secondary meaning will be found. As the Court of Customs and Patent Appeals stated:

> No hard and fast line can be drawn and no general rule can be enunciated by which one can determine precisely where a word such as JOY acquires such distinctiveness that it can function as a mark indicating a particular producer as a source or origin of such goods. Each case must stand on its own record.[67]

---

[58]   *Plough, Inc. v Florida Tan Prods. Co.*, 174 USPQ 46 (TTAB 1972).

[59]   *In re Colgate-Palmolive Co.*, 149 USPQ 793 (TTAB 1966).

[60]   *In re Polytop Corp.*, 167 USPQ 383 (TTAB 1970).

[61]   *Brookfield Communications, Inc. v W. Coast Entm't Corp.*, 174 F.3d 1036 (9th Cir. 1999).

[62]   *Blisscraft of Hollywood v United Plastics Co.*, 294 F.2d 694 (2d Cir. 1961).

[63]   *Colgate-Palmolive Co. v House for Men, Inc.*, 143 USPQ (TTAB 1964).

[64]   See Federal Trademark Act of 1946, as amended (the 'Lanham Act') §2(f), 15 USC §1052(f).

[65]   *Two Pesos, Inc. v Taco Cabana, Inc.*, 505 U.S. 763, 769 (1992).

[66]   *Inwood Labs., Inc. v Ives Labs., Inc.*, 456 U.S. 844, 851 n.11 (1982) ('To establish secondary meaning, a manufacturer must show that, in the minds of the public, the primary significance of a product feature or term is to identify the source of the product rather than the product itself').

[67]   *Clinton Detergent Co.*; *see also In re Hollywood Brands, Inc.*, 214 F.2d 139 (CCPA 1954) (no set standard of proof for distinctiveness under the Lanham Act).

That said, the general rule is that, the more descriptive a term, the greater is the evidentiary burden of establishing secondary meaning.[68] Like the determination of descriptiveness, the existence of secondary meaning is a question of fact that cannot be reversed on appeal unless the finding was 'clearly erroneous'.[69]

3. INFRINGEMENT DEFENCES: DESCRIPTIVE USE OF A DESCRIPTIVE MARK

3.1 Plaintiff's Mark not Entitled to Protection

The rule is well established that a business should be permitted to describe its products accurately, even if a competitor claims trade mark protection in the description. In 1920 the United States Supreme Court explained:

> [T]he law would not secure to any person exclusive use of a trade mark consisting merely of words descriptive of the qualities, ingredients, or characteristics of an article of trade. . . . [T]he function of a trade mark is to point distinctively . . . to the origin or ownership of the wares to which it is applied, and words merely descriptive of qualities, ingredients, or characteristics, when used alone, do not do this. Other like goods, equal to them in all respects, may be manufactured or dealt in by others, who, with equal truth, may use, and must be left free to use, the same language of description in placing their goods before the public.[70]

The above quotation thus reflects the view that, in the absence of secondary meaning, a descriptive term cannot distinguish the goods or services of just one seller in the marketplace and that 'for policy reasons, descriptive words must be left free for public use'.[71] As the Ninth Circuit has explained, 'one competitor will not be permitted to impoverish the language of commerce by preventing his fellows from fairly describing their own goods'.[72]

If a court views a trade mark – even a federally registered trade mark – as a common descriptive term or a descriptive term lacking secondary meaning,[73] it will not be accorded protection. This being so, the court will not

---

[68] *American Heritage Life Ins. Co.; In re Boston Beer Co.*, 47 USPQ 2d 1914 (TTAB 1998), *aff'd*, 198 F.3d 1370 (Fed. Cir. 1999).
[69] *Zatarains, Inc. v Oak Grove Smokehouse, Inc.*, 698 F.2d 786 (5th Cir. 1983).
[70] *Estate of P.D. Beckwith, Inc. v Comm'r of Patents*, 252 U.S. 538, 543–44 (1920).
[71] *In re Colonial Stores, Inc.*, 394 F.2d 549 (CCPA 1968).
[72] *Bada Co. v Montgomery Ward & Co.*, 426 F.2d 8 (9th Cir. 1970).
[73] In theory a descriptive term without secondary meaning cannot obtain federal registration. However, a registration will issue if the examiner is persuaded that the mark is suggestive, not descriptive.

examine the nature and quality of the defendant's use of the challenged term, attempting to distinguish between use as a mark as opposed to use as a merely descriptive use. Because the plaintiff's mark is unprotectable, it does not matter what use the defendant makes of it.

3.2   Defendant's Use is Not a 'Trade Mark' Use

3.2.1   Classic fair use

A closely-related defence is that of 'classic fair use'. That defence succeeds when the court finds that the defendant is using the phrase at issue not in a trade mark sense but merely to describe its goods or services.[74] The rationale for the defence is that:

> [W]hen the plaintiff chooses a mark with descriptive qualities, the fair use doctrine recognizes that he cannot altogether exclude some kinds of competing use, particularly those which use words in their primary descriptive and non-trade mark sense.[75]

These principles are reflected in *M.B.H. Enterprises, Inc. v WOKY, Inc.*,[76] a case involving radio stations. The plaintiff, having registered I LOVE YOU as a service mark for the provision of promotional campaigns to radio stations, licensed that mark to various radio stations, including one in Milwaukee. A direct competitor, WOKY, decided that it would 'say in an organized and persistent manner' that it 'loved' Milwaukee.[77] It adopted three verbal formulations to express its affection for Milwaukee and displayed them on billboards and bumper stickers, broadcast them and used them in television advertisements. Holding that WOKY had established a 'fair use' defence, the court found that WOKY used its call letters and broadcast frequency, but not its slogans, to identify itself to the public and had not intended to cause confusion between its services and those of its competitor. Because WOKY had made a descriptive use of the slogans, and not a trade mark use, its use was fair,

---

[74]   See Federal Trademark Act §33(b)(4), 15 USC §1115(b)(4) (providing that it is a defence to infringement of a federally registered mark if 'the use of the name, term, or device charged be an infringement is a use, otherwise than as a mark . . . of a term or device which is descriptive of and used fairly and in good faith only to describe [the defendant's] goods or services'). Federal Trademark Act §33(b)(4) is the 'statutory restatement of the corresponding common law defence': *Venetianaire Corp. of Am. v A & P Import Co.*, 429 F.2d 1079 (2d Cir. 1970); *King-Size, Inc. v Frank's King Size Clothes, Inc.*, 547 F. Supp. 1138 (SD Tex 1982).

[75]   *United States Shoe Corp. v Brown Group, Inc.*, 740 F. Supp. 196, 198 (SDNY) (quotations and citations omitted), *aff'd without op.*, 923 F.2d 844 (2d Cir. 1990).

[76]   633 F.2d 50 (7th Cir. 1980).

[77]   Ibid. at 51.

notwithstanding that it 'intended to derive commercial advantage from its declarations of love for Milwaukee'.[78]

The courts are divided over whether the fair use defence is available only against a plaintiff's descriptive, as opposed to a suggestive, use of a trade mark. One view is that the defence may be raised only if the plaintiff is using a descriptive mark.[79] The other view is that one can make a non-infringing, descriptive fair use even if the plaintiff is not using the phrase in a descriptive sense.[80] The latter view seems more persuasive because a plaintiff's use of the mark has little apparent relevance in determining whether the defendant is making a non-trade mark use of the same mark.

In *KP Permanent Make-Up, Inc. v Lasting Impression I, Inc.*[81] the United States Supreme Court held that 'some possibility of consumer confusion must be compatible with fair use' and further held that because 'the burden of proving likelihood of confusion rests with the plaintiff, . . . the fair use defendant has no free-standing need to show confusion unlikely'. The Supreme Court's conclusion that some amount of consumer confusion is compatible with fair use flies in the face of the view that 'it is inconsistent to find both likely confusion and a fair use'.[82] Before *KP Permanent Make-Up*, a minority of courts suggested that confusion and fair use could coexist. For example, the Second Circuit opined that, '[i]f any confusion results, that is a risk the plaintiff accepted when it decided to identify its product with a mark that use[d] a well-known descriptive phrase'.[83] After *KP Permanent Make-Up*, courts may well follow the position expressed in the *Restatement (Third) of Unfair Competition* that a defendant who uses another's mark fairly and in good faith to describe its goods or services is not an infringer 'even if some residual confusion remains likely'.[84]

Although *KP Permanent Make-Up* clarified the relationship between a plaintiff's burden in proving a likelihood of confusion and the classic fair use

---

[78]   Ibid. at 54.

[79]   See, for example, *Cullman Ventures, Inc. v Columbian Art Works, Inc.*, 717 F. Supp. 96 (SDNY 1989); *Inst. for Sci. Info., Inc. v Gordon & Breach, Sci. Publ'rs, Inc.*, 931 F.2d 1002 (3d Cir.), *cert. denied*, 502 US 909 (1991).

[80]   See, for example, *Sunmark, Inc. v Ocean Spray Cranberries, Inc.*, 64 F.3d 1055 (7th Cir. 1995); *Seaboard Seed Co. v Bemis Co.*, 632 F. Supp. 1133 (ND Ill 1986); *DowBrands, L.P. v Helene Curtis, Inc.*, 863 F. Supp. 963 (D. Minn. 1994).

[81]   125 S. Ct. 542, 550 (2004).

[82]   2 J.T. McCarthy, *McCarthy on Trademarks and Unfair Competition* §11:47 (4th ed. & Supp. 2005) (expressing the view that '[a] court should never find that a likelihood of confusion exists but refuse to enjoin it because defendant's use is "fair"').

[83]   *Cosmetically Sealed Indus., Inc. v Chesebrough-Pond's USA Co.*, 125 F.3d 28, 30 (2d Cir. 1997).

[84]   *Restatement (Third) of Unfair Competition* §28 comment b (1995).

defence, the Supreme Court declined to address a number of other important questions. For example, even though some degree of consumer confusion may now co-exist with fair use, the Court indicated that there might be a limit on the amount of confusion that must be accepted before the defence becomes available.[85] The Court declined, however, to offer any guidance on how much confusion is too much. The Supreme Court also recognized that two courts of appeals have found that likelihood of confusion 'bears not only on the fairness of using a term, but even on the further question whether an originally descriptive term has become so identified as a mark that a defendant's use of it cannot realistically be called descriptive'.[86] Nevertheless, the Court declined to address the issue.

Surprisingly, the Court failed to offer guidance on the factors, other than a likelihood of confusion, that may legitimately be considered in determining whether a use is 'fair'. The United States, as *amicus curiae*, argued that the 'used fairly' requirement in Section 1115(B)(4) demands only that the descriptive term describe the goods accurately. In response the Supreme Court merely noted that '[a]ccuracy of course has to be a consideration in assessing fair use, but the proceedings in this case so far raise no occasion to evaluate some other concerns that courts might pick as relevant, quite apart from attention to confusion'.[87]

3.2.2 Nominative fair use

'Classic fair use' is distinguished from 'nominative fair use' in that the classic fair use analysis applies when a defendant has used the plaintiff's mark only to describe the defendant's own product.[88] By contrast, the nominative fair use analysis 'is appropriate where a defendant has used a plaintiff's mark to describe the plaintiff's product, even if the defendant's ultimate goal is to describe his own product'.[89]

A nominative use may occur in various situations. For example, a manufacturer of Brand X cola might engage in comparative advertising by announcing that, '[i]n blind taste tests, consumers preferred Brand X to

---

[85] *KP Permanent Make-Up,* 125 S. Ct. at 550 ('It suffices to realize that our holding that fair use can occur along with some degree of confusion does not foreclose the relevance of the extent of any likely confusion in assessing whether a defendant's use is objectively fair'.).

[86] Ibid. at 550–51.

[87] Ibid. at 551.

[88] In *Ty, Inc. v Publ'ns Int'l, Ltd.*, 2005 WL 464688 at ¶5 (ND Ill Feb. 25, 2005), Judge Zagel noted that '[t]he term "nominative fair use" might just as easily have been labeled "denominative fair use", "proper name fair use", "reference fair use", [or] "signifying fair use"'.

[89] *Cairns v Franklin Mint Co.*, 282 F.3d 1139 (9th Cir. 2002).

COCA-COLA'.[90] Alternatively, a third party may refer to a trade mark without using it in a trade mark sense. For example, in *New Kids on the Block v
News America Publishing, Inc.*,[91] a newspaper conducted a survey asking
readers to identify their favourite member of a particular pop music group,
which the survey named. To vote, readers had to call a 900 telephone number,
from which the newspaper earned a toll. The band reasoned that the newspaper had used its service mark without permission and, having profited from
it, sought to recover infringement damages. However, the Ninth Circuit Court
of Appeals held that the newspaper's use of the mark was a non-infringing
'nominative use' that did not imply sponsorship or endorsement by the
trade mark owner. Accordingly, the use was fair.

In *New Kids*, the Ninth Circuit held identified three elements necessary to
satisfy the defence:

> First, the product or service in question must be one not readily identifiable without
> use of the trade mark; second, only so much of the mark or marks may be used as
> is reasonably necessary to identify the product or service; and third, the user must
> do nothing that would, in conjunction with the mark, suggest sponsorship or
> endorsement by the trade mark holder.[92]

The *New Kids* policy has been applied to allow the parodic use of a trade mark
to denote the target of the parody. For example the use of BARBIE was
permitted in a song that made fun of the vacuous image associated with
Mattel's famous BARBIE doll.[93] The nominative fair use defence also
protects retailers who use brand names on websites to advise visitors that they
sell the branded product,[94] or to describe the site owner's former affiliation
with the mark owner.[95] However, the nominative fair use defence will not
protect someone who uses a trade mark so frequently in a website or its
metatags as to cause search engines to direct internet users there instead of to
the plaintiff's site,[96] or protect a use so prominent as to cause confusion.[97]

---

[90]   See *J.K. Harris & Co. v Kassel*, 253 F. Supp. 2d 1120 (N.D. Cal. 2003) (holding that a company could mention a competitor's trade mark on its website to compare
and criticize).
[91]   971 F.2d 302 (9th Cir. 1992).
[92]   Ibid. at 308.
[93]   *Mattel, Inc. v MCA Records, Inc.*, 46 USPQ 2d 1407 (C.D. Cal. 1998), *aff'd
on other grounds*, 296 F.3d 894 (9th Cir. 2002).
[94]   *Patmont Motor Werks, Inc. v Gateway Marine, Inc.*, 1997 WL 811770 (N.D.
Cal. 1997).
[95]   *Playboy Enters., Inc. v Terri Welles, Inc.*, 78 F. Supp. 2d 1066 (S.D. Cal.
1999), *aff'd in part, rev'd in part on other grounds*, 279 F.3d 796 (9th Cir. 2002).
[96]   *Horphag Research Ltd. v Pellegrini*, 337 F.3d 1036 (9th Cir. 2003).
[97]   *Brother Records, Inc. v Jardine*, 318 F.3d 900 (9th Cir. 2003); *Liquid Glass
Enters., Inc. v Porsche AG*, 8 F. Supp. 2d 398 (DNJ 1998).

In an opinion widely criticized as confusing, the Third Circuit adopted a different formulation of the nominative fair use defence following *KP Permanent Make-Up*.[98] Over a stinging dissent, the Third Circuit proposed a 'burden shifting' test. Preliminarily, a plaintiff in a nominative use case would have to prove a likelihood of confusion before the defendant is required to raise the defence.[99] Because the 10-factor likelihood of confusion test ordinarily applied in the Third Circuit would make no sense in determining whether the defendant's use of the plaintiff's mark to describe the plaintiff's product caused a likelihood of confusion, the Third Circuit suggested that a trial court focus primarily on (i) the price of the parties' goods and other factors indicative of the care exercised by consumers in making a purchase; (ii) the length of the defendant's use of the mark without actual confusion; (iii) the defendant's intent in adopting the mark; and (iv) evidence of actual confusion.[100] Assuming the plaintiff proved a likelihood of confusion, the burden would shift to the defendant to demonstrate the fairness of its use by showing that (i) the use of the plaintiff's mark was necessary to describe both the plaintiff's product or service and the defendant's product or service; (ii) the defendant used only so much of the plaintiff's mark as was necessary to describe the plaintiff's product; and (iii) the defendant's conduct or language reflected the true and accurate relationship between the parties' products or services.[101] The dissent, although critical of the *New Kids* test, characterized the newly enunciated Third Circuit test as 'judicially unmanageable' and likely to increase confusion.[102]

Not every circuit has adopted the nominative fair use defence[103] and it remains unclear whether the Supreme Court's likelihood of confusion analysis in *KP Permanent Make-Up* applies to that defence.[104] A leading commentator, Professor Joseph McCarthy, has observed, for example, that the 'use of another's trade mark to identify, not the defendant's goods or services, but the

[98] See *Century 21 Real Estate Corp. v. Lending Tree, Inc.*, 425 F.3d 211 (3d Cir. 2005).
[99] Ibid. at 222.
[100] Ibid. at 224.
[101] Ibid. at 222.
[102] Ibid. at 233, 238.
[103] The Sixth Circuit refused to adopt the 'nominative fair use defence', finding that its traditional likelihood of confusion test sufficiently captures the potential for trade mark misuses: *PACCAR, Inc. v Telescan Techs., L.L.C.*, 319 F.3d 243, 256 (6th Cir. 2003), *overruled in part*, *KP Permanent Make-Up, Inc. v Lasting Impression I, Inc.*, 125 S. Ct. 542, 547 (2004). The Seventh Circuit has not yet ruled on the applicability of the nominative fair use defence.
[104] In *KP Permanent Make-Up*, 125 S. Ct. at 546 n.3, the Supreme Court specifically declined to address the 'nominative fair use' defence.

plaintiff's goods or services, is not an infringement so long as there is no like-lihood of confusion'.[105]

However, *Ty, Inc. v Publications International, Ltd.*,[106] the only case to consider the issue post-*KP*, held that the Supreme Court's logic in *KP* 'applies with similar force to defendants pursuing the defence of nominative fair use despite the almost certain likelihood of confusion regarding the source of the mark'. There the maker of well known Beanie Babies plush toys sued the publisher of a series of books and magazines designed as collectors' guides to the plaintiff's products, for infringing use of its BEANIE BABIES and Ty heart logo marks.

In considering the third prong of the *New Kids* test (that is, suggestion of sponsorship or endorsement), the court distinguished between 'confusing use and misleading use'.[107] It suggested that so long as the defendant has not used the plaintiff's mark to mislead consumers into believing that the plaintiff has sponsored or endorsed the defendant's product, the existence of a likelihood of confusion does not in itself negate a nominative fair use defence. The court recognized that this 'does not mean that consumer confusion is not relevant to the issue of fair use'.[108] However, like the Supreme Court, it declined to suggest how much weight should be given to this factor. It thus remains to be seen whether other federal courts will apply the *KP* analysis to the nominative fair use defence and, if so, whether they will provide any guidance as to the evaluation of fair use in this context.

---

[105]   3 J.T. McCarthy, *McCarthy on Trademarks and Unfair Competition* §23:11 (4th ed. & Supp. 2005) (emphasis in original).
[106]   2005 WL 464688 at ¶6 (ND Ill 25 Feb 2005).
[107]   Ibid. at ¶8.
[108]   Ibid. at ¶6.

13. Interim relief, final injunctions and freedom of speech: the French *Greenpeace* and *Danone* litigation

Grégoire Triet

1. INTRODUCTION

Article L 713-1 of the French Intellectual Property Code lays down the principle according to which 'registration of a mark shall confer on its owner a right of property in that mark for the goods and services he has designated'. This conception of the trade mark right as a proprietary right explains why, under French law, trade marks have traditionally enjoyed very high status and strong protection. The French Supreme Court has on several occasions held, in wording which has become classic, that 'the right in a mark is absolute over the whole territory and confers on its proprietor the right to bring an infringement action against any person who violates it, whether in good or bad faith'.[1]

The only statutory exceptions to this pure monopoly are contained in Articles L 713-4 (inability to prevent parallel imports of EEA origin) and L 713-6 (inability to prevent use of a similar sign as (a) a company name, trade name or sign, where such use is either earlier than the registration or made by another person using his own surname in good faith; (b) a reference which is necessary to state the intended purpose of the product or service, in particular as an accessory or spare part, provided no confusion exists as to their origin).

For a long time, French case law has appeared most reluctant to admit the possibility that the trade mark right might be limited by exceptions other than those mentioned above. A series of recent decisions has however modified this framework by admitting, or at least suggesting, that other elements might constitute a limit to trade mark protection: these decisions are known collectively as the *Danone/Greenpeace* cases.

---

[1]   Cass. Com. 26 June 1973, *Carel*, D. 1974. 558; see also Cass. Com. 23 Nov. 1993, *Coup de cœur*, PIBD 1994, III, p. 115.

The common background to *Danone* and *Greenpeace* was the existence of a conflict, bringing major commercial corporations into conflict with non-profit organizations and citizens' groups which launched online campaigns against those corporations' social or environmental policies. In order to maximize the visibility of their websites and the impact of their critical message, they made use of the corporations' names and logos by distorting them by means of a pastiche. For instance, in *Danone*, a free speech organization created a website in order to protest against relocations operated by the Danone group by calling for a boycott of its products. The address of the website was 'jeboycottedanone' ('iboycottdanone') followed by '.com' and '.net' suffixes. On each page of the site, the Danone logo was represented, preceded by the expression 'I boycott'. Danone attempted to obtain the banning of the website on the ground that the reproduction of its Danone word mark and the imitation of its Danone logo mark infringed its trade marks. The Tribunal de Grande Instance (court of first instance) Paris, ruling both in interim relief proceedings and in proceedings on the merits, upheld the claim based on the infringement of the logo mark, but the Cour d'appel (Court of Appeal) reversed the judgment.

In the *Greenpeace* cases, the oil company Esso and the leading international nuclear energy company Areva complained that the famous environmentalist organization had used their trade marks, with or without distortion, to illustrate a number of web pages dedicated to the denunciation of these corporations' environmental policy. Greenpeace had entitled a page 'Stop Esso', this expression also being used as a metatag keyword in the source code of the page. Greenpeace also made abundant use of the ESSO logo, distorted into E$$O. In similar fashion Greenpeace illustrated its anti-nuclear web pages by incorporating the Areva logos into gruesome images (for example: an 'A' projecting a skull-shaped shadow, dead fish covered with a blood-stained 'A', nuclear bombs and so on).

Before the President of the Court, sitting in chambers in interim relief proceedings, Esso's claim, based on the alleged infringement of its logo mark, succeeded, the company obtaining provisional prohibition of the website. However, the Cour d'appel reversed the injunction. The Tribunal de Grande Instance and the Cour d'appel, subsequently ruling on the merits of the case, also rejected Esso's claim. For its part, Areva failed in all its actions grounded on trade mark law. The Court, however, when called to rule on the merits of the case, eventually held Greenpeace liable on the ground of general civil liability.

The litigation stakes were high since these confrontations pitched a highly protective idea of the trade mark right on the one hand against a doctrine of freedom of speech, emancipated from the trade mark right, on the other.

2. SOME FRENCH LEGAL BACKGROUND

For readers who might be unfamiliar with the French legal system, it is necessary to mention a few procedural specificities of French trade mark law.

Article L 716-6 of the French Intellectual Property Code provides for an interim relief proceeding commonly called 'référé-interdiction'. This allows a trade mark proprietor to obtain interim injunctive measures without having to prove a situation of urgency. The conditions are that he has first filed a suit for infringement on the merits, that such action appears well-grounded and that it was filed within a short time after the day on which the alleged infringement became known.

This proceeding was used by the claimants in the *Danone/Greenpeace* cases, which explains the high number of decisions rendered up till now, given that there were injunctions,[2] appeals concerning injunctions,[3] judgments on the merits[4] and appeals against judgments on the merits.[5] We shall distinguish between the judgments rendered before 2 August 2002, which found the 'critics' liable on the ground of trade mark infringement, and those rendered after this date, which rejected such analysis and have attracted much public attention, being the most interesting decisions. It is generally only the latter judgments which are designated *Danone/Greenpeace* case law.

In order to better understand these decisions' contribution to trade mark law, it is necessary to go back over French case law before *Danone/Greenpeace*. We shall then analyse the solutions brought by this case law.

3. FRENCH CASE LAW PRIOR TO THE *DANONE/GREENPEACE* DECISIONS

In spite of its monopolistic conception of trade mark rights, French case law has never completely ignored the difficulties which may arise from potential

---

[2]   *Danone*: TGI Paris, 23 April and 14 May 2001, [2003] ETMR 26; *Esso/Greenpeace*: TGI Paris, 8 July 2002, PIBD No. 756.III. p. 49, [2003] ETMR 35; *Areva/Greenpeace*: TGI Paris, 2 Aug. 2002, *Propriété industrielle* – Oct. 2002, p. 20.

[3]   *Danone*: Paris, 28 Nov. 2001, unpublished; *Esso/Greenpeace*: Paris, 26 Feb. 2003, Dalloz 2003, No. 27, p. 1831; *Areva/Greenpeace*: Paris, 26 Feb. 2003, Dalloz 2003, No. 27, p. 1831.

[4]   *Danone*: TGI Paris 4 July 2001; Petites Affiches 18 Sept. 2001, No. 186, p. 11; *Esso/Greenpeace*: TGI Paris 30 Jan. 2004, [2004] ETMR 1216; *Propriété industrielle* – Oct. 2004, p. 20; *Areva/Greenpeace*: TGI Paris 9 July 2004, *Propriété industrielle* – Oct. 2004, p. 18.

[5]   *Danone*: Paris 30 April 2003, Dalloz 2003, No. 26, p. 1760; *Esso/Greenpeace*: Paris 16 November 2005, *Lextenso.com Propriété intellectuelle*, November 2005.

conflicts between the exercise of such monopoly and third parties' freedom of expression. However, the taking into account of such fundamental right was circumscribed by being confined to very specific situations and came up against its limits when the use of the mark went beyond 'necessary reference'.

3.1 Freedom of Speech: a Concept Not Unknown to Trade Mark Law . . .

French case law conceded long ago that a trade mark proprietor may not prevent and control every reference to his mark by third parties, at the risk of unduly interfering with their right to freedom of expression. For instance, well-established case law considers that trade mark rights may not prevent use of the sign constituting the mark in its common and general meaning.[6] Similarly, French case law found no difficulty in admitting the right of an author to use a mark in a literary or artistic work.[7] It also recognizes the right of third parties to use a mark for information purposes,[8] the right to criticize falling within the scope of such information-related purposes.

One would therefore be mistaken if one were to believe that, before the *Danone/Greenpeace* case law, French case law was blind to the necessity to conciliate trade mark law and freedom of speech. It was indeed concerned about striking a balance between these two rights and sought not to interfere unduly with freedom of speech and trade by preventing third parties from referring to a mark when such reference was necessary for the exercise of such freedom.

It is in the application of this jurisprudence that, in *Danone* and *Greenpeace*, the major claimants did not succeed in their claims grounded on the infringement of their word marks. For instance, Danone and Esso lost their actions grounded on the reproduction, without modification, of the word marks DANONE and ESSO respectively as domain names ('jeboy-cottedanone') and as metatag keywords ('stop esso'). At every level, the courts have considered that reference to the marks was necessary to inform internauts of the contents of the web pages and that the words 'Danone' and 'Esso' were understood by internauts as designating the Danone or Esso companies, not their products.

This protection of third parties' freedom of speech, when reference to the mark is necessary, may implicitly be related to a statutory text, in that Article L 713-6 (b) provides for a 'necessary reference' exception. The term 'necessary' is of the utmost importance here: for we shall see that case law was

---

6   For example: Cass. Com. 6 May 1996, Ann. 96, 25, *Louisiane*.
7   Paris, 3 Nov. 1987, Ann. 88, p. 236.
8   Paris, 22 February 1995, PIBD 95, III, p. 257.

much less inclined to let critics of trade mark holders escape liability when use of the mark was not strictly indispensable for the expression of the critic's message.

3.2   . . . But a Concept Applied in a Very Restrictive Way

In practice, the problem arose for figurative marks such as logos. Indeed, if it is impossible to express an opinion about a product without mentioning its name, it seems hardly necessary, in order to convey one's ideas about that product, to reproduce the figurative elements of the mark.

Now, imagine a citizens' group wanting to express its (negative) opinion of a corporation by using a striking message which will impress itself on the minds of consumers (which in itself is perfectly lawful). It may seem quite tempting to use humour as a weapon and to parody or caricature that corporation's logo, since it stands as the corporation's identifying element *par excellence*. Following the old saying 'un bon dessin vaut mieux qu'un long discours' ('a good drawing is better than a long speech'[9]), one may argue that a striking 'graphical distortion' will reach a larger target and will have greater impact than a written account, however well-expressed. This is why anti-smoking groups, among others, have on several occasions tried to launch anti-smoking campaigns based on the parody of the trade dress of cigarette packets (for example a camel's skeleton, the Gitane dancer with crab claws instead of feet, a skull wearing the Gauloise helmet). These attempts have been almost routinely condemned by the courts on the ground that trade mark law does not recognize the right to caricature a mark.[10]

In 2000, things seemed to evolve when the Cour de Cassation rendered a decision which is sometimes presented as having, to a certain extent, recognized a right of parody in trade mark law.[11] The CEO of the automotive company Citroën took offence at being repeatedly targeted in a satirical TV programme. He could not complain about the satire directed at him personally, as it fell within the scope of free-speech protection. However, since Citroën cars were also subject to humorous jibes, the CEO hit on the idea of suing his persecutors for the harm done to the company's trade marks and product image. The French Supreme Court, after a lengthy proceedings, eventually rejected such action by ruling that

---

[9]   The French equivalent of the English saying 'One picture is worth a thousand words'.

[10]   See notably Cass. Com. 21 Feb. 1995, Dalloz 1995, IR p. 97

[11]   Cass. Plenary Session. 12 July 2000, Dalloz 2001 No. 3, J., p. 259 *Guignols de l'info*.

the jokes about the branded vehicles were uttered within the context of a satirical programme . . . and may not be dissociated from the caricature of [the CEO], so that the allegedly offending statements come under the free-speech scope of protection, and are unlikely to raise confusion between the satirical programme and reality.

We think that, even though this case deals with the issue of freedom of caricature in a trade mark-related matter, it does not go so far as to recognize a right of parody in trade mark law. The court's decision was rendered on the ground of general civil liability, not trade mark law, and the court did not directly rule on the right to parody a mark. It actually evaded the issue by finding that the criticism against the mark was not, on the facts, separable from the criticism against the CEO as a person, which enabled the court to place the entire litigation within the scope of the freedom to criticize people.

Case law on trade mark parody has not fundamentally changed since this case, as is evidenced by the first *Danone* and *Greenpeace* (Esso) decisions, which did not allow the imitation of the logos on the ground that such imitation was not strictly necessary to the expression of its authors' ideas.[12] This is the context in which the *Danone/Greenpeace* decisions (that is the post-2 August 2002 case law) were delivered.

4. ANALYSIS OF *DANONE/GREENPEACE*

Analysis of the *Danone/Greenpeace* case law reveals that it is articulated around two notions. One is external to trade mark law: the right to parody as an expression of freedom of speech; the other belongs to trade mark law, being the commercial or non-commercial destination of the allegedly infringing use.

4.1 An External Criterion: the Right to Parody as a Support to Freedom of Speech

Article L 122-5 of the Intellectual property Code, which deals with copyright,

---

[12]   See TGI Paris 4 July 2001 (*Danone*) cited above: 'Neither the right to inform, nor the right to freedom of expression may justify this wrongful imitation and this infringement of Danone's property rights in its semi-figurative marks, while such imitation of the mark, even if it accompanies remarks made freely on the website, is not *necessary* to the expression of such opinion and serves only to illustrate screen pages which could have been illustrated differently.'

TGI Paris, 8 July 2002 (*Esso*) cited above: 'In conclusion, the appropriation of the mark in a presentation using large-size colour font for the imitated titles and logos, does not *exclusively* partake of the necessity to communicate [Greenpeace's] opinions and objectives' (free translation, emphasis added).

provides that, 'once a work has been disclosed, the author may not prohibit: ... (4) parody, pastiche and caricature, observing the rules of the genre'. No written provision provides for a similar defence under trade mark law. In the *Danone* and *Greenpeace* litigation, the defendants expressly based their plea of defence on parody and caricature 'which imply a burlesque magnification of the mark which is held up in ridicule for the purpose of criticism',[13] thus arguing purely and simply for the transplant of this copyright law notion into trade mark law.

While traditional case law, as we have seen, strictly confined this defence within copyright law, some legal commentators, relying on *Guignols de l'info*,[14] favoured the recognition, under certain conditions, of such a defence in trade mark law. This found an echo in one of the judges called to rule in one of the *Greenpeace* cases. In the first decision to rule in favour of the defendant (the order of 2 August 2002 in *Areva*), Judge Belfort rejected Areva's action on the ground that

[t]here is reason to question the relevance of Article L 713-3(b)[15] in this case ... whereas, firstly, these imitations are not located on commercial ground but *on the ground of free speech which falls within the scope of the right to criticize and carica-ture* and, secondly, the likelihood of confusion is problematic. ... (emphasis added)

It results from this wording that the judge was willing to accept, in trade mark law, an exception of parody, stemming from the right to freedom of speech. This decision has, however, remained isolated on this point; and it clearly appears from *Danone/Greenpeace* at its final stage that the right to parody remains unrecognized in French trade mark law. Indeed, none of the decisions made after the order of 2 August 2002 recognizes any exception in favour of parody. In fact in *Greenpeace/Esso* the judgment on the merits rendered on 30 January 2004 takes care expressly to recall that 'trade mark law ignores excep-tions of parody'. The other judgments on the merits implicitly dismissed such exception and examined the infringement issue strictly in accordance with two of the criteria of trade mark law, similarity and likelihood of confusion.

Having said that, we must now examine why the courts have all taken care to make reference to freedom of expression[16] while refusing to recognize this

---

13   Greenpeace's brief in response in TGI Paris, 8 July 2002.
14   See note 11 above.
15   Art. L 713-3(b) prohibits confusingly similar use of a mark.
16   'Considering that the principle of free speech, which has constitutional value, implies that the association ... may ... denounce [the claimant companies' policy] under the form it deems appropriate to its purpose; that even though such freedom is not absolute, it may however only suffer the restrictions that are rendered necessary by the respect of third parties' rights.'

fundamental right as a direct limitation upon trade mark law. In doing so we shall contrast the decisions rendered on 26 February 2003 by the Paris Cour d'appel in the interim relief actions with the subsequent decisions that were rendered on the merits.

4.1.1   The interim relief appeal judgments of 26 February 2003

In the appeal judgments rendered in the interim relief actions, the freedom of speech principle is not applied directly as an exception to trade mark law. On the contrary, the Cour d'appel expressly mentions that freedom of speech is not absolute and that it must suffer the restrictions that are rendered necessary by respect for third parties' rights,[17] which include trade mark rights. In the cases in dispute, the court considered that those trade mark rights are questionable (given the problematic issue of the likelihood of confusion), which in itself could provide sufficient cause for rejection of the application for interim relief. However, the court went further, stating that, had the action appeared better-grounded, it would still refuse injunctive relief because damage to the claimants' mark could easily be compensated by damages at the end of the proceeding on the merits, without the need for any interim prohibition injunction.

The court actually uses the principle of free speech *not* for the purpose of ruling upon the merits of the case but in order to assess the relevance of interim relief. It seems that the court applied a 'balance of interests' test and concluded that, between the damage that would be sustained by Greenpeace if its freedom of speech were unduly restricted and the damage suffered by Esso and Areva if the Greenpeace websites were operating until the end of the proceedings, the balance tilted towards Greenpeace.

4.1.2   The subsequent judgments on the merits

In the judgments later rendered on the merits, freedom of speech also lay at the heart of the debate. This debate, however, did not take place at the level of the trade mark infringement action. It took place solely, once the infringement action was dismissed, at the level of the subsidiary action grounded on common civil liability law. For the purpose of such an action, the judges examine whether, when exercising their right to free speech, the defendants committed any abuse that would amount to a civil tort. As the Tribunal said in *Greenpeace/Areva*: 'freedom to criticize should be exercised with respect for the general obligation of prudence and objectivity'.

In concrete terms, in the *Greenpeace/Esso* and *Danone* cases, the judges eventually ruled that the defendant critics had not abused their right to criticize and had not denigrated the companies' products. On the contrary, in

---

[17]   See note 16.

Greenpeace/Areva, the Tribunal considered that the systematic association of the Areva trade marks with symbolic representations of death had the effect of conveying the thought that 'Areva spreads death around', which was too much a final and simplistic view, proceeding from a purely denigrating process and not from a debate of ideas.

4.1.3 Post-*Danone/Greenpeace* litigation

In post-*Danone/Greenpeace* litigation involving trade mark parody, trade mark holders have generally brought legal proceedings only on the ground of general civil liability and have generally won their cases. For instance, there was an unusual case about a humorist who, in a radio programme, told a joke in which the famous Nutella chocolate spread played a part in paedophile and incestuous practices. Following this programme, the proprietor of the Nutella trade mark sought compensation before the courts for the damage sustained by its mark.

The Tribunal de Grande Instance rejected the claim on the ground that, given the satirical style of the programme, as well as the provocative and outrageous nature of the joke, the reference to the Nutella product, obscene as it was, was necessarily devoid of any real impact and unlikely to raise in the mind of the audience any association of the mark with the practices mentioned by the comedian. The Tribunal also considered that the allusion to the Nutella product, which aimed at rendering the joke more suggestive, did not proceed from a desire to trespass on the mark's notoriety for commercial purposes or to harm the trade mark owner's reputation.

The Cour d'appel reversed the judgment and ruled that

> freedom of speech and the supposedly humorous nature of the joke did not authorize [the humorist] to quote the name of a product known to be destined to children by associating it to child abuse and incestuous practices, which has necessarily harmed its image; besides that, such use of the notoriety of the name in order to ensure the success of the programme has enabled the defendants to benefit unduly from the means used by the trade mark owner to maintain its notoriety.[18]

A second case concerns an anti-smoking campaign using the trade dress of the Camel cigarette packet. The Cour d'appel de Paris, having recited that freedom of speech is a principle with constitutional value which must be exercised with respect for other people's rights, held that the campaigner was civilly liable in that 'reference to a specific brand of cigarette, even parodically, . . . has the consequence of discrediting one manufacturer to the detriment (sic) of the others whose image has not been used'.[19]

---

[18] Paris 7 May 2004, *Lextenso.com. Propriété intellectuelle* – June 2004.
[19] Paris 14 Jan. 2005, PIBD 2005, III, p. 242.

It results from this that we consider that the contribution of the *Danone/Greenpeace* case law does not reside in the irruption of freedom of speech into trade mark law as an exception to the trade mark owner's monopoly. Its real innovation lies in the effective taking into account of a criterion belonging to trade mark law: the destination of the allegedly infringing use.

4.2 An Internal Criterion: the Destination of the Allegedly Infringing Use

After the courts, explicitly or implicitly, refused to admit the existence of a right to parody in trade mark law, the Tribunal (in the *Greenpeace* cases) and the Cour d'appel (in *Danone*), ruling on the merits, rejected the infringement actions on the ground that the allegedly infringing use did not meet the conditions of trade mark infringement, which implies the use of a confusingly similar sign for identical or similar products (the principle of speciality) and a use in the course of trade.

4.2.1 Application of the principle of speciality

The initial *Greenpeace* and *Danone* decisions, which had condemned the 'critics', had made a classical application of trade mark law when assessing whether the modified logos had been used for products or services identical or similar to those designated in the registration and whether there resulted a likelihood of confusion. In order to reach a positive answer, the courts had forced the wording of the law in a questionable manner. For instance in *Danone* the Tribunal relied on the fact that the website listed the products to be boycotted, in finding that 'the allegedly infringing sign is used, if not to designate identical products, at least in relation therewith' and that 'such use of the imitated sign cannot fail to lead the internaut to associate this sign with the marks at stake which are furthermore very well-known by the public, and therefore to raise confusion'. In *Greenpeace/Esso* the order inferred the likelihood of confusion from the finding that the perception of the allegedly infringing sign 'cannot fail to call to mind the products and services offered by this famous mark'.

The reasoning of the courts was flawed in two ways. First, when the law prohibits the use of a mark for identical products, it means products of the same nature, marketed by a competitor of the trade mark owner. In these cases, however, the marks were not used in relation with competing products but in relation to the owner's own products, without any act of marketing by the alleged infringer. Secondly, faced with the problem of proving actual likelihood of confusion, the judges contented themselves with finding a mere likelihood of association, which they simply assimilated to a likelihood of confusion. However, European case law is perfectly clear: a mere likelihood of association is insufficient of itself to prove a likelihood of confusion.[20]

The first contribution of the *Danone/Greenpeace* case law is to have broken with this traditional trend, which extended trade mark monopoly much beyond – or even against – the wording of the law, and to have ruled in a manner closer to its spirit. These decisions held that there could be no likelihood of confusion between the products and services at stake since the alleged infringers did not trade in any products or services at all and since the consumer was unlikely to believe, given the unambiguous content and presentation of the websites, that they were operated by Danone, Esso or Areva. The second *Danone/Greenpeace* contribution lies in the place given to the criterion of use in the course of trade.

4.2.2 Use in the course of trade

In the *Danone/Greenpeace* cases the judges found, dismissing the allegation of infringement, that the allegedly infringing use was a 'usage polémique étranger à la vie des affaires' ('a polemical use made outside the course of trade'). This 'course of trade' notion is familiar to European trade mark law since it is contained in Article 5 of the European Trade Mark Harmonisation Directive, which limits the trade mark proprietor's exclusive right to preventing third parties from using certain signs 'in the course of trade'. This notion is not expressly contained in the French Intellectual Property Code, although trade mark law is supposed to be the result of the implementation of the Directive.

It could be argued that such a notion exists indirectly and implicitly through the principle of speciality, which defines infringement as the use of a trade mark for identical or similar products. Indeed, a non-commercial use does not *prima facie* have any bearing on products or services. It appears to this author, however, that the principle of speciality does not perfectly reflect the 'course of trade' notion. This chapter has shown how certain decisions had distorted this principle to the point of considering that certain non-commercial types of use were confusingly similar. The *Danone/Greenpeace* case law is therefore outstanding in that it expressly makes, of non-commercial use, an exception to the trade mark proprietor's monopoly. This is where its novelty lies and why it deserves to be counted among the important decisions in French trade mark law.

Interesting as it is, this jurisprudence still presents unresolved issues. For instance, it would be useful if the scope of the 'course of trade' notion were

---

[20]   *Sabel v Puma* Case C-251/95 [1998] ETMR 1 and *Marca Mode v Adidas* Case C-425/98 [2000] ETMR 561.

better defined. Indeed, the judgment of 9 July 2004 seems to have assimilated the 'course of trade' notion to 'competition between commercial entities'. This seems unnecessarily restrictive since certain types of use by a non-competing commercial entity, or by a non-commercial entity, may fall within the 'course of trade'. These decisions also lack coherence in the legal articulation of the assessment of the infringement. Indeed they seem either to add the 'non-commercial use' condition to the 'likelihood of confusion' and the 'similarity between the products and services' conditions, or to imply non-commercial use from the absence of likelihood of confusion and similarity. It results however from the Directive that the condition of 'non-commercial use' should be assessed first and that similarity and likelihood of confusion should be examined only after, and if, the allegedly infringing use has been held to be in the course of trade.

In spite of these minor reservations, the *Danone/Greenpeace* case law undeniably constitutes a milestone in French trade mark law. Future case law will have the opportunity to clarify the application of the 'course of trade' notion and any developments in it will be followed with great interest.

14. Trade mark issues in the financial services industry

Steven Weiner and Frank Azzopardi

The recent innovation of new financial products, such as derivatives, hedge funds and other investments, has caused creators of financial products and portfolio managers alike to ask: 'What's in a name?' Some find the answer more complicated than they may have first imagined.

Trade mark rights arise when a trade mark is used in commerce, regardless of whether the user has sought to register the mark. However, registration with the United States Patent and Trademark Office ('USPTO') and/or one or more Secretaries of State expands the scope of protection and creates a presumption of when the registrant first used the mark.[1]

Just as in many other industries, financial service providers use branding as a strategically important way to distinguish their products or fund. This chapter focuses on some of the trade mark issues confronting the financial services industry in the United States. First, some issues facing portfolio managers seeking to start up and name a fund are considered, especially in light of the difficulty of confidently assessing the likelihood of confusion between marks in the financial services sector. Secondly, this chapter discusses the extent to which the creators of derivative financial products and the promoters of secondary market trading in them can make referential use of another party's mark under trade mark law – such as in the context of promoting and selling index-linked derivative products – without a licence from the trade mark owner.

1.   THE INVESTMENT FIRM'S DILEMMA

Once the initial capital is raised by a portfolio manager, one might think that most of the work necessary for starting up a fund has been done. However,

---

[1]   In addition to federal trade mark registration, most states in the United States allow a user of a trade mark in that state to register its rights with the relevant Secretary of State (or other administrative figure). See J. Thomas McCarthy, *McCarthy on Trademarks and Unfair Competition* §22:10 (4th ed. 2005).

finding a name is one of the toughest and most important tasks a portfolio
manager must tackle, an increasingly difficult task for many firms. For example,
the number of hedge funds has doubled over the past five years to more than
8000.[2] Figure 14.1 highlights the rapid growth in the number of hedge funds.[3]

With so many participants, the financial community becomes increasingly concerned that the pool of available names has dried up. A portfolio
manager pointed out in an article in the *Wall Street Journal*: '[a]ll the Greek
gods were taken' and '[s]o were many animals, mountain ranges, rivers,
roads – even solar systems'.[4] The portfolio manager quipped that the task
of finding a name for his fund 'was harder than naming [his] children'.[5]

How does trade mark law limit the ability of portfolio managers to find a
suitable name for their funds? Trade marks and trade names offer protection
against any use of a similar mark or name by another party that causes a likelihood of confusion.[6] Consequently, trade mark attorneys run numerous
trade mark searches for newly-formed hedge fund clients and recently
spunoff private equity firm arms of large investment banks in the seemingly
impossible pursuit of a name that conjures the right image within the investment community without leading to a likelihood of confusion with an earlier
trade mark or trade name.

Some investment firms find the process so frustrating and difficult that
they opt for a name that incorporates the personal name and/or initials of the
portfolio manager. This is typically a much safer way to proceed for many
firms, given that use of a personal name by itself is considered to be descriptive unless a party claiming trade mark rights can show that it has acquired
a secondary meaning or the distinctiveness required for protection.[7]
However, for the same reasons, this approach provides less protection
against subsequent adoption of similar-sounding names by unauthorized
third parties.

---

[2]   Ianthe Jeanne Dugan, 'Why Hedge Funds Hunt for Animals, Search the Stars
– As Firms Proliferate, Finding The Right Name Is Tough', *Wall St. J.*, Jul. 25, 2005 at
A1. See also *Staff Report to the United States Securities and Exchange Commission,
Implications of the Growth of Hedge Funds* (2003) where it was suggested that based
on then current estimates, 6000 to 7000 hedge funds operated in the United States
managing approximately $600 to $650 billion in assets and that in five to ten years
from the date of the report (September 2003), hedge fund assets were predicted to
exceed $1 trillion.
[3]   Ibid.
[4]   Ibid.
[5]   Ibid.
[6]   See *McLean v Fleming*, 96 US 245, 24 L. Ed. 828 (1878), Lanham Act §32,
15 USCA §1114(1). See also McCarthy, §23:1.
[7]   Lanham Act §2, 15 USCA §1052(e).

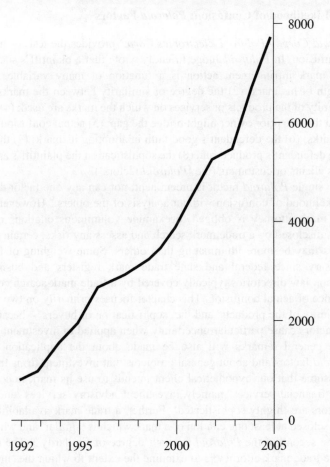

Note: The number of hedge funds has skyrocketed.

Source: Hennessee Group.

Figure 14.1 Stiff competition

Portfolio managers wanting something more novel or auspicious will often be in the difficult position of having to choose a name the defence of which may pose some risk. Litigation is an unattractive option to an investment firm about to commence operations. In assessing the risk of infringement, an attorney must assess those same factors that a court will consider when resolving whether there is a likelihood of confusion. As explained below, the application of these factors raises particular uncertainty and difficulty in the context of investment services.

1.1 Likelihood of Confusion: *Polaroid* Factors

Polaroid Corp. v Polaroid Electronics Corp.[8] provides the test for likelihood
of confusion. In *Polaroid* Judge Friendly wrote that a plaintiff's success in a
trade mark infringement action is a function of many variables: (1) the
strength of his mark; (2) the degree of similarity between the marks; (3) the
proximity of the products or services on which the marks are used; (4) the likelihood that the prior owner might bridge the gap; (5) actual confusion between
the marks; (6) the defendant's good faith in adopting its mark; (7) the quality
of the defendant's products and (8) the sophistication the plaintiff's and defendant's clients or customers (the '*Polaroid* factors').

No single *Polaroid* factor is preeminent; nor can any one factor determine
the likelihood of confusion without analysis of the others.[9] However, when a
trade mark attorney is obliged to examine voluminous citations of earlier
marks disclosed by a trade mark search and assess any risks, certain *Polaroid*
factors may be more illuminating than others. Some weighing of factors is
necessary since federal and state trade mark registers and business and
common law directories typically covered by a trade mark search contain no
evidence of actual confusion. This chapter focuses primarily on two factors –
'proximity of the products' and the 'sophistication of buyers' – because these
two factors cause particular uncertainty when applied to investment services.
Some general remarks will also be made about the application of other
Polaroid factors and about general problems that investment firms face.

Assume that our hypothetical client intends to use its mark in connection
with 'financial services, namely investment advisory services' and that its
investors are 'highly sophisticated'. Further, a trade mark availability search
has disclosed at least one citation of a mark which is 'similar' and which satisfies the second of the *Polaroid* factors ('degree of similarity'). The next step
for the trade mark attorney is to examine the extent to which the 'investment
advisory services' are proximate to the cited user's products or services.

1.2 Proximity of Products and Sophistication of Buyers

The proximity of products inquiry 'concerns whether and to what extent the
two products compete with each other'.[10] This inquiry leads to an examination
of 'the nature of the products themselves and the structure of the market'.[11]

---

[8]   287 F.2d 492 (2d Cir. 1961).
[9]   *Lever Bros. Co. v American Bakeries*, 693 F.2d 251, 253 (2d Cir. 1982).
[10]   *Cadbury Beverages v Cott*, 73 F.3d 474, 480 (2d. Cir. 1996). See also *The
Morningside Group Limited v Morningside Capital Group*, (n. 21), 140.
[11]   Ibid. See also *Lexington Management Corporation v Lexington Capital
Partners*, (n. 15), 284.

However, in undertaking this inquiry the courts have noted that '[t]he products or services need not compete with one another'[12] since 'confusion, or the likelihood of confusion, not competition, is the real test of trade mark infringement'.[13] Moreover, in resolving the question of proximity, proximity of products should be considered in conjunction with 'sophistication of buyers' because the latter 'recognizes that the likelihood of confusion between the products at issue depends in part on the sophistication of the relevant purchasers'.[14]

Applying these principles to specific facts, it is important to survey some cases that have considered these principles in the context of investment services. While investment firms are located across the breadth of the United States, the Second Circuit is arguably the most appropriate circuit upon which to focus, given the large number of investment firms located in the New York area. In reviewing some of the more pertinent Second Circuit cases one may gain an appreciation of the difficulty confronting the investment firm seeking an available name for its fund and of the problem trade mark attorneys face in giving an opinion that the client's preferred choice has a 'clean bill of health' and is available for use. This is because the courts in the Second Circuit have often been reluctant to distinguish between seemingly different types of investment services. Thus, even though the client believes that there is a sufficient delineation between its investment services and the investment services of a cited user, it may prove difficult convincing a court of that fact.

A case which applied the proximity test in the area of investment services is *Lexington Management Corporation v Lexington Capital Partners*.[15] The plaintiff, a registered investment advisor, managed a family of 18 mutual funds marketed under the Lexington name. The Lexington funds were designed to provide a variety of investment options for retail investors, financial planners and intermediaries and for the defined benefit and contribution marketplace. The defendant, a broker/dealer registered with the NASD, the SEC and other regulatory bodies, was not a registered investment advisor and derived most of its revenue from commissions on stock transactions in which it acted as a retail broker and from underwriting activities as well as its market-making activities.

The district court held that the nature of the parties' respective services supported a finding that the proximity of products requirement had been satisfied in this case:

---

12   *Lexington*, 285.
13   *Mobil Oil Corp. v Pegasus Petroleum Corp.*, 818 F.2d 254, 257–58 (2d Cir. 1987).
14   *Cadbury Beverages v Cott*, 73 F.3d 474, 480 (2d. Cir. 1996). See also *Lexington*, 284.
15   10 F.Supp.2d 271 (2d Cir. 1998).

... both companies seek individuals with disposable income who desire investment opportunities. Presumably, individuals likely to invest in individual stocks would also be likely to invest in mutual funds; indeed, mutual funds themselves are composed of shares of various companies. Indeed, defendant itself even deals in mutual funds. Although defendant derives less than one percent of its revenue from this source, the fact that it sells the very products offered by plaintiff demonstrates clearly how close their products are to one another. While the companies here perform different specific services, they each compete for the same investor dollars and hence deal in the same markets. [16]

Finding a proximity of products essentially because both companies seek individuals who desire investment opportunities and thus compete for the same investment dollars casts the net very wide over the area of investment services as to which a prior user can assert rights. The court noted that, though the plaintiff and the defendant did not perform identical services or offer identical products, 'because they both operate in the same discrete "investment securities" field, the likelihood of confusion – especially by association – is great'.[17]

Notably, the court added 'the sophistication of the potential customer class does not change the result'.[18] The court referred to the decision in *In re United California Brokers, Inc.*,[19] where the Patent and Trademark Office Trademark Trial and Appeal Board rejected the argument that potential investors of the plaintiff and the defendant were so 'sophisticated and wise' that they would know the parties 'could not become involved in [each other's] activities without running afoul of SEC regulations'.[20] Therefore, even if the trade mark attorney receives advice from counsel specializing in financial institutions regulation that involvement or association of the parties is impossible from a regulatory point of view, that fact will not necessarily indicate that the products or services are not proximate.

Another case which considered the proximity test in the area of investment services is *The Morningside Group Limited v Morningside Capital Group*.[21] The plaintiff engaged in financial activities including structured and financed investments in a broad range of United States companies and assisting in managing its acquisitions, often soliciting co-investors in those endeavours. The defendant, an investment firm, first generated meaningful publicity when it advertised an acquisition of Carson Products Company in the *Wall Street*

---

[16] *Lexington*, 285.
[17] Ibid., 286.
[18] Ibid.
[19] 222 USPQ 361.
[20] Ibid. See also *In re United California Brokers, Inc.*, 222 USPQ 361, 362.
[21] 182 F.3d 133 (2d Cir. 1999).

Journal. In its advertisement, the defendant identified itself as Morningside Capital Group of Westport, Connecticut. That morning, the plaintiff's officers received several phone calls from financial professionals congratulating them on the Carson Products acquisition or inquiring as to why they had not been informed of the deal. In response to the *Wall Street Journal* advertisement and the ensuing inquiries about the acquisition of Carson Products, the plaintiff filed a Lanham Act suit.

The court found that the plaintiff and the defendant were in competition as 'they both seek out direct investment opportunities for themselves and others', even though they 'had focused their investment efforts on somewhat different industries'.[22] The court emphasized that confusion in the financial investment context is particularly troubling because of the 'personal nature of the investment market'.[23] The United States Court of Appeals noted:

> High-level investment business is commonly conducted based on trust and personal relationships among individuals. If any investor reads about a Morningside Capital investment – such as the Carson Products acquisition – and mistakes that transaction for a Morningside Group investment of which it was not aware, it may well feel 'cut out' of a potentially lucrative deal. Unless it communicates with someone at Morningside Group to express its displeasure and thus discovers its mistake, its business relations with Morningside Group could be soured. In that market, then, even positive publicity for Morningside Capital could cause business problems and lost opportunities for Morningside Group. And it is of course obvious that adverse consequences for Morningside Group could also flow from a converse scenario – unfavorable publicity attendant on a Morningside Capital transaction.[24]

The court reiterated the principle in *Lexington* that, when 'there is a high degree of similarity between the parties services and marks, "the sophistication of the buyers cannot be relied on to prevent confusion" '.[25]

Both *Lexington* and *Morningside* underline the importance of taking a relatively conservative approach when reviewing the results of a trade mark search and assessing the likelihood of confusion with respect to particular citations in the investment services area. Assuming the cited mark is similar and the cited user conducts business in the financial investment market, any distinction made between the types of investments offered by the client and the cited user may be tenuous. At least in the Second Circuit, courts appear more inclined to find that the plaintiff satisfies the 'proximity of products' factor even when the parties' investment efforts may be targeted at substantially

---

22   *Morningside*, 140.
23   Ibid., 141.
24   Ibid., 140.
25   Ibid., 143. See also *McGregor-Doniger Inc. v Drizzle Inc.*, 599 F.2d 1126, 1137 (2d Circ. 1979).

different industry segments, due in part to the 'personal nature of the invest-ment market'.[26] In this regard, the degree of sophistication of investors appears insufficient *per se* to negate a finding of confusion.

Even so, in both *Lexington* and *Morningside* at least some overlap may arguably be found between the services of the respective parties (albeit minor in *Lexington*). A defendant may therefore still successfully defend its right to use a particular mark by establishing that a clear, sharp delineation exists between the plaintiff's and the defendant's investment services. In some Second Circuit cases the defendant appears to have been given this latitude and has successfully contended that the services are not proximate.

In *Haven Capital Management, Inc. v Havens Advisors, LLC*[27] the plain-tiff provided investment advice to its clientele, managed funds for them on a separate account basis and operated the Haven Fund, a mutual fund in which clients purchased shares. The investments were in marketable equity and fixed income securities, primarily in investment grade domestic companies. It promoted itself as a conservative investment management firm, advocating long-term growth at a reasonable price. The defendants provided advice and management services to its clientele in 'event based' investing – primarily in risk arbitrage, in hedges and in distressed securities.

The court found that the 'proximity of product' factor weighed against the likelihood of confusion. The plaintiff being a 'conservative investment advi-sor' offering 'growth at a reasonable price', coupled with its admission that, after the defendants commenced business, 'no existing investor accounts had been lost', plus the continued significant growth of new accounts over that period, led the district court to conclude that there was insufficient proximity. The court also cited the testimony of a defence witness who said: '[It] would be almost impossible that you could confuse someone doing risk arbitrage with someone doing traditional investments ... These are vastly different asset classes'.[28]

Moreover, in addressing 'sophistication of buyers', the court emphasized that 'substantial amounts of money' are involved in the defendants' business, as in the plaintiff's business: '[t]hese are not simple financial transactions'. The court also cited the testimony of one of the defendants that the investors with whom she deals 'know everyone who does risk arbitrage, they know everyone who does distress, they know everyone who does small growth companies'.[29] Accordingly, the court held that:

---

26 Ibid., 141.
27 965 F.Supp. 525 (2d Cir. 1997).
28 *Haven*, 532.
29 Ibid., 534.

There is a vast difference in objectives between conservative investing and the financial engineering involved in risk arbitrage or hedging, let alone the financial engineering in bringing companies back from the brink of bankruptcy . . . I cannot conclude that investors who are attracted to or could be attracted to conservative investing would be or might be lost to plaintiff because there is a small financial engineering firm using the name 'Havens' that invites real risktakers to do business with it.[30]

Similarly, in *Franklin Resources, Inc. v Franklin Credit Management Corporation*[31] a mutual fund company that used the 'Franklin' mark commenced trade mark infringement and dilution actions against a finance company using the name 'Franklin Credit.'. The district court held that, 'while there is very limited overlap between the commercial activities of Franklin Resources and Franklin Credit', application of the proximity of products factor and the analogous 'sophistication of the buyers' factor 'militate strongly against a likelihood of consumer confusion between the trade marks'.[32] The court continued:

As for the proximity of the parties' products, while to a limited extent Franklin Resources pursues other ventures, its primary business has been since its inception and remains today the marketing and administration of mutual funds. As for Franklin Credit, its business has been since its inception and remains today the purchasing at discount of non-performing loans from the original lenders (typically banks or the receivers of failed banks) and then pursuing the borrowers in efforts at collection. The proximity between these products, services, or activities (however one chooses to characterize them) is virtually nil.[33]

The court concluded that 'possibility of confusion against which the trade mark laws protect must be characterized as remote', adding: 'It is hard to imagine a more sophisticated, street-wise, savvy buyer (or more precisely, conduit) of Franklin Resources' products and services than professional broker-dealers'.[34] Accordingly 'it is not likely that a broker-dealer, who happens to learn that a company called Franklin Credit is engaged in the loan collection business, would confuse that company with Franklin Resources, linked to the broker-dealer as participants in the mutual funds business'.[35]

Admittedly, it is hard to explain why the *Lexington* and *Morningside* went one way while *Haven* and *Franklin* went the other. Therein lies the difficulty

---

30   Ibid.
31   988 F.Supp. 322 (2d Cir. 1997).
32   *Franklin*, 329.
33   Ibid.
34   Ibid., 330.
35   Ibid.

facing anyone who relies on distinctions between different types of investment services. These decisions can however be reconciled: in *Haven* and *Franklin* one party operated in a highly specialized area of investment services (in *Haven* the defendant performed risk arbitrage; in *Franklin* the plaintiff acquired distressed debt). Perhaps where the specialization of one party is so sharply defined, offering a clear point of distinction between its own services and those of a similarly-named party, the courts are less inclined to find trade mark infringement. However, the broad findings of proximity articulated in cases like *Lexington* and *Morningside* show that reliance on distinctions between investment services can be fraught with risk.

A client who is especially eager to use a particular name and who seeks additional insight should note *Beneficial Corporation v Beneficial Management Corporation*,[36] cited in both *Lexington* and *Franklin*. Neither party in *Beneficial* provided investment services. However, they both offered financial services. The plaintiff offered consumer loans to individuals only while the defendant offered loans for business purposes only (only a few of the defendant's loans being to individuals). Moreover, the plaintiff's loans averaged $1500 while the defendant's averaged $54 000. Concluding that the defendant's clients were sophisticated, the court noted:

> The plaintiffs may or may not be correct in arguing that the general public does not distinguish between different kinds of loan companies. However, trade mark laws do not protect against the possibility that a member of the general public might fall under the mistaken impression that the companies are related. Rather, the trade mark laws are intended to protect those members of the public who are or may become customers of either from purchasing the products of one of them under the mistaken assumption that they are buying the product produced or sponsored by the other ... In view of the pronounced differences between the loans made by plaintiffs and those made by defendant, and the convincing evidence of the sophistication of defendant's customers, we conclude that the possibility of the confusion against which the trade mark laws protect must be characterized as remote.[37]

Given that the court distinguished between the average loan amounts and the clientele of the parties, it is reasonable to suggest that a court will apply the reasoning in *Beneficial* where both parties offer investment services. In particular, if there are material differences in the level and types of investments that the parties make as well as the investors from whom they seek funds, one may argue that in these circumstances the possibility of confusion is remote.

For example, assume that both parties are private equity firms. The plaintiff

---

[36]   529 F.Supp. 445 (2d Cir. 1982).
[37]   *Beneficial*, 450.

focuses exclusively on early-stage venture investments and its average investment is $1 million and the minimum subscription stake for participants in the plaintiff's fund is $100 000. The defendant however focuses on acquiring businesses through mergers and acquisitions. Its average investment is $100 million and the minimum subscription stake for participating investors is $10 million. In this example the investments of each firm differ markedly both in terms of type and amount and their respective clienteles are therefore also likely to differ in terms of net worth and risk profile.[38]

A Second Circuit court *might* consider these differences analogous to the facts in *Beneficial*. Indeed, the court in *Franklin* cites *Beneficial* as supporting a similar proposition, suggesting that it was useful to quote the *Beneficial* reasoning 'at some length', that case being 'equally applicable to the case at bar':[39]

> Those who invest in mutual funds, even in relatively minor amounts and under the guidance of a broker-dealer, are individuals with discretionary income, prompted by concerns for their financial security, and determined to do something about it. Those who suddenly encounter [the defendant] do so because they own homes of sufficient value to stand as security for a mortgage loan, whose terms the individual borrowers presumably negotiated with the original lending bank. These circumstances bring the case at bar within Judge Lasker's analysis in *Beneficial* . . ., which considered possible confusion among borrowers from two lending companies.[40]

However, despite clear approval in *Franklin* of the reasoning in *Beneficial*, a court might distinguish the reasoning in *Beneficial* in that, where the facts before it fall squarely within the financial investment context, a more conservative approach is warranted due to the 'personal nature of the investment market'.[41] In this regard, the *Franklin* court appeared to characterize the plaintiff's activities narrowly as 'purchasing at a discount non-performing loans' and 'pursuing the borrowers in efforts at collection'.[42] Assessing the likelihood of confusion, the court observed:

> If one focuses upon the individuals involved, the fund shareholders *vis-à-vis* [the defendant] and defaulting mortgagors *vis-à-vis* [the plaintiff], the plaintiff fares no

---

[38] In the cited example, because the minimum investment is relatively large, since each of the plaintiff's and defendant's customers is likely to be highly sophisticated, the sophistication requirement should not be problematic for the defendant. In *Beneficial* the court placed a lot of emphasis on the sophistication of the defendant's customers in reaching its finding. See *Beneficial*, 449–450.

[39] *Franklin*, 329.

[40] Ibid., 330.

[41] *Morningside*, 141.

[42] *Franklin*, 329.

better. There is no evidence that individuals who have fallen behind on their home mortgage payments are at the same time pursuing investment strategies in mutual funds, and the absence of such proof is not surprising.[43]

However, the court has apparently ignored the fact that firms who focus on distressed debt, like the plaintiff in *Franklin,* raise funds from investors to pursue such 'troubled loans'. The court did so even after observing that the plaintiff 'raised funds to pursue this business through the use of "Limited Partnerships" whose names included the [word] "Franklin . . ." '.[44] Firms investing in distressed debt are typically still considered investment firms. That being so, a more relevant comparison in *Franklin* was arguably between the 'fund shareholders' of the defendant and the investors in the Limited Partnerships of the plaintiff. By narrowly characterizing the plaintiff as a debt collection agency, the court did not specifically address the 'personal nature of the investment market' concern raised in some other cases.[45] Therefore, even though the disputants in *Franklin* were both investment firms, it is imprudent to rely too heavily on *Franklin* as supporting the application of *Beneficial* in the investment services context.

It is unclear whether the defendants in *Lexington* and *Morningside* explicitly sought to extend the reasoning in *Beneficial* to apply to the facts in their cases, there being no discussion of this argument in the judgments. A possible explanation for this is that *Lexington* and *Morningside* did not manifest a pronounced difference between the plaintiff's and the defendant's levels of investment and the investors from whom they sought funds. Rather, the only difference appears to have been in the types of investments or the activities undertaken by the parties. However, as the courts held, the parties in those cases were competing for the same investment dollars from substantially similar clientele.

Arguments can be made for and against the application of *Beneficial* in the investment services area. If the facts suggest that the investments of the client and a cited user 'appeal to different customers, are sold in different markets [and] exist for different purposes',[46] a court may be persuaded that those services are in no sense proximate. A trade mark attorney, in assessing the risks posed by the use of a similar name in connection with different investment services, may therefore usefully investigate whether there exist material differences between the net worth and risk profile of the

---

43 Ibid., 330.
44 Ibid., 325.
45 See *Morningside*, 141; *Lexington*, 285.
46 *Information Clearing House, Inc. v Find Magazine*, 492 F.Supp. 147 (SDNY 1980). See also *Franklin*, 330 and *Beneficial*, 449.

clientele of the cited user and those of the client, and to determine whether the investment services of each firm are marketed through different channels.

1.3 The Other *Polaroid* Factors – Some General Remarks

The analysis so far has focused on 'proximity of products' and 'sophistication of buyers' primarily because several other *Polaroid* factors can only be resolved with the necessary facts in hand. For example, neither general assumptions concerning other *Polaroid* factors – such as evidence of confusion or the defendant's state of mind in adopting a particular mark – nor the sort of analysis described may be of much assistance. The resolution of these issues will be greatly fact-based and those facts will vary from case to case.

However, it is important to consider the strength of any cited mark when assessing the likelihood of confusion. A mark's strength is its 'distinctiveness' or, more precisely, its tendency to identify the goods sold or services provided under the mark 'as emanating from a particular . . . possibly anonymous source'.[47] In assessing its strength, a mark can be classified as one of four types, in ascending order of protectability and strength: (1) generic, (2) descriptive, (3) suggestive and (4) arbitrary or fanciful.[48]

Depending on the nature of the mark sought, the identification of a prior user of that mark may not necessarily constitute a 'knock out' blow to a later user, even if the prior user appears to use that mark in connection with products or services that are proximate to the client's investment services. In assessing the risk of confusion, one should attempt to classify the mark within the four categories identified above: if it is generic or descriptive, the risk of infringement is relatively low.

The terms 'generic' and 'descriptive' are self-explanatory and there are cases where a prior user has failed to prevent a party making later use of a mark because it lacked the requisite strength. In *Sterling Acceptance Corporation v Tommark, Inc., d/b/a Sterling Associates*[49] the plaintiff alleged infringement on the basis that the defendant used the word 'Sterling' as a trade name. The court held that the plaintiff's mark STERLING lacked commercial strength, being 'used by a large number of businesses which provide financial services'; the word, 'which is commonly used in the term 'Pound Sterling', ordinarily refers to money'.[50] The court also mentioned that the USPTO's

47 *W.W.W. Pharmaceutical Co. v Gillette Co.*, 984 F.2d. 567, 581 (2d Cir. 1991).
48 *Estee Lauder, Inc. v The Gap, Inc.*, 108 F.3d 1503, 1508 (2d Cir. 1997).
49 227 F.Supp.2d 454 (D. Md. 2002).
50 *Sterling*, 462.

records disclosed 'eighteen registrations in the financial services class . . . and over three hundred and fifty registrations in other classes' containing the same word.[51]

Similarly, in *Citizens National Bank of Meridian v Citizens Bank of Philadelphia*[52] the plaintiff's mark 'Citizens' was considered to be very weak, deserving little protection regardless of its classification. The court referred to the presence of 168 registered businesses in the plaintiff's home state of Mississippi that used 'Citizens' in their name, including seven banking institutions: '[e]xtensive use of a word, particularly in a similar industry, reduces the likelihood of confusion among consumers and drastically weakens a mark'.[53]

However, the existence of numerous cited users does not necessarily imply that a mark is weak. In *Lexington* the district court said: 'the significance of third party trade marks depends wholly upon their usage';[54] 'the existence of third party use alone will not sap the strength of an otherwise robust mark'.[55] In *Lexington* itself the fact that 125 businesses (60 in New York City alone) incorporated the word 'Lexington' into their name did not defeat the plaintiff's claim. The court observed:

> While this evidence suggests that there is, indeed, significant third-party use of the word 'Lexington,' it is not competent evidence because it does not demonstrate that these marks are 'actually used by third-parties, that they were well promoted or that they were recognized by consumers.' . . . Because this evidence is devoid of any descriptive information apart from the companies' names, it does not show what these third-party businesses do.[56]

In classifying a mark as 'suggestive' or 'arbitrary or fanciful', the courts have applied the following definitions. A 'suggestive mark' is one that 'employs terms which do not describe but merely suggest the features of the product, requiring the purchaser to use "imagination, thought and perception to reach a conclusion as to the nature of the goods" '.[57] McCarthy cites CITIBANK as an example of a suggestive mark as it only suggests 'a modern

[51] Ibid.
[52] 35 Fed.Appx. 391 (5th Cir. 2002).
[53] *Citizens*, 392. See also *Sun Banks of Fla. Inc. v Sun Fed. Sav. & Loan Ass'n*, 651 F.2d 311, 316 (5th Cir. 1981).
[54] *Lexington*, 281; *Scarves by Vera, Inc. v Todo Imports Ltd.*, 544 F.2d 1167 (2d Cir. 1976); *Sunenblick v Harrell*, 895 F.Supp. 616, 627 (SDNY 1995).
[55] Ibid.
[56] Ibid., 282.
[57] *W.W.W. Pharmaceutical Co.*, 572 (citing *Thompson Medical Co. v Pfizer Inc.*, 753 F.2d 208, 213 (2d Cir. 1985).

or urban bank'.[58] An 'arbitrary mark' however has 'an actual dictionary meaning, but that meaning does not describe the product' (for example, 'The Apple Bank') and a 'fanciful mark' is 'a made up term'.[59]

Accordingly, the nature of the mark must be considered, taking note of the number of citations produced by the trade mark search. If the mark is superficially generic or descriptive, a third party may struggle to assert rights without showing that the mark has acquired a secondary meaning. As for the number of citations, noted in *Citizens*, extensive third party use can dilute a mark's strength[60] because '[t]hird party uses of a mark on similar goods are relevant for the purposes of showing a 'crowded field' and that the mark is therefore weak'.[61] The trade mark search is thus just an initial step in the information-gathering process; further investigations should be conducted to confirm whether the mark is truly weak.

Even if the search report indicates a 'crowded field' with respect to a particular mark in the investment services area, this preliminary view being supported by more comprehensive investigations, the client must be reminded that extensive third party use can be a double-edged sword. It may defuse a trade mark infringement claim against the client, but the client may be unable to assert any meaningful trade mark rights against other third parties that later choose to conduct business under similar names. Moreover, from an operational and reputation perspective, a risk abounds that the conduct of third parties could 'taint' the client's business – that is, the conduct of a third party under a particular mark could generate adverse publicity which would in turn damage the client's goodwill and business even though the parties are completely unrelated.

Where, for example, the client establishes a hedge fund named ACME Investments, the register and the relevant business directories are then searched and so many uses of ACME are found in the financial services area that, on a preliminary view, the mark is weak and no one party can assert exclusivity. This view is subsequently supported by field investigations. The client invests heavily in positioning ACME Investments as a highly reputable, successful hedge fund based in New York. Two years later a scandal erupts, relating to an unrelated entity also called ACME Investments but located in California. The media reveal that the principals of ACME Investments in

---

[58]   McCarthy, *supra*, §11:05. *See also Citibank, N. A. v Citibank Group, Inc.* 724 F.2d 1540, 222 USPQ 292 (11th Cir. 1984); *Citigroup Inc. v City Holding Co.* 171 F. Supp. 2d 333 (S.DNY 2001).

[59]   *Arrow Fastener Co. v Stanley Works*, 59 F.3d 384, 391 (2d Cir. 1995).

[60]   *Citizens*, 392.

[61]   *Nikon, Inc. v Ikon Corp.*, 1992 US Dist. LEXIS 6299, No. 89 Civ. 6044 (KMW)(NG), 1992 WL 114509.

California have embezzled millions of dollars of investor funds. Publicity of this kind can be very damaging to the client even though it has nothing to do with the firm in California. At the very least, the red-faced client may have to explain to its investors that the firm in California is a completely unrelated third party.

1.4   The Dilemma and Some Rays of Hope

The application of the *Polaroid* factors to investment services highlights the dilemma confronting investment firms. Typical investment firms are worried that courts (at least in the Second Circuit) are reluctant to distinguish between different types of investment services. The standard identified by the courts in determining the proximity of investment services ('do both companies seek individuals who desire investment opportunities and compete for the same investment dollars?') potentially casts the net very wide, making it harder for defendants to argue persuasively that their services are distinguishable from those of prior users.

Thus firms seeking new names face a dilemma: should they limit themselves to novel, fanciful names (as, for example, car makers often do) or to personal proper names (as professional firms often do); or should they adopt names and brands with more traditional feel and appeal in the financial investment industry generally? The dilemma is real, but the picture is not one of unalleviated gloom. While Second Circuit courts have been reluctant to distinguish between different types of investment services, they have shown willingness to take a commonsense view about whether confusion is likely, when circumstances permit. If the specialization of one party is so sharply defined – such as risk arbitrage or distressed debt collection – a court may be more likely to find that the likelihood of confusion is remote. Similarly, where client and cited user offer investment services which appeal to different customers, are sold in different markets and exist for different purposes, a court should accept that the services are in no sense proximate. In this regard, significant differences in the average spend and types of investments made by the firms and differences in the clientele of the firms (whether in terms of net worth, risk profile, or both) may be important.

Finally, in assessing the likelihood of infringement, assessment of the strength of cited marks is vital. Comprehensive field investigations will determine the nature and extent to which third parties have used the client's preferred choice of mark. Bear in mind, however, that even if the trade mark attorney considers that the mark is available since the cited mark is weak, the presence of other users has its own set of pitfalls, which may be far more damaging than any claim for trade mark infringement.

2.   AN INDEX BY ANY OTHER NAME?

Derivative products are extremely popular as investors seek investments
which enable them to tailor their risk profile so that their exposure most
closely matches their view of the financial markets and their preferences for
holding and managing risk. A derivative product can be either a high- or low-
risk investment. So-called 'derivative' financial products come in many forms,
including swaps, options (both exchange traded and over-the-counter), futures,
exchange traded funds ('ETFs') and index-linked debt instruments.

2.1   Trade Mark Laws and Derivative Products

A common feature of all derivative products is that their value is based upon
the performance of another instrument or commodity or, frequently, a financial index. The fact that derivative products are dependent on the performance
of another instrument or commodity means that the creator of such products
and the promoter of any secondary market trading in them must be able to
refer to that underlying instrument or commodity when describing and
promoting the derivative product. Trade mark laws limit the manner in which
these products can be advertised and described. If the underlying instrument
or commodity on which the value of the derivative product is based is
protected by trade marks, any unlicensed references to third party marks must
be carefully tailored to avoid the false impression that the trade mark owner
has authorized the use of its mark.[62]

Derivatives are often complex but they must be properly understood before
undertaking trade mark analysis. This section focuses primarily on index-
linked financial products because it is mostly in that field that litigation has
arisen and they provide the clearest illustration of how trade mark laws affect
the marketing of such products. To give the analysis some context, a simple
illustration of an index-linked derivative product is an index-linked guaranteed
investment contract ('GIC'), where the capital invested is guaranteed and the
return on the capital is dependent on the performance of an underlying index.
For the purposes of this analysis, the underlying index is the S&P500 and the
return on capital will be assessed over a five-year period. This product will
appeal to investors who want to preserve their capital but are willing to risk
growth opportunities.

The tension that trade mark laws present to the creators of index-linked

---

[62]   *Standard and Poor's Corporation v Commodity Exchange, Inc.*, (n. 84),
708–710; *The Nasdaq Stock Market, Inc. v Archipelago Holdings, LLC*, (n. 69),
303–305.

GICs is the extent to which they may refer to the fact that the product is linked to an index like the S&P500. To avoid the risk of trade mark infringement, the sponsors of such products generally obtain a licence from the enterprise that prepares the index such as Standard & Poor's Corporation, so that those marks can be used in marketing and promoting the derivative product without risk of infringement. Sometimes, however, products have been promoted and traded without a licence from the trade mark owner and occasionally, this has led to litigation. The cases have not just focused on trade mark infringement: the courts have had to consider a number of intellectual property issues when addressing the plaintiff's claims, including copyright and misappropriation claims. However, this analysis is confined to trade mark infringement and, in particular, the application of the 'fair use' defence.

2.2 Trade Mark Fair Use

Trade mark law recognizes that a third party may make a 'fair use' of another party's mark without infringing that party's rights. There is a statutory fair use provision in the Lanham Act, as well as a nominative fair use defence, recognized by the courts, which is an accepted part of the common law. The Lanham Act provides a defence to a claim of trade mark infringement where:

> the use of the name, term, or device charged to be an infringement is a use, otherwise than as a mark . . . of a term or device which is descriptive of and used fairly and in good faith only to describe the goods or services of such party, or their geographic origin.[63]

The courts have noted that '[t]he defence is available only in actions involving descriptive terms and only when the term is used in its descriptive sense rather than its trade mark sense'.[64] Thus the purpose of the statutory fair use defence is to allow a party other than the owner of a trade mark to describe accurately its own goods or services.

The nominative fair use defence differs from the statutory defence because it involves the descriptive use of another's mark to describe or identify the trade mark owner's goods or services, not the goods or services of alleged infringer. In *New Kids on the Block v News America Publishing, Inc.*,[65] the court said that three requirements must be met if use of another's mark is 'nominative' and therefore non-infringing:

---

[63] Lanham Act §33(b)(4), 15 USCA §1115(b)(4).
[64] *Zatarains, Inc. v Oak Grove Smokehouse*, Inc., 698 F.2d 786 (5th Cir. 1983). See also *Soweco, Inc. v Shell Oil Co.*, 617 F.2d 1178, 1185 (5th Cir. 1980).
[65] 971 F.2d 302 (9th Cir. 1992).

First, the product or service in question must be one not readily identifiable without use of the trade mark; second, only so much of the mark or marks may be used as is reasonably necessary to identify the product or service; and third, the user must do nothing that would, in conjunction with the mark, suggest sponsorship or endorsement by the trade mark holder.[66]

In applying the *New Kids* test, the Ninth Circuit has not considered the likelihood of confusion because doing so 'would lead to the incorrect conclusion that virtually all nominative uses are confusing'.[67] At the time of writing, however, the Third Circuit modified the test by adopting a two-step approach: applying the *Polaroid* factors (other than the 'strength of the mark' and the 'similarity of the mark' since those factors do not 'fit' in the nominative use context) and once the plaintiff has met its burden of proving confusion, the burden shifts to the defendant to show that its nominative use of the plaintiff's mark is fair.[68] Thus there is a circuit split on the application of the *New Kids* test.

2.3   The Approach Taken by the Courts

Cases involving promotion and trading in index-linked derivatives are likely to turn on the nominative fair use defence since they arise from the use of a mark to describe an index or derivative product prepared by the trade mark's owner. While the application of this defence in this context is far from settled, some general principles have emerged from the case law. The decisions are of limited precedential value in that most are from trial courts, the opinions sometimes being given in the context of requests for temporary restraining orders or other interim relief.

A recent case in point is *The Nasdaq Stock Market, Inc. v Archipelago Holdings, LLC.*[69] A district court hearing of a motion to dismiss, the decision helpfully sought to review earlier cases in the same context and furnished a clearer statement as to how nominative fair use applies to index-linked derivatives. Archipelago made unlicensed use of the name of Nasdaq's QQQ product (an ETF sponsored product based on the Nasdaq-100 Index), 'QQQ' being merely the ticker symbol for that ETF. Evidence was submitted that the Nasdaq-100 Index is generally perceived as a valuable indicator of broader market performance, leading to the creation of numerous investment products,

---

[66]   *New Kids*, 308.
[67]   See *Cairns v Franklin Mint Co.*, 292 F.3d 1139, 1151 (9th Cir. 2002); *Playboy Enterprises, Inc. v Welles*, 279 F.3d 796, 801 (9th Cir. 2002).
[68]   See *Century 21 Real Estate Corp. v Lending Tree Inc.*, 3rd Cir., No. 03-4700, 10/11/05.
[69]   336 F. Supp. 2d 294 at 296 (SDNY 2004).

such as QQQ, that attempt to track its operation.[70] Archipelago ran a competing exchange platform, gaining SEC approval to establish 'ArcaEx' as a new
ETF. Having been previously licensed to use the plaintiff's marks,
Archipelago cancelled its licence to trade the QQQ product in the month
ArcaEx began trading. However, Archipelago continued to facilitate trade in
the QQQ product on the ArcaEx exchange platform and it became the most
actively traded product by volume.

Nasdaq argued that Archipelago, in advertising its ability to trade the QQQ
product, engaged in unfair competition and false designation of origin in violation of federal trade mark laws, citing as an example an advertisement which
stated 'We've Got QQQ Out the Wazoo'.

There is no discussion in the judgment of whether the *New Kids* test
replaces the likelihood of confusion test. However, the court cited the 'eight-
factor, fact intensive test' of *Polaroid* as the appropriate measure of likelihood
of confusion.[71] It noted, however, that the defendant's use would be considered 'nominative, non-infringing use' if the three requirements listed in *New
Kids* were met.[72] In doing so, the court appears to be endorsing a two-step
approach similar to that taken in the Third Circuit.

The court did not dismiss Nasdaq's Lanham Act claims, even though it
thought such claims seemed weak, but said that the statements in
Archipelago's advertising sufficed to meet the lenient standards for defeating
a motion to dismiss for failure to state a claim. The court noted a successful
motion to dismiss must show that, even when the complaint is liberally
construed, the plaintiff can prove no set of facts which would entitle him or
her to relief.[73] Here 'the defendant's nominative use defence requires evaluation of whether its use of the plaintiff's marks suggests sponsorship or affiliation in the minds of the relevant purchasers – an analysis based on a factual
inquiry inappropriate on a motion to dismiss'.[74] At the time of writing, this
case still awaits trial.[75] If a trial takes place, assuming the court adopts an
approach similar to that taken in the Third Circuit, Nasdaq will need to establish that the *Polaroid* factors support a finding that the use of its marks is likely
to cause confusion. In response, Archipelago must then satisfy the *New Kids*
requirements for nominative fair use. But even if Nasdaq succeeds, there is

---

[70]   The court also noted that the Nasdaq Stock Market is the only stock market or
exchange to create and maintain a leading financial index.

[71]   *Nasdaq*, 304.

[72]   Ibid.

[73]   Ibid., 301.

[74]   Ibid., 305.

[75]   The case was stayed on 17 May 2005 and a status letter was due to be filed
with the court by 31 March 2006.

nothing to stop Archipelago continuing to use trade marks such as QQQ when advertising its ability to trade such shares so long as it does nothing to create the false impression that it holds a licence to trade QQQ shares.

It is thus open to Archipelago to limit further its use of the QQQ trade mark in its advertisements and promotional materials, combining such use with suitable disclaimers.[76] Some earlier decisions emphasize the importance of such disclaimers in assessing whether there is a likelihood of confusion,[77] especially where such likelihood can be characterized as 'minimal or moderate' or 'far less than substantial'.[78] However, where the likelihood of confusion is 'more substantial'[79] the Second Circuit courts have taken a more 'skeptical view of disclaimers as a remedy for reducing customer confusion',[80] placing the burden of proving the effectiveness of the disclaimer on the defendant.[81]

In the context of index-linked derivatives, the use in question is typically some form of referential use. That being so, the risk of confusion usually rises only to a 'minimal or moderate' level since the creator of an index-linked derivative product or the promoter of secondary market trading of an index-linked derivative product is using another's mark to describe that product. If the user is not doing anything to suggest sponsorship or endorsement by the trade mark owner, the use of disclaimers is one way to reduce the likelihood of confusion. To be effective, however, the disclaimers should be conspicuously placed in any advertisements and promotional material. If disclaimers are buried in the fine print they are likely to be ignored by consumers and no court is likely to place much emphasis on them.[82]

In *Nasdaq* the court examined two earlier decisions which also addressed nominative fair use. The court attempted to put these decisions into some kind of context. In doing so, it followed the decision in *Golden Nugget, Inc. v American Stock Exchange, Inc.*[83] and distinguished *Standard & Poor's*

---

[76] Ibid., 304.
[77] *Chicago Board of Trade v Dow Jones, Inc.*, No. 82 L 4067 (Cir. Ct. Cook County 4 June 1982); *National Football League v Governor of Delaware*, 435 F. Supp. 1372, 1381 (D.Del. 1977).
[78] *Soltex Polymer Corp. v Fortex Industries, Inc.*, 832 F.2d 1325, 4 USPQ2d 1785 (2d Cir. 1987).
[79] *ProFitness Physical Therapy Center v Pro-Fit Orthopedic and Sports Physical Therapy P.C.*, 314 F.3d 62, 65 USPQ2d 1195 (2d Cir. 2002).
[80] McCarthy, §23:51 (McCarthy has remarked that the Second Circuit's view of disclaimers is less than clear or uniform).
[81] *ProFitness*. See also *Home Box Office, Inc. v Showtime/Movie Channel, Inc.* 832 F.2d 1311, 4 USPQ2d 1789 (2d Cir. 1987).
[82] *International Kennel Club, Inc. v Mighty Star, Inc.*, 846 F.2d 1079, 6 USPQ2d 1977 (2d Cir. 1988).
[83] 828 F.2d 586, 591 (9th Cir. 1987).

Corporation v Commodity Exchange, Inc.[84] These were both handed down
without the benefit of *New Kids* and thus mention neither that decision nor
'nominative fair use'.

Unlike *Nasdaq*, *Golden Nugget* did not involve index-linked securities.
Golden Nugget, a corporation active in gaming and hotels sued the American
Stock Exchange when it began issuing, listing and trading put and call options
on Golden Nugget stock without first obtaining consent. Golden Nugget
claimed that this conduct amounted to a violation of trade mark laws and
unfair competition. The court rejected the claim:

> Surely a dealer in a product can describe it accurately by its trade name – shares of
> Golden Nugget common stock are not unlike second-hand BMWs or Chevrolets.
> Describing the product nondeceptively and by name brand has never been a viola-
> tion of a manufacturer's trade mark. We see no distinction between shares of stock
> and second-hand cars in this regard. We reject [the] argument that Golden Nugget
> options are a new product, distinct and separate from Golden Nugget stock, that has
> appropriated the Golden Nugget name. [Golden Nugget] suggests that the fact some
> Golden Nugget options are not exercised is significant to the analysis. It apparently
> sees this as proof that the option is a separate product. We think this is reaching. An
> option at most is a right to buy or sell Golden Nugget shares.[85]

The *Nasdaq* court suggested that the plaintiff had not explained how the
listing of the QQQ product on Archipelago's exchange differed in any material way from the facts addressed in *Golden Nugget*:[86] there appeared to be no
substantive difference between listing and trading put and call options on the
American Stock Exchange and listing the QQQ on the ArcaEx so that
investors wishing to sell their QQQ shares or to buy QQQ shares from other
investors may do so.

In *Standard & Poor's*, the defendant wanted to create and trade futures
contracts based upon the Comex 500 Index. The Second Circuit observed that
the Comex 500 Index 'would "essentially duplicate" the Standard & Poor's
500 Index, using the same 500 stocks as the Standard & Poor's 500 Index and
the identical method of compilation . . . the settlement price for the Comex 500
contract would be the then current Standard & Poor's 500 Index value'.[87] The
defendant had sought a licence to use the Standard & Poor's 500 Index as an
integral part of a stock index futures contract to be traded under Comex's
auspices. The parties were not however able to reach agreement. S&P sued for
trade mark infringement and false designation of origin, seeking a preliminary

---

[84] 683 F.2d 704, 704 (2d Cir. 1982).
[85] *Golden Nugget*, 591.
[86] *Nasdaq*, 303.
[87] *Standard & Poor's*, 706.

injunction. The plaintiff's claims were considered in the context of whether it had established a likelihood of success on the merits and whether on the balance of hardships it was entitled to such relief.

Again, the court considered the *Polaroid* factors in light of the facts, which included the similarity of the 'Comex 500 Index' to the 'Standard & Poor's 500 Index'. The judge held that 'the terms '500' and '500 Index' have a secondary meaning which would cause persons familiar with stock indices to think of S&P'. The Court of Appeals concluded that 'this finding was not clearly erroneous . . . [a]lthough the "Comex 500" mark is devoid of any explicit reference to the S&P mark, the use of "500", often followed by the words "stock index", may well create the possible inference that the Standard & Poor's 500 Index is the sponsor of the Comex 500 contract'.[88] This inference was bolstered by the fact that 'Comex advertisements and promotional brochures were "calculated to cause, and will cause, the reader to believe that there is a relationship between S&P and Comex, and that S&P at least endorses the trading of futures contracts based on the Comex 500"'.[89]

The decision in this case was however principally focused on the preliminary injunction issue; the court emphasized this, stating that the public interest concerns 'weigh heavily in favor of maintaining the status quo pending prompt resolution of the merits'.[90] It was on this basis that *Nasdaq* distinguished it.[91] Thus the extent to which a plaintiff may rely on the reasoning in *Standard & Poor's* as a basis for a decision on the merits under the Lanham Act is questionable. As a matter of conjecture, S&P's trade mark infringement claim would most probably not have succeeded, had the case been decided on its merits. In response to the defendant's argument that it had commenced using disclaimers, the court observed: '[w]hile it is apparent that prominent and adequately displayed disclaimers of any affiliation with S&P in Comex's promotional material might substantially reduce the likelihood of source confusion, and accordingly reduce S&P's chance for success on the merits of the Lanham Act claims', it did not need to address this issue as S&P's motion for a preliminary injunction was adequately supported by its other claims. Moreover, the defendant did not explicitly raise this claim before the trial court, nor did it present any proposed written promotional materials containing disclaimers.[92]

At the time of writing, the district court had just handed down its decision

---

88   Ibid., 708.
89   Ibid., 709.
90   Ibid., 712.
91   *Nasdaq*, 303.
92   *Standard & Poor's*, 710.

in *McGraw-Hill*.[93] The matter was heard in the context of an application for
preliminary injunction by the plaintiffs and a motion to dismiss brought by the
defendants. This case was similar to *Nasdaq*. The plaintiffs created and owned
securities indexes – the S&P500 and the 'Dow Jones Industrial Average'
('DJIA'). The plaintiffs claimed that the defendants, two minor stock
exchanges, among other things, infringed the plaintiffs' trade marked intellectual property by offering for trade ETFs that were tied to the S&P500 and
DJIA respectively. The relevant ETFs were called 'Standard & Poor's
Depository Receipts' (SPDRs) and DIAMONDS respectively.

The court had no need to decide on the application for preliminary injunction filed by The McGraw-Hill companies because, before the hearing, the
parties made a temporary licensing arrangement that allowed the defendants to
trade SPDRs options while the case was pending. Thus the matters before the
court were Dow's application for preliminary injunction and the defendants'
motion to dismiss. The court rejected Dow's application since Dow had not
shown 'the requisite irreparable harm or either a likelihood of success or a
serious question going to the merits of the claims to meet the burden necessary
to warrant preliminary relief'.[94] The court noted that *Golden Nugget* and
Nasdaq establish that 'Dow has no property right in the physical shares of
DIAMONDS once they are sold to the investing public, and therefore has no
right to prevent the public from trading on the exchange of their choice'.[95]

The court also granted the defendants' motion to dismiss with respect to the
claims asserted by the McGraw-Hill companies. Unlike *Nasdaq*, the court did
not undertake a comprehensive analysis of the nominative fair use defence.
However, the court noted:

> To describe a product non-deceptively is not a violation of trade mark law . . . So
> long as [the defendant] merely lists SPDR options by using the terms 'SPDR' or
> 'Standard & Poor's Depositary Receipts,' there is no infringement of [the plain-
> tiff's] marks.[96]

Though the motion to dismiss was limited to the claims brought by the
McGraw-Hill companies the court observed that, if a similar motion was made
with respect to Dow's allegations against the defendants, it would likely reach
the same result.[97]

---

[93]   *The McGraw-Hill Companies v International Securities Exchange, Inc.* and
*The Options Clearing Corporation, and Dow Jones & Company, Inc. v International
Securities Exchange, Inc. and The Options Clearing Corporation* 2005 US Dist.
LEXIS 18674 (SDNY 2005).
[94]   *McGraw-Hill*.
[95]   Ibid.
[96]   Ibid.
[97]   Ibid.

2.4 The Lessons Learned

Although the precedents in this area are not definitive, the nominative fair use defence and, in particular, the three part test of *New Kids*, are widely accepted.[98] The courts that have considered the issue have not required licensing from the owner of an index-related trade mark for the creation of trading of options linked to the price of that index or the secondary market trading of derivative products linked to that index. The courts have emphasized that to describe a product non-deceptively is not a violation of trade mark law. However, if either the creator of an index-linked derivative product or the promoter of secondary market trading of an index-linked derivative product wishes to refer to a popular and widely available stock index, it should be careful to satisfy the three requirements of *New Kids*. In this regard, the creator or promoter of such products should do nothing to suggest sponsorship or endorsement by the trade mark owner but should strongly consider including appropriate disclaimers to dispel any affiliation with the trade mark owner.

---

[98]   *Nasdaq*. See *Cairns v Franklin Mint Co.*; *Playboy Enterprises, Inc v Welles*; *Century 21 Real Estate Corp. v Lending Tree Inc.* See also *Liquid Glass Enters. v Dr. Ing. h.c.F. Porsche AG*, 8 F. Supp. 2d 398 (3d Cir. 1998); *Mattel Inc. v Walking Mt. Prods.*, 353 F.3d 792 (9th Cir. 2003); *Horphag Research Ltd. v Pellegrini*, 337 F.3d 1036 (9th Cir. 2003); *Brother Records, Inc. v Jardines*, 318 F.3d 900 (9th Cir. 2003).

15. The impact of permitted use on trade mark valuation

Mark Bezant

WORKING WITH KIDS AND ANIMALS

One afternoon when I was puzzling over this topic, my youngest son Edward wandered into my study. 'Dad', he asked, 'Why is it that people sponsor different breakfast cereals?' Thrown by the question, I ducked behind one of my own. 'Why do you think it is?' I asked. 'Because that's just the way it is', he replied instantly. Outclassed, inevitably, by an eight year old, I asked him which were his favourite cereals. He obligingly reeled off a long list of names: 'Cinnamon Grahams'; 'Golden Nuggets'; 'Honey Nut Cheerios'; 'Cookie Crisp'; 'Chocolate Weetabix'; 'Ricicles'.

I was struck by several things: the common use of compound trade marks, trade marks that had descriptive prefixes, branding based on attributes such as flavours and product names containing common or everyday terms. Curiosity aroused, I pushed on with the conversation. It turned out he'd heard of companies like Nestlé ('they make food') and Kellogg's ('they make breakfast cereals'). But in his mind the 'sponsors' were someone else: the characters and images on the packets such as monkeys, a wolf, a prospector and 'a man wearing glasses' (it turned out he was 'a scientist').The use of trade marks and branding to promote breakfast cereals is clearly complex and illustrates the situation more broadly. Brands are stretched (new flavours; new product sizes), repositioned or relaunched (health-oriented; concentration-enhancing for children), and promoted using a barrage of visual devices such as ancillary trade marks (for example the WHOLEGRAIN mark in the case of cereals, which itself is owned by cereal manufacturers), colours, characters and packaging. This is all in the name of protecting or enhancing brand value. Trade mark law clearly has a role to play in all of this. The challenge is to understand the limits (and limitations) of trade mark law and their implications for value.

WHERE DOES THE VALUE LIE?

A starting point, when examining the boundaries of trade mark law on the value of intangibles, is to consider what exactly is being valued. This can be important when considering 'trade marks' and 'brands', in that the terms are often used interchangeably or loosely. But rather like an elephant, brands and trade marks are often easier to identify than to define, as legislators and courts have discovered. In some cases the valuation is of a specific registered trade mark under a licence in which the rights and obligations of the parties are documented. In others, the valuation relates to a branded business and thus reflects the brand's impact on customers, staff, suppliers and financiers. Between these two positions lies a brand, which is considered as a collection of intangibles related to a product or service (or a portfolio of them) such as trade names and marks, trade dress, packaging, copyright, design rights and domain names.

In addition, value commonly associated with brands and trade marks may derive (in the eyes of consumers at least) from other forms of intangible asset such as:

- *trade secrets or patents* underpinning a recipe or food product. SPLENDA, the low-calorie sweetener, and QUORN, the mycoprotein-based meat substitute, are cases in point;
- *technological innovations*, protected by patents, know-how and design rights, such as the DYSON vacuum cleaner; and
- *distribution rights*, or access to channels to market, which can underpin the value attaching to the trade mark. For example, CHARLES CHURCH, an upmarket UK housebuilding brand, was known nationally as a result of extensive advertising in the colour magazines of the quality Sunday papers and similar publications. But its housebuilding activities were confined to a few parts of the country, reflecting the small size of the business. Some years later the business was acquired by Persimmon, a national housebuilder, who was able to tap into this broad awareness of the brand and exploit it more widely.

Companies increasingly use a portfolio of interlocking, or overlapping, IP rights – trade marks, design rights, copyrights and patents. In parallel, they continue to test the limits of trade mark law on issues such as the registrability of shapes, colours, packaging and compound trade marks or slogans. This has a bearing on valuation, given the different degrees of legal protection afforded to the various components of a brand and the limits of each of those forms of protection. The combination of different intellectual property rights to project and protect brands rather resembles climbers roping themselves together for safety. If one climber slips, it is hoped that the others will stop him falling. But any detrimental impact through the permitted use of a trade mark may well affect the value of other components of the brand, with the result that all the climbers are swept off the mountain by an avalanche of customer rejection. So, for the purposes of this chapter, I use the umbrella term 'brand'.

THE VALUATION OF BRANDS

To understand the implications of the limits of trade mark law for brand value, it is necessary to understand the levers or drivers of value. The value of an intangible asset derives from its incremental effect on a business, relative to the position of the same business without that intangible asset. The impact varies with the characteristics of the intangible and its specific use; it can be wide-ranging. Figure 15.1 illustrates the different potential impacts both for demand-side and supply-side factors. The primary focus of brand valuation consists of demand-side or consumer-related factors. The benefits most readily associated with brands are a price premium or additional volume of sales, which translate into incremental profit streams through enhanced margins (compensation for infringement of trade marks examines the same issues, covering price erosion and loss of sales volumes through diversion of customers). Other demand-side factors relate more to longer-term value, such as customer loyalty and the option to exploit the brand more widely through brand extensions or licensing.

Supply-side factors affect operating costs such as:

- *Customer acquisition and retention costs.* In industries such as financial services, customer set-up costs can be high relative to customer maintenance costs. This partly reflects regulatory requirements for financial services products as well as industry practices such as the payment of fees to intermediaries and brokers. High churn, through the cancellation of policies or the rapid switching of savings and mortgage accounts, can be expensive for the provider;
- *Economies of scale in purchasing.* For leading confectionery products such as MARS bars, the stability and scale of demand allows Mars to negotiate favourable supply agreements for ingredients;
- *Staff retention.* Personnel costs are typically a large part of the cost base. Attracting and retaining talented staff can be critical to value, given the disruptions and costs (not least the loss of knowledge and experience) caused by ongoing staff turnover and a disaffected workforce;
- *Marketing costs.* These include both the sales and marketing costs of current products and the costs of new brand launches. Research suggests

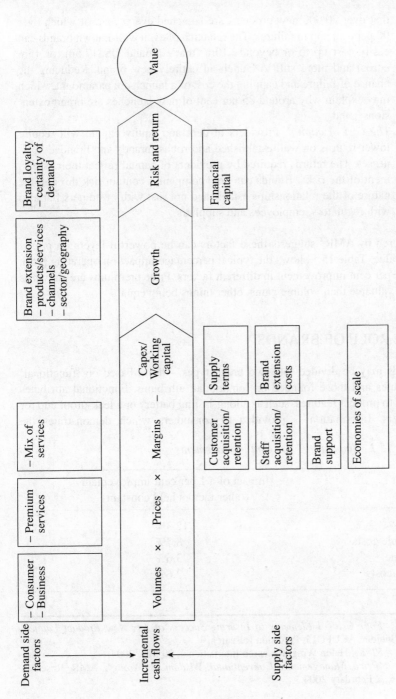

Figure 15.1 How demand-side and supply-side factors affect brand value

that over 20 000 new products are launched every year, of which over 90 per cent end in failure.[1] The relaunch of even well-known brands can easily cost up to or beyond £10m (that's around US$17.5m, or 15m euros) and more still to launch an entirely new brand. Reducing the chance of failure and capping the cost of a launch are paramount, which may explain why around 85 per cent of new launches are brand extensions[2]; and

- *The cost of capital.* Providers of debt and equity capital will require lower returns on well-established and robust brands and branded businesses. The returns required by providers of capital reflect their assessment of the risks. Brands can help companies contain risk through the nature of the relationships established not just with customers but also with regulators, employees and suppliers.

Research by AMR[3] suggests these factors can be powerful levers on profits and value. Table 15.1 shows the typical percentage impact on operating profit of a 1 per cent improvement in different factors. Price premiums are shown as more valuable than volume gains, other things being equal.

THE ROLE OF BRANDS

Brands may be divided into two broad types – those based on 'functional' attributes and those founded on 'emotional' attributes. Functional attributes relate to product features, such as a long-lasting battery or a leak-proof cup for toddlers. Information is provided to consumers which demonstrates the

Table 15.1   Impact of 1 per cent improvements

Factor	Impact of a 1 per cent improvement (other factors held constant)
Price	12.3%
Variable costs	8.7%
Volume	3.6%
Fixed costs	2.6%

[1]   *Four Critical Elements to Insuring Success of Any New Product Launch*, Mark Sneider, ACUPOLL Precision Research.

[2]   *RISK!*, Helen Wing, Research International, 20 May 2004.

[3]   *'Price Management: Conventional Wisdom is Wrong'*, AMR Research Outlook, 2 February 2004.

brand's attributes; this sort of information can often be examined or validated. Emotional attributes relate to the alignment of the brand's stated values and aspirations with those of the customer. The two attribute types are not mutually exclusive (hence the widely-held assumption that a closer shave will boost a man's sex appeal). Ultimately, both classes of attribute concern trust between the brand and the consumer. Value depends on that level of trust being maintained by the brand delivering on its promises, thus persuading consumers to pay for actual or perceived value.

Historically, many branded products were manufactured and provided solely by the brand owners themselves and contained proprietary technology or ingredients (or were marketed as though they did). This is no longer the case, as both companies and brands have unravelled in the following ways:

- *innovations are replicated rapidly among competing businesses*, to the point at which products are often functionally equivalent. Brand names are used to differentiate similar products rather than to identify different product qualities or attributes;
- *manufacturing has been outsourced*, typically to developing economies where production costs are lower;
- *exploitation occurs, either additionally or exclusively, through third parties* via licensing, franchising, or merchandising;
- *brand endorsement is devolved to celebrities* (who subsequently turn out to be all too human after all) or involves association with other brands, such as the recommendation of washing powders by white goods manufacturers and the promotion of products containing branded ingredients (ranging from foodstuffs to computers, for example INTEL INSIDE). Brand endorsement is also sought by affiliation with independent certification marks, such as the FAIRTRADE mark or the RAINFOREST ALLIANCE. For example, Nestlé has recently launched its NESCAFÉ PARTNERS BLEND under the FAIRTRADE mark. Some supermarket own-label brands are also badged as FAIRTRADE products and the number of FAIRTRADE marked products continues to grow rapidly;
- *customer care is outsourced to call centres*, again often located in developing economies, and aftersales activities such as maintenance and servicing may be contracted to third parties.

The significance of these developments is they result in both greater flexibility and an enhanced opportunity for exploiting brands, but they increase the dependency of brand owners on third parties. There is far greater transparency around the branded product, in terms of who made it, how and where it was made and what it contains. Consumers may not like what they see. It is bad enough to discover the emperor has no clothes. It is worse still to find out they weren't even stitched by the palace seamstress.

LAND – THEY AIN'T MAKING IT ANY MORE

The growth of consumer-oriented economies and branding has led to a crowded roster of brand names. All the good names seem to have been taken already (attempts to identify or even create new names – an industry in itself – seem to have an uncanny knack of selecting words that mean something unfortunate in another language, or which are already registered for another class of goods or services or in another territory). This has led to increased use of compound trade marks (in some cases a result of brand extensions, such as the cereals my youngest son is so familiar with). These compound trade marks can lack distinctiveness, both in a trade mark sense and to consumers.

Many brands depend in part on their relationship with distributors and retailers, such as the leading supermarkets and retail chains. Retailers may offer own-label alternatives to branded products and can control the pricing and display both of branded products and their own-label analogues. Retailers can therefore present their products alongside brands but use the branded good as a price reference point to encourage consumers towards their (usually cheaper) offering. Own-label products may also echo the 'look and feel' of branded products and may benefit accordingly, given the use by busy consumers of visual cues as brand identifiers.

Brand differentiation, both for established and new brands, is becoming more challenging. Differentiation may take the form of technology advances, such as an improved formulation of washing powder. It may also focus on visual features such as colour combinations or the shape of the packaging or of a dispenser. Registration of 3-D objects is resisted by trade mark offices and courts[4] where the shapes have no distinctive character. The European Court of Justice (ECJ) considers that the public's perception of a colour mark, shape mark or slogan is not the same as that of a word mark, unless there is strong evidence of prior use giving rise to distinctive character.[5] So trade mark law may be of limited assistance where ornate brand architecture is used if competitors can launch similar looking or badged offerings, thus reducing any distinctiveness and advantage to the original brand.

---

[4]   See for example *Koninklijke Philips v Remington* Case C-299/99 [2002] ECR I-5475, [2002] ETMR 81. *Linde and Others* Joined Cases C-53/01 to C-55/01 [2003] ECR I-3161, [2003] ETMR 78, *Eurocermex* Case C-286/04 P [2005] ETMR 95.
[5]   See, for example, *Libertel* v *Benelux Merkenbureau* Case C-104/01 [2003] ECR I-3793, [2003] ETMR 63.

Branding activity and greater brand complexity may have the effect of diffusing the goodwill attaching to the trade mark across other aspects of the brand architecture. However colours, imagery and shapes used as part of brand architecture may not be afforded (equivalent) trade mark protection. In effect, some value migrates from the core registered trade mark, where the owner can be confident in asserting its legal rights in this monopoly, to brand indicia where trade mark rights are less clear or less powerful (other forms of protection, such as design rights and copyright may however be available).

GREEN IS THE NEW BLACK

In the early days of the motor industry, Henry Ford purportedly offered his customers 'any colour they wanted, so long as it's black'. Nowadays, the customers call the shots. The demands on companies and brands to demonstrate responsibility and integrity have never been higher. Branded goods owners have responded vigorously, declaring their credentials in the following ways:

- *environmental responsibility* – products are identified as 'organic', 'ozone friendly', 'GMO free', 'energy efficient', 'recyclable', 'biodegradable' and so on;
- *social responsibility* – consumers are reassured that products are not tested on animals, or manufactured under unacceptable working conditions in third world factories. Confectionery manufacturers offer vouchers for schools and sponsor active lifestyles programmes to appease parents' concerns over rising levels of child obesity. The development of industry voluntary codes of conduct (albeit under the shadow of threatened regulation) is accelerating, such as restrictions on advertising to children and removing vending machines from schools, or removing items from vending machines seen as unhealthy. In the US Wal-Mart is fighting accusations that its stores drive out local enterprise and diminish the flavour and fabric of communities;[6] and
- *personal responsibility* – ethical banking and investment products are common examples. Nearly all foodstuff manufacturers offer ranges incorporating 'low calorie'; 'high fibre'; 'low sugar'; 'lower salt'; 'cholesterol reducing', 'fat free' or 'vitamin enriched' products. Concerns over obesity have led to reduced portion sizes (or their renaming – 'for sharing' – to put responsibility back on the consumer). The

---

6   *Financial Times*, 26 October 2005.

UK Food and Drink Federation estimates that, by the end of 2006, 97 per cent of products made by its members will provide full nutrition information to consumers.[7]

MORE IS LESS

In many respects none of this is new. Certain brands, such as BODY SHOP and the CO-OP bank, have always positioned themselves as socially and environmentally responsible but such behaviour is now almost obligatory for all brands. Brand owners try to demonstrate their integrity by providing detailed and precise information (under the gaze of industry regulators – for example, a recent FDA notice on food labelling, amending the definition of sodium levels permitted in those products permitted to be identified as 'healthy', ran to 32 pages).[8]

Information relating to technical performance, such as vacuum cleaner suction or the absorbent qualities of kitchen towels or nappies, is ever more available. In addition to information generated by companies, consumer associations and regulators provide further analysis. Information asymmetry, which allowed brand owners to cultivate particular brand images, is becoming a thing of the past.

Specialist websites compare and contrast not just brands but different retailers' pricing of brands. Information on consumer preferences is also accessible to brand owners from surveys, electronic point of sale data. Customer Relationship Management systems and website traffic permit more insightful qualitative and statistical analysis.

The mood of consumers is also avidly gauged. YouGov, a UK online pollster, has recently announced a daily online survey (brandindex), where consumers are asked to rate brands on different dimensions.[9] In a media-led and media-fed society, this will probably lead to rapid swings in approval ratings and volatile rankings. Coca-Cola's DASANI brand, launched in the UK at a cost of £7 million, came in for widespread media lampooning when it became known that the brand, which was marketed on the basis of high technology purification techniques, was based on tap water taken from the unfashionable town of Sidcup. The fact that the brand was promoted on the purification process and not on the source had no bearing on the critics' delight in attacking the brand as 'false', mainly because it was felt that Coca-Cola was

---

[7]   http://www.fdf.org.uk/manifesto_survey.aspx.
[8]   *Food Labeling; Nutrient Content Claims, Definition of Sodium Levels for the Term 'Healthy'*, Food & Drug Administration, 29 September 2005.
[9]   http://www.brandindex.com.

deceiving consumers by using an exotic brand name and charging a high price for what was seen as glorified tap water.[10]

THE PERMITTED USE OF TRADE MARKS AND THE IMPLICATIONS FOR BRAND VALUE

The function of trade marks is to identify or guarantee the origin of the product or service.[11] Trade mark law is not generally concerned with guarantees of quality, lifestyle statements or 'promises' to consumers. This, though, is the heart of branding. But many brands now operate in a complex network of interdependencies with third parties that include consumers, competitors, suppliers, regulators and opinion formers. Although the value of a brand is influenced by these relationships, brand owners may not be able to use trade mark law to protect value when these relationships break down (or indeed restore value, if financial compensation is also limited in nature or difficult to determine).

PERMITTED USE OF TRADE MARKS BY COMPANIES AND COMPETITORS

Permitted use of trade marks by companies can take several forms, principally:

- *use by independent businesses*, such as providers of ancillary services covering a range of items from spare parts to repairs and maintenance and software;
- *use by competitors* who produce compatible products, and who need to refer to competitor trade marks to provide information to customers about their product; and
- *comparative advertising*.

Brand owners who cannot prevent third parties from using their trade marks to advertise their own goods and services may be able to distance themselves from association with third parties. Consumers are unlikely to mark down a brand as a result of dissatisfaction with a third party affiliated with the brand owner's offering, unless the consumer assumes or believes that the brand owner is responsible to consumers for the quality of these other parties (for

---

10   *Things get Worse with Coke*, *The Guardian*, 20 March 2004.
11   *Hoffmann-La Roche*, Case 102/77[1998] ECR 1139.

example where the servicing of household appliances is only permitted by a
third party stipulated by the brand owner). The use of authorised dealers,
accredited distributors and training programmes allows brand owners (and
consumers) to identify the boundaries between the brand owner and third party
providers of related goods and services. Having said that, the benefit of
endorsement is likely only to flow one way – from the brand owner to the
provider of ancillary products and services. The cost of policing these relationships and bridging quality gaps may constrain brand value.

Many pricing strategies involve selling an initial product at a low margin,
or a loss, to attract the customer. Once the customer is captured, subsequent
related goods and services are sold at a profit (such as mobile handsets sold at
heavily subsidised prices to persuade customers to sign up to tariff schemes).
The ECJ's decision in *Gillette* [12] may cause companies to reconsider their
product and pricing strategy. The case involved a third party's use of trade
marks to confirm compatibility of its blades with Gillette's razors. The permitted grounds for such use, namely 'honest use' and 'being necessary' to provide
information to consumers are potentially narrow (although of course open to
interpretation). But the presence of another party's products in such circumstances will constrain the brand owner's opportunity for higher volumes and
price premiums (if the products are compatible, why buy the more expensive
one?), and recouping the cost of investment (whether in the technology or the
marketing of the brand). Permitted use following *Gillette* may also help
competitors accelerate their market entry through product association with
existing brands. Permitted use under these circumstances may arise more in
business-to-business brands where technical specifications are often an important consideration.

In a related development, as the trade mark arena becomes more crowded
(such as through the enlargement of the European Union), the potential arises
for honest use of confusingly similar marks. This may present particular difficulties for trade marks not accorded 'well-known' or 'famous' trade mark
status.

Comparative advertising is on the rise in Europe and presents a threat to
brand owners and brand value. The increasing transparency of brands and
branded goods companies provides plenty of reference points for competitors
to use. But, if brands are reduced to competing checklists of ingredients and
specifications, they may lose so much of their cachet that consumers will
become less willing to pay extra for the brand. Attempts to reposition or
refresh brands (through new recipes, healthier ingredients and so on) may be

---

[12]   *The Gillette Company and Gillette Group Finland Oy v LA-Laboratories Ltd
Oy*, Case C-228/03, [2005] ETMR 67.

expensive. Service-based and emotion-based brands are less exposed to deval-
uation through deconstruction, but are still at risk regarding their social and
environmental credentials (gas-guzzling sport utility vehicles being a case in
point).

Where a brand does not do 'exactly what it says on the tin', comparative
advertising may be used to expose and undermine the brand's standing.
Although comparative advertising in principle allows one business to explain
why its offering is better than a competitor's, it may be more likely that the
brand under comparison will be talked down rather than the other brand will
be talked up.

Comparative advertising might focus directly on the product or service
content or indirectly on the business practices of the brand owner (that is the
percentage of inputs sourced from domestic suppliers). Manufacturers and
supermarkets launching FAIRTRADE products may be criticised for
perceived unethical behaviour across their entire supply chain, and of double
standards. This may be exploited by newer, smaller rivals, or by protest groups
such as disgruntled suppliers.

A further difficulty arises if comparative advertising is found to be unfair
or damaging. Compensation may be based on the difference (in economic
terms) between an honest and dishonest comparison, which might be slight.

USE BY CUSTOMERS AND OPINION FORMERS

In some instances, brands can be hijacked by a subgroup of customers against
the intentions of the brand owners. For a period, DR MARTENS footwear
became identified with right wing extremists[13] and, more recently, the upmarket BURBERRY brand has become associated with downmarket 'Chavs'.[14]

These developments are relatively rare and may not always damage the
brand's value if they reflect (or confirm) a brand's iconic status. The
BURBERRY brand does not seem to have been overly tainted by the Chavs'
adoption of the label as their signature clothing. Other groups of consumers
still find the brand's cachet appealing.

More damaging are uses by dissatisfied consumers or protest groups.
Greenpeace has successfully resisted attempts by Esso and others to have
parodies of registered trade marks removed from Greenpeace's website (E$$O
being the offending parody in Esso's case),[15] not least given freedom of

---

[13]   www.drmartens.com
[14]   http://www.open2.net/money/briefs_20051028branding.html.
[15]   *Association Greenpeace France v SA Societe ESSO* [2003] ETMR 867 (Cour
d'appel de Paris).

speech considerations. Greenpeace has recently published on its website, with accompanying trade marks, its ranking of UK supermarkets' policies for sourcing seafood and the implications for destruction of fishing stocks.[16] The Friends of the Earth's website lists, again embellished by trade marks, companies and specific activities which are considered to be environmentally damaging.[17]

Litigation following the publication of the spoof diaries of former UK Government Minister Alan Clark explored the notions that the parody must be such to avoid confusion over origin.[18] It remains unclear if there are any limits to what is seen as acceptable parody, as the *'Black Label'/'Black Labour'* case in South Africa has shown.[19]

Opinion formers can confer considerable benefit or damage on brands. Morgan Spurlock's documentary 'Supersize Me', examining the impact on his well-being of a McDonald's-only diet for one month, has probably done more damage to the value of the McDonald's brand than the vast sums of money incurred on marketing by competitors such as Burger King and KFC.

Blogs and protest websites (amexsux.com, Walmart-blows.com, and verizonpathetic.com bearing testimony to the imagination of enraged customers) provide a basis for customers to undermine the value of brands, given the wide reach and long memory of the internet.

There will always be dissatisfied customers and protest websites are a modern mechanism for venting frustration. Their impact on brand value is likely to be small. The actions of organisations such as The World Wildlife Fund and Greenpeace, which are not seen as motivated by commercial objectives, are far more likely to influence brand value (both positively and negatively).

HONEY, I SHRUNK THE BRAND

Brand value depends on a combination of price factors, cost effects and the stability or growth in long run demand. There will always be one-off or unusual situations in which the permitted use of a particular trade mark interferes with these factors and damages brand value. These cases are likely to

---

16 http://www.greenpeace.org.uk/oceans/supermarkets/recipe_for_disaster.cfm.
17 www.foe.co.uk/campaigns/corporates/case_studies/index.html.
18 *Clark v Associated Newspapers* [1998] 1 All ER 959.
19 The ruling in *South African Breweries International (Finance) BV v Laugh it Off Promotions* (2003) WTLR 28 May 2003 that imposed such limits has since been reversed: see Daniel Greenberg, 'To Dilute Your Trade Mark – Just Add Parody' [2005] EIPR 436.

attract the headlines, if only in the legal world. But there are some underlying themes.

Brands based on functional attributes may be squeezed by permitted use of trade marks, through comparative advertising, and honest use. This could result in price pressures as well as rising product, quality and branding costs. Service-based brands and brands sold on emotional attributes may be less vulnerable as comparisons are harder to make, and in the case of emotional attributes-based brands less pertinent.

The broader protection afforded to 'well-known' or 'famous' marks, against damage to reputation, may provide additional comfort to brand owners. This may also explain the rapidly growing interest in acquiring this status in jurisdictions worldwide.

The main additional threat from permitted use of trade marks, which is true for all brands, is loss of customer trust and loyalty where brands fail to maintain high standards of environmental, social and personal integrity. The trigger for this could well be comparative advertising, but is more likely to be a result of criticism by protest groups and commentators. In these cases, loss of brand value could be severe. The risk of such events happening may also act to drag brand value down.

Postscript: back in the world of breakfast cereals, I noticed two additions to our collection: Honey Nut Shredded Wheat and supermarket own-label Honey Nut Flakes!

16. Unauthorised use of trade marks: a trade mark proprietor's perspective

Bruce Proctor

This chapter was originally provisionally entitled 'Hey, That's MY Trade Mark', or 'How I Learned to Stop Worrying and Love (Or At Least Tolerate) the Unauthorised Use of My Trade Marks'. From that, the reader may glean that my purpose here is to give a sense of what it feels like to be a trade mark owner faced with the relentless and unauthorised use of 'my' trade marks (or, more accurately, trade marks owned by companies for whom I have had the pleasure of working) and what I do about it.

I believe, before I offer my point of view, that the reader should have full disclosure and understand the biases and prejudices of the author. These are some of mine: I entered the world of trade marks and intellectual property about 24 years ago as a litigator handling intellectual property cases in the United States. I have since spent almost 19 years in an in-house capacity, principally handling intellectual property matters. Eight of those years have been spent within US-based companies with significant global business interests. Eleven have been spent within non-US-based companies, also with significant global business presence.

BACK TO BASICS

As I reflect on how to best describe my point of view, I am struck by the fact that I've consistently kept to basics when it comes to trade marks and the scope of protection one should expect and seek. These basics have informed and continue to inform my strategies and actions around third party use of 'my' trade marks.

The two basics (and I do admit they are basic) I keep uppermost in my mind are that

(i)   trade marks are not rights in gross but, rather, are reputational rights and
(ii)   there needs to be a 'taking' of some of that reputation or goodwill before a trade mark owner has anything to complain about.

While these propositions may appear obvious, I have always viewed trade marks as reputational rights which derive life, full meaning and vitality only by virtue of the goodwill and reputation which they engender. Or, to restate the same proposition in the negative, trade marks are not absolute property rights or 'rights in gross' that have any existence independent of their underlying goodwill. This statement, while not overly controversial on its face, may have significant consequences in an enforcement context, as I seek to explain below.

It is conceded that there are exceptions to the absolute statement that trade marks are solely creatures of focused goodwill. Clearly the many civil law jurisdictions accord a status to trade mark registrations that appears more like an absolute property right than a right appertaining solely to underlying goodwill. However, in an enforcement context in civil law jurisdictions, the principles which are applied look more and more like common law notions. Additionally, non-use provisions in civil law jurisdictions are arguably an acknowledgement that trade mark rights are not absolute property rights but are living, breathing things that require use and reputation to give them meaning and validity.

Further, some marks become so well-known that third party use in most contexts, including use in relation to wholly unrelated goods, presents the real risk of damage to holders of such marks in a dilution context and otherwise. For example, it seems to me that if a third party uses the COCA-COLA trade mark in a commercial context, the massive amount of goodwill residing in that trade mark will be implicated. Failure by the owners of the COCA-COLA trade mark to use and register it in association with all goods, in all service categories, in every country, will not and should not preclude protection, given the tremendous fame of that mark. While this is not an exception to the view of trade marks as reputational, it does represent a broadening of the traditional concept of trade marks and the territorial nature of their validity.

A further 'back to basics' proposition that I keep before me is this: trade marks and trade mark jurisprudence operate in parallel with the broader law of unfair competition. Once we are confident that a trade mark is imbued with the requisite goodwill, it must be determined whether any specific third party use constitutes either fair or unfair competition. In particular, has the third party unfairly taken any of that trade mark's reputation? This inquiry into fair versus unfair competition is an area of intensive activity, given that the line between them is shifting all the time. Whether the cause of this change is technological or is simply the consequence of jurisprudence developing, notions of what constitutes fair competition are ever-changing. Examples of such changes include the treatment of famous and well-known marks, comparative advertising standards, the standards governing parody and, broadly, the internet.

There are some activities which we would term 'unfair competition' and are often revealed to us by an intuitive feeling that the party in question did something a bit sleazy or untoward. However there are no bright lines which make all commercial acts recognisable as being fair or unfair. As noted by Professor Thomas McCarthy in the US, the ideal to be achieved is 'commercial morality' and unfair competition encompasses a whole host of practices that we can describe as being less than commercially moral.[1] It has been suggested that certain behaviour is unfair because it is contrary to 'good conscience'.[2] However, as the variety of acts which are contrary to good conscience is nearly infinite, the law of unfair competition requires to be continually moulded and reshaped.

The recognition that a near-infinite number of ways exist to compete unfairly, along with the corresponding need for flexible jurisprudence, has informed thought in relation to trade mark law for some time. One of my favourite expressions of this concept was put forth in 1925 by the American jurist, Learned Hand: '[t]here is no part of the law which is more plastic than unfair competition, and what was not recognized an actionable wrong twenty-five years ago may have become one today'.[3]

Certainly the plastic law of unfair competition has been moulded and reworked many times since Judge Hand's era, though we no longer need to wait 25 years for noticeable shifts.

THE COMMON LAW VIEW OF TRADE MARKS MAKES UNCOMMONLY GOOD SENSE

To expand on the concept of trade marks as reputational rights: the common law view holds that a trade mark is a commercial signature, or a mere shorthand means by which consumers are enabled to recognise those traders with whom they wish to conduct business. These traders beam their reputation at the consuming public's consciousness in the form of trade marks, which become mere repositories of business reputation or image. Unfair competition, in the form of trade mark infringement, is, at its essence, the utilisation of another's commercial reputation/goodwill for commercial benefit with the effect being the creation of a likelihood of confusion. As has been stated long ago, with greater eloquence than this author can muster:

---

[1]   See J.T. McCarthy, *Trademarks and Unfair Competition* Section 1:10.
[2]   Supra, note 1, citing *International News Service v Associated Press*, 248 US 215, 63L. Ed. 211, 39 S.Ct. 68 (1918).
[3]   *Ely-Norris Safe Co. v Mosler Safe Co.*, 7 F.2d 603 (2d Cir. 1925), rev'd on other grounds, 273 US 132 (1927).

The protection of trade marks is the law's recognition of the psychological function of symbols. If it is true that we live by symbols, it is no less true that we purchase goods by them. A trade mark is a merchandising short-cut which induces a purchaser to select what he wants, or what he has been led to believe he wants. The owner of a trade mark exploits this human propensity by making every effort to impregnate the atmosphere of the market with the drawing power of a congenial symbol. Whatever the means employed, the aim is the same – to convey, through the mark, in the minds of potential consumers, the desirability of the commodity upon which it appears. Once this is attained, the trade mark owner has something of value. If another poaches upon the commercial magnetism of the symbol he has created, the owner can obtain legal redress.[4]

It is consonant with this view to say that, where a person owns a trade mark and a third party makes unauthorised use of it, that third party must be found to have appropriated some of the 'commercial magnetism' or to have 'poached' it in order to conclude that an actionable event had occurred. In a legal context we explore whether such unauthorised use creates a likelihood of confusion, mistake or deception, constitutes passing off, dilutes, creates an association, constitutes taking unfair advantage and so on.

However, the use of one's trade mark by a third party, without the attendant use of that mark's reputation for the purposes of poaching commercial magnetism, should not give a trade mark owner any right to relief as no confusion or its likelihood would be present, no dilution would have occurred, no association would be created, nor would any other transgression have transpired. While a legal analysis might refer to the existence of some variety of fair use, the fact that the use at issue was merely descriptive, or perhaps a parody, the heart of the matter lies in the absence of commercial immorality. In other words, the use of the trade mark was fair.

We live in a world of commerce and in societies that are intent on borrowing things from others all the time. In the overlapping worlds of commerce and culture, music is passed around and 'sampled' by its incorporation into other pieces; visual art appropriates commercial symbols (a famous example is that of Warhol's Campbell soup cans); some products are used to provide cues for competing products while other products are used to deliver political and social messages; these are all instances of borrowing that appear to lack any hint of commercial immorality. We take and borrow commercial images and messages all the time (see, for example, the provisional title of this chapter, mentioned in its introductory paragraph).

To those who devote their lives and energies to imbuing commercial symbols with goodwill and reputation, all in furtherance of selling their products and

---

[4]   *Mishawaka Rubber and Woolen Mfg. Co. v S.S. Kresge Co.*, 316 US 203 (1942).

services, these third party uses can look a lot like theft. Whether the aggrieved parties complain of confusion, tarnishment, association, dilution, taking unfair advantage, infliction of detriment, or any other grounds of objection, they are invoking violation of 'commercial morality' in seeking to apply the plastic law of unfair competition to fit their grievance, or to mould it towards the achievement of that purpose.

THE MESSAGE FOR IN-HOUSE PROTECTORS OF TRADE MARKS

Although this may be difficult to believe, the concept that one cannot preclude all third party uses of one's trade mark – that one cannot mould the law of unfair competition to remedy all unauthorised third party trade mark uses – is troubling to some people. In-house stewards of trade mark portfolios are often placed in a position of having to deliver the bad news that not all third party uses of trade marks are actionable (though as is suggested below, such stewards may themselves be at fault if they find themselves delivering such 'bad' news sufficiently often).

It is important to keep in mind that trade marks are, perhaps appropriately, generally regarded as highly sacred objects within commercial entities. The process of ideation, followed by consumer acceptance testing, searching and clearance, can be punishing. I have participated in and witnessed this process over many years and can testify that it has become increasingly difficult. The commercial playing field has only become more crowded and the challenges have continued to grow, particularly with the emphasis on global or near-global trade mark clearance and the explosion of internet material that one might search. All this leaves those who participate in the trade mark clearance process feeling as though they have actually given birth.[5]

Then there is the not insignificant fact that trade marks are truly the engines that drive the business activities of many companies. Consumer products companies live and die on the backs of their trade marks. This valuation equation is illustrated by the oft-repeated trade mark parable about the Coca-Cola Company: should some catastrophic event strike the company and destroy all its assets in one fell swoop, they could, the next day, borrow more than enough

---

[5] The author wishes to clarify that he has not actually given birth. However, as a father he has experienced the process, at least vicariously. This chapter should not be understood as stating by implication that the male of the species either can give birth or fully comprehends what it is like to do so.

money to rebuild everything lost, based solely on the value of the COCA-COLA trade mark.[6]

The combination of (i) feelings of trade mark maternity/paternity along with (ii) the immense and almost unimaginably great value residing in trade marks results in the creation of intense passion for one's brands. Companies promote this passion and rely on it. Examine any high-performing company, or any high-performing team within a company, and you will feel this passion.

I know how I feel about the trade marks entrusted to my care. They come to be like friends, children, loved ones. Indeed, involvement in the clearance process does make us feel as though we have in some sense helped give them life. When these well-loved marks are infringed, once we have done our legal analysis and believe that the line of commercial morality has been crossed, we enter into full battle mode. The easy bit is the identification of a clear – or at least likely – wrong, which can be addressed with a clear remedy. It is however far more difficult when others treat your marks in an unkindly manner, disparage them in comparative advertisements by claiming their products are superior, insult them by giving them prominence on a commentary website or ridicule them by parodying them. However, one must, often, turn the other cheek and find comfort in the knowledge that commercial morality was not offended (in a legal context, no confusion or association was created, no dilution took place, there was no taking of unfair advantage) even if you were.

Again, I think that it is necessary for we defenders of trade marks to return continually to basics: has commercial morality been offended, has something of value been taken or am *I* merely offended that someone has called my baby ugly? This is a key distinction. It is important not only because it neatly reflects the correct balance between property rights and unfettered competition and is likely to mark the dividing line between winning and losing trade mark cases; it is important because ignoring this balance can jeopardise the legitimate rights of all trade mark owners.

While the pressures brought to bear by a client or one's management to pursue third party uses of trade marks can be compelling, the cumulative impact of 'bad cases making bad law' demands that all practitioners give serious thought to the consequences of all actions they commence and of all the letters before action they send.

One need only keep abreast of case law to detect a real distaste for (or even a backlash against) the perceived improper expansion of trade mark rights by rights holders. I, for example, would disagree with the assertion that third party trade mark usage on memorabilia was intended, and understood, as a

---

[6] Interbrand has estimated the value of the COCA-COLA trade mark as in excess of euro 56 billion: see *Business Week*, 1 August 2005.

badge of support, loyalty or affiliation, not as a badge of origin, because in my view a purchaser will believe a trade mark holder is ultimately originating, or at least approving, products bearing its trade mark.[7] However, this issue causes me to ponder whether the trade mark-owning community, collectively, has lost a level of support among some members of the judiciary by over-reaching in certain areas.

I do not think that the point has been lost on members of the judiciary that, while patents and copyrights fade away over time, trade marks have the capacity to become immortal. I believe that the prospect of this commercial immortality can produce real concerns among those who have been asked to ratify it. Thus I think it entirely appropriate that trade mark owners who seek redress should be put to their proofs and demonstrate that third party use of their marks has crossed the line between commercial morality and immorality, that commercial magnetism has been poached. I believe that the effort exerted in this direction represents a fair price to pay in return for immortality.

I recall being on a panel about five years ago, taking part in a discussion among in-house practitioners. While discussing the subject of 'sucks' sites on the internet, I volunteered that my then employer would not pursue such sites through the courts. This was because, though we were less than pleased by them, since they were legitimate expressions of opinion they were covered by free speech principles and did not constitute infringement of our trade mark rights (the baby had definitely been called ugly, indeed *very* ugly, but commercial immorality/poaching/confusion was nowhere in evidence).[8]

I was pleased when, following that panel discussion, I was complimented by an audience member – a member of the judiciary – for the sensible nature of this view (and with his opinion that I was doing a real service for my client by exercising such good judgment). However, I was chagrined by his feeling that trade mark owners do, too often, overreach and by his accompanying suspicion regarding the motives of many trade mark owners who commence legal proceedings in respect of unauthorised third party use. Indeed, this perceived overreaching had caused him to regard concepts like dilution with suspicion, as further attempts by the trade mark owning fraternity to overexpand their monopoly.

---

[7]   See *Arsenal Football Club plc v Reed* [2003] ETMR 73 (CA), where the Court of Appeal indicated their support for this view and reversed the judgment of the lower Court, holding that a substantial number of consumers regarded defendant's unauthorised use of Arsenal Football Club logos as designating the origin of those goods.

[8]   The author can envision uses of trade marks on commentary sites that would constitute infringement, but they are, in his view, in the very small minority.

DOING THE RIGHT THING IS ALSO THE SMART THING

Notwithstanding the comments that have been articulated above, this chapter does not seek to suggest that a widespread backlash against trade marks is imminent, or even likely. The sky is not falling and all weather reports are favourable in that regard. I do however believe that all practitioners need to understand the limits of the law and adhere to them. However, this is one of those instances where doing the right thing, and uniformly acting in ways that are consonant with the proper function of the trade mark, should turn out to be a good career and professional move.

Although it has been glossed over in this chapter, it is rather important to remember that the balance between property rights and unfettered competition is the issue relied upon by judges in most jurisdictions when determining who wins or loses trade mark cases. Accordingly even a trade mark proprietor who is not particularly interested in, or who does not subscribe to, the view that it is wise to be cognisant of the interests of all trade mark owners, to be conscious of self-interest and to avoid of looking foolish, should concede that those factors are strong motivators. In my experience, trade mark-owning clients feel no better about their lawyers when they commence actions that do not succeed. Indeed, the displeasure that trade mark owners experience on account of the 'heinous' nature of allegedly infringing third party use of their mark can easily become even greater displeasure with their legal advisers once it becomes clear that the grounds upon which their unsuccessful action were founded were questionable in the first place.

Whether a legal adviser is in-house, or out-house, I would suggest that the following points be emphasised:

- Significant time needs to be spent educating clients as to how their trade marks will be treated both in the worlds of commerce and of court-rooms. For example, if a client has not been assisted in being able to tell the difference between a descriptive trade mark and a fanciful one, and which one will receive a greater scope of protection, his legal adviser will have done him a disservice.
- The adviser's educative function must extend to issues relating to the securing of those rights necessary for underpinning investment in a project. If a client is planting its commercial flags in sand and does not know how to plant them in concrete which happens to be nearby, plentiful and just as easy to utilise, the legal adviser has not done his job.[9]

---

[9] 'Trademark Selection – Raising Your Commercial Flag', Bruce N. Proctor, *Remarks*, Trademark News for Business, Volume 4 No. 1 (1991).

- An adviser who works in-house but does not spend a significant portion of his time educating and re-educating his employer's marketeers on trade marks, also learning from them how he can help them more effectively sell the company's products and services, is not fulfilling an essential role: he must learn how to transcend his job description as lawyer/trade mark attorney and become fully focused on promoting the objectives of his team and ultimately his employer's needs.

The key message here is that there is no silver bullet. Whether an adviser works in-house or in private practice the structure for being an effective partner in the marketing of a branded product, making the correct calls and being listened to, is built one brick at a time. Counsel needs to take the time building client relationships, interacting with clients, providing meaningful education and gaining credibility. Merely possessing the legal knowledge to make the correct call, regarding a third party use of a trade mark, or anything else, will be of little assistance if the possessor of that knowledge does not have the ear – and the confidence – of the trade mark owner.

CONCLUSION

As this chapter has probably made clear, I am an unashamed lover of trade marks and care deeply about the important role they occupy in commerce and society. My time in the trenches has however impressed upon me the importance of restraint. While in the past any third party use of 'my' trade mark may have produced a flash of anger and an uncontrollable urge to right the terrible wrong, this has been replaced by a knowing acceptance that third party use is inevitable. Such use can be flattering, amusing, insulting or infringing. When the infringing variety occurs, a take-no-prisoners approach is not only cathartic but may be appropriate and required. In instances where such use is absolutely upsetting but objectively 'fair', the best advice is this: no matter how objectionable that use is, keep in mind what all parents know – one's own baby is never ugly, no matter what others might say.

17. Unauthorised permitted use in a multilingual jurisdiction

Thierry Calame

1. INTRODUCTION

The increased mobility of humans and the diminishing importance of national boundaries have led to a mixing of different cultures and languages. This development has also had an impact on trade mark law. First, increased internationalisation is reflected in legal arrangements and conventions embracing numerous countries and languages. Secondly, as a result of increased mobility and migration across national boundaries, not only multilingual countries but most trade mark systems are faced with a multitude of languages. The problems associated with multilingualism arise, therefore, in almost all trade mark jurisdictions.

Multilingualism enables businesses, in creating brands, to draw from an enlarged pool of terms which can be understood by at least some of the relevant average consumers. Such terms are particularly favoured in brand creation because they enable trade mark owners to communicate ideas solely by virtue of the meaning which is inherent in these terms. Conversely, the grant to single traders of exclusive rights in terms which other traders may wish to use raises problems. This issue arises frequently in multilingual jurisdictions where the number of terms which can be understood by at least some of the relevant average consumers is particularly large.

This chapter seeks to analyse some of the effects of multilingualism on registrability and the scope of trade mark protection as well as unauthorised permitted use. Although this analysis is based on a number of selected multilingual jurisdictions,[1] it ultimately applies to any jurisdiction where multiple languages are spoken.

---

[1]   The analysis is based on the Community Trade Mark Regulation (CTMR) and Trade Mark Directive and the trade mark laws of the USA, Canada, Benelux, UK, Spain and Switzerland.

2. REGISTRABILITY

2.1 Introduction

An application to register a trade mark may be refused where public interest objections or earlier conflicting rights of another person are raised. These grounds of refusal are referred to as absolute and relative bars to registration. The absolute bars to registration are applied by the trade mark office *ex officio*,[2] while the relative grounds of refusal may generally be raised by opponents only.[3] Absolute grounds of refusal may relate to whether the meaning of a trade mark is descriptive or generic,[4] whether it is deceptive[5] or immoral,[6] whether a product shape results exclusively from the nature of the goods themselves and whether a product shape consists exclusively of the shape of goods which is necessary to obtain a technical result.[7]

Descriptive, deceptive and immoral signs all communicate to the public a certain message the contents of which establish the bar to registration. This

----

   [2]   As to absolute grounds of refusal, see Article 7 CTMR; Article 3 Trade Mark Directive; §1052 Lanham Act for trade marks and §1053 Lanham Act for service marks with reference to §1052; s.12 Canadian Trade-Mark Law; Article 49(1) and (2) and Article 6[bis] (1)(1) Benelux Trade Mark Act; s.3 UK Trade Marks Act 1994; Article 5 Spanish Trade Mark Act; Article 2 Swiss Trade Mark Act. In some jurisdictions, including the UK, relative grounds may be raised *ex officio*: see for instance Jeremy Phillips, *Trade Mark Law: a Practical Anatomy* (2003), para. 4.179; William Cornish and David Llewelyn, *Intellectual Property: Patents, Copyright, Trade Marks and Allied Rights* (2003), para. 17.06.
   [3]   As to relative grounds of refusal, see Article 8 CTMR; Article 4 Trade Mark Directive; §1052(d) Lanham Act; s.12(d) Canadian Trade-Mark Law; Article 3 Benelux Trade Mark Act; s.5 UK Trade Marks Act 1994; Article 6 Spanish Trade Mark Act; Article 3 Swiss Trade Mark Act.
   [4]   Article 7(1)(b), (c) and (d) CTMR; Article 3(1)(b), (c) and (d) Trade Mark Directive; §1052 Lanham Act; s.12 (1)(b) et seq. Canadian Trade-Mark Law; Article 6[bis](1)(a) Benelux Trade Mark Act in connection with Article 6[quinquies] B (2)(2) PVÜ; s.3(1)(b), (c) and (d) UK Trade Marks Act 1994; Article 5(1)(b), (c) and (d) Spanish Trade Mark Act; Article 2(a) Swiss Trade Mark Act.
   [5]   Article 7(1)(g) CTMR; Article 3(1)(g) Trade Mark Directive; §1052 (a) Lanham Act; s.12(1)(b) Canadian Trade-Mark Law; Article 4(2) Benelux Trade Mark Act; s.3 (3)(b) UK Trade Marks Act 1994; Article 5(1)(g) Spanish Trade Mark Act; Article 2(c) Swiss Trade Mark Act.
   [6]   Article 7(1)(f) CTMR; Article 3(1)(f) Trade Mark Directive; §1052(a) Lanham Act; s.12(1)(e) in connection with s.9(j) Canadian Trade-Mark Law; Article 4(1) Benelux Trade Mark Act; s.3(3)(a) GB – TMA; Article 5(1)(f) Spanish Trade Mark Act; Article 2(d) Swiss Trade Mark Act.
   [7]   Article 7(1)(e) CTMR; Article 3(1)(e) Trade Mark Directive; s.3(2) UK Trade Marks Act 1994; Article 5(1)(e) Spanish Trade Mark Act; Article 2(b) Swiss Trade Mark Act.

message is communicated primarily through words and only rarely through figurative elements. These absolute grounds of refusal are, therefore, of particular importance in multilingual jurisdictions.

2.2 Descriptive Signs

2.2.1 Principles
Descriptive signs lack inherent distinctiveness and, therefore, cannot be registered. Descriptive marks, although not inherently distinctive, can acquire distinctiveness as a result of the use which the trade mark owner has made of it.[8] Signs are descriptive if they designate specific characteristics of the goods or services.[9] In this context, signs or indications which may serve to designate the kind, quality, quantity, intended purpose, value or geographical origin of the goods and services are relevant.[10] In determining whether a sign is descriptive, it is necessary to consider the meaning of that sign in the eyes of the relevant average consumer.[11]

In order for registration to be precluded, the sign must be exclusively descriptive, that is all the elements must have a descriptive capacity. It is possible to register marks which consist of descriptive and non-descriptive elements and are, therefore, distinctive if taken as a whole. Conversely, if a sign only consists of descriptive elements, it cannot be registered unless the applicant proves distinctiveness acquired through use.

2.2.2 Eyes of the relevant average consumer and significance for absolute bar to registration
In multilingual jurisdictions, the increasing number of terms understood by the relevant average consumer not only leads to a larger pool of potentially attractive marks, it also leads to an increase in number of terms which may potentially have a descriptive capacity. The meaning of a significant number of

---

[8]   Such acquired distinctiveness is also referred to as secondary meaning. See Section 2.2.3 below and Article 7(3) CTMR; Article 3(3) Trade Mark Directive; §1052(f) Lanham Act; s.12(2) Canadian Trade-Mark Law; s.3(1) UK Trade Marks Act 1994; Article 5(2) Spanish Trade Mark Act; Article 2(a) Swiss Trade Mark Act.

[9]   See for instance Phillips, para. 4.128 et seq.; Cornish/Llewelyn, para. 17.35 et seq.

[10]   See Article 7(1)(c) CTMR and Article 3(1)(c) Trade Mark Directive.

[11]   See for *European Community law*: ECJ, 31.1.2001, Case T-193/99 *Doublemint*, n.29 et seq.; similarly the conclusions of the Advocate General, 31.1.2002, Case C-363/99 *Postkantoor*, n.41; for *Switzerland*: RKGE, sic! 1997, 559 *Eco-Speedster*; Eugen Marbach, *Markenrecht, Schweizerisches Immaterialgüter- und Wettbewerbsrecht III* (1996), at 37; Lucas David, *Markenschutzgesetz*, 2nd ed. (1999), MSchG 2 n.9.

signs will only be understood by some of the relevant average consumers, while other consumers will imagine that the marks are merely fanciful and therefore distinctive. Thus the question arises as to whether and possibly how such signs need to be excluded from protection as a result of their descriptive capacity.

For multilingual jurisdictions the territory of which is partitioned in a clear manner, such as the EU, one may consider limiting the refusal of trade mark protection for signs which only some of the relevant average consumers understand as being descriptive to the places where the language in which the sign is descriptive is spoken. Such a solution would, however, cause problems where a clear partitioning of the jurisdiction is not possible. Moreover a geographical division of trade mark protection would be incommensurate with the principle of territoriality. According to this principle, the trade mark protection granted by a particular jurisdiction extends to the whole territory of such jurisdiction. As a result, if a sign is understood by at least some of the relevant average consumers as being descriptive, registration must be precluded for the jurisdiction as a whole.

In determining whether a sign is of an exclusively descriptive character, the multilingual jurisdictions analysed in this context generally consider the meaning of that sign in each of the operative languages in such jurisdiction.[12] The ground of refusal, therefore, applies if the sign is descriptive in only one of the operative languages. The perception of linguistic minorities is usually not taken into account by trade mark offices in this context. Signs which are only descriptive in minority languages are generally registered. They can, however, be removed from the registry in cancellation proceedings if the court considers a descriptive meaning in one minority to be sufficient. In one case in Switzerland, for instance, the Swiss Federal Supreme Court held that in determining the descriptive capacity of the term YENI RAKI – a Turkish

---

[12]   See for *European Community law*: s.2.3 and s.8.1.3 Examination Guidelines; the same applies in *Switzerland*: Federal Supreme Court, PMMBl 1990 I 46 *Membra*; RKGE, sic! 2001, 28 *Levante*; Christoph Willi, *Markenschutzgesetz* (2002), MSchG 2 n.15 et seq.; Marbach, at 32; David, MSchG 2 n.9; depending on the relevant average consumer, a foreign language may, therefore, be relevant; see Swiss Federal Supreme Court decision ATF 120 II 150 *Yeni Raki*. In Benelux, trade mark protection for a term in one of the national or regional countries extends *ex lege* to the translation of such term in all of these other languages, according to Article 13C Benelux Trade Mark Act. Consequently, the trade mark examination must extend to all of these languages; see ECJ, 12.2.2004, Case C-363/99 *Postkantoor*, n.60. In Canada s.12 (1)(b) Canadian Trade-Mark Law provides that in determining descriptive character one has to consider only the French and English language, whereas the direct designation of goods and services is exempted from protection in every language, not only French and English, according to s.12 (1)(c).

brandy – the members of the Turkish minority in Switzerland were the relevant average consumers and the term 'Yeni Raki' was accordingly precluded from registration.[13]

2.2.3 Proof of acquired distinctiveness

Signs which consist exclusively of descriptive elements may be registered if the trade mark applicant can prove distinctiveness acquired through use. Since in multilingual jurisdiction all signs which are descriptive in only one of the operative languages are precluded from protection, the number of signs which require proof of acquired distinctiveness increases in such jurisdictions. One could say, therefore, that the acquisition of trade mark protection through use is more difficult in a multilingual jurisdiction.

Proving distinctiveness acquired through use has some particularities in a multilingual jurisdiction. Generally speaking, the descriptive meaning of a sign can only be understood by such consumers as are capable of speaking the language in question. In a multilingual jurisdiction the need to keep a specific word free for general use only exists in relation to some of the relevant average consumers. In multilingual jurisdictions the territory of which is partitioned in a clear manner, it is, therefore, appropriate to limit the required evidence of acquired distinctiveness to the regions where the trade mark is effectively understood as being descriptive. Such a solution takes into account both the interests of the trade mark owner and those of the relevant average consumers and therefore reflects a good balance between their interests. Unlike in the case of a geographical division of trade mark protection, the principle of territoriality is not an impediment to proceeding in this manner. It is only for the purpose of establishing registrability that a geographical distinction is made; after registration the trade mark enjoys protection for the whole territory of that jurisdiction.

2.3 Deceptive and Immoral Signs

Deceptive and immoral signs are also precluded from registration. Signs are deceptive if they are of such a nature as to deceive the public, for instance as to the nature, quality or geographical origin of the goods or services.[14] Signs

---

[13] Swiss Federal Supreme Court decision ATF 120 II 144 *Yeni Raki.*

[14] See for example Article 7(1)(g) CTMR; Article 3(1)(g) Trade Mark Directive; partly deviating §1052(a) Lanham Act; similar, however, s.12 (1)(b) Canadian Trade-Mark Law; Article 5(1)(d) Spanish Trade Mark Act; s.3 (3)(b) UK Trade Marks Act 1994; Cornish/Llewelyn, n.17.49; Phillips, n.4.41 et seq.; Willi, MSchG 2 n.216; Marbach, at 68; Paul Ströbele/Franz Hacker, *Markengesetz*, 7th ed. (2003), MarkenG 8 n.550; Karl-Heinz Fezer, *Markenrecht*, 3rd ed. (2001), MarkenG 8 n.298; Fuchs-Wissemann in Friedrich Ekey/Diethelm Klippel, *Markenrecht* (2003), MarkenG 8 n.67.

are immoral if they have political, religious or sexual clearly offensive content and, as a result, are contrary to public policy or to accepted principles of morality.[15]

In determining whether a sign is deceptive or immoral, it is necessary to consider the meaning of that sign in the eyes of the relevant average consumer.[16] In a multilingual jurisdiction, all languages spoken in such territory must be equally taken into account. As in the case of descriptive signs, the number of signs communicating a certain message increases with each additional language that is spoken in a given territory. Conversely, the number of registrable signs decreases.

The legal position is, however, different from descriptive signs in relation to the acquisition of trade mark protection. First, the absolute ground of refusal does not only apply to signs which consist *exclusively* of deceptive or immoral elements. The combination of deceptive or immoral elements with other elements which are not deceptive or immoral does not overcome the absolute bar to registration.[17] Secondly, it is not possible to overcome this bar to registration by furnishing evidence of distinctiveness acquired through use. Deceptive and immoral signs accordingly are exempted from trade mark protection without limitation.

3. THE SCOPE OF PROTECTION

Signs including descriptive or generic elements may be registered if they contain further elements which are not descriptive. In addition, signs consisting exclusively of descriptive elements can be registered if they have acquired distinctiveness as a result of the use which the trade mark applicant has made of it. In this context, the question as to the scope of protection of such marks arises. As in the case of registrability, in determining the scope of protection one must equally consider the multiple languages that are spoken in a given territory. To decide otherwise would seriously undermine the basic principle of congruence of requirements and effects of protection in intellectual property law.

---

[15]   Cornish/Llewelyn, para. 17.48; Phillips, para. 4.32 et seq.; Willi, MSchG 2 n.262; Marbach, at 92; Ströbele/Hacker, MarkenG 8 n.548; Fezer, MarkenG 8 n.353; Fuchs-Wissemann, in Ekey/Klippel, MarkenG 8 n.73.

[16]   Cornish/Llewelyn, para. 17.48; Phillips, para. 4.34; Marbach, at 92; Ströbele/Hacker, MarkenG 8 n.548, 610; Fezer, MarkenG 8 n.301, 353; Fuchs-Wissemann in Ekey/Klippel, MarkenG 8 n.67, 73.

[17]   See for example Swiss Federal Supreme Court, PMMBl 1972 I 67 *Week-End-Sex*; Willi, MSchG 2 at 264.

3.1 Trade Marks Consisting of Descriptive and Non-descriptive Signs

In multilingual jurisdictions, the number of potentially descriptive signs increases with every additional language that is spoken in a territory. Since the descriptive character of one trade mark element is no impediment to protection of the mark as a whole, the number of trade marks consisting of such descriptive signs also increases with every additional language.

In relation to the scope of protection of such marks, descriptive elements of marks have little, if any, inherent distinctiveness.[18] In determining the scope of protection, one must take into account mainly their non-descriptive element, although their descriptive and therefore less distinctive elements must not be disregarded altogether.[19] The distinctiveness of a mark may be acquired and enhanced as a result of continuing and intensive use.[20] The mark is generally used as a whole, thereby enhancing the distinctiveness of the mark as a whole. However, the use of the mark as a whole may enhance the distinctiveness of an individual element, at least insofar as such element is to some extent independent.[21] But, even in this case, the distinctiveness of the inherently distinctive element will generally surpass the distinctiveness of the descriptive element because the use of the mark uniformly affects the distinctiveness of all elements. Even if a mark consisting of descriptive and non-descriptive elements is used intensively, the scope of protection is, therefore, determined mainly by the non-descriptive and more distinctive element.

Due to the comparably low distinctiveness of the descriptive elements, the owner of a mark consisting of descriptive and non-descriptive elements will hardly ever be in a position to exclude third parties from using the descriptive elements unless such descriptive elements have acquired distinctiveness through use.[22] The extension of the number of descriptive signs, therefore, leads to a reduction of the scope of trade mark usage reserved to the trade mark proprietor, whereas third parties have access to more elements of protected trade marks for (unauthorised) permitted use.

3.2 Trade Marks Consisting of Exclusively Descriptive Signs

In multilingual jurisdictions the number of signs consisting exclusively of

---

[18]   Willi, MSchG 3 n.113; Ströbele/Hacker, MarkenG 9 n.281; Fezer, MarkenG 14 n.298.

[19]   Willi, MSchG 3 n.133; Ströbele/Hacker, MarkenG 9 n.331.

[20]   Willi, MSchG 3 n.115; Ströbele/Hacker, MarkenG 9 n.20; Fezer, MarkenG 14 n.302.

[21]   Fezer, MarkenG 8 n.43.n.

[22]   See below Section 3.2.

descriptive elements increases with each additional language that is taken into account. However, unlike in the case of marks consisting of descriptive and non-descriptive elements, the number of protected signs containing descriptive elements does not increase. To the contrary, as a result of multilingualism there are more signs precluded from registration and only registrable if evidence of acquired distinctiveness is furnished.

As for every mark, a mark which is initially descriptive but acquires distinctiveness as a result of extensive use confers on its owner the right to exclude others from using, in the course of trade, identical or confusingly similar marks for the claimed goods and services. Marks that have acquired distinctiveness through use generally enjoy a normal scope of protection unless high reputation and corresponding distinctiveness lead to an extended scope of protection. To the extent such marks can be protected, multilingualism does not lead to any peculiarities in relation to scope of protection.

4. NON-INFRINGING ACTS

4.1 Introduction

The above comments have shown that in multilingual jurisdictions, descriptive or generic signs can be protected by trade marks in various ways. The protection of signs which consist of descriptive and non-descriptive elements is not so much of a problem, to the extent that the descriptive element is not protected in itself and, as a result, third parties who wish to use such an element are permitted to use it.

The protection of signs consisting exclusively of descriptive elements, however, may be problematic. Two types of situations can be envisaged in this context. First, signs consisting exclusively of descriptive elements may be registered as marks, if evidence of distinctiveness acquired through use is furnished. Secondly, descriptive signs can be registered if they are descriptive in a language which was not taken into account by the trade mark office for the purpose of determining registrability. In either situation, the question arises as to whether the trade mark owner may prohibit the members of a particular language group to use a sign which is descriptive in their language or whether such (unauthorised[23]) use is permitted by law.

---

[23]   In this context, 'unauthorised' means 'not authorised by the trade mark owner'.

4.2   Unauthorised Permitted Use of Descriptive Signs

The concept of permitted but unauthorised use of another's trade mark is well established. Article 17 of TRIPs permits Member States to provide limited exceptions to trade mark infringement such as 'fair use of descriptive terms, provided that such exceptions take account of the legitimate interests of the owner of the trade mark and of third parties'.

European trade mark law explicitly provides for such an exception to infringement. Both Article 12(b) CTMR and Article 6(1)(b) Trade Mark Directive provide that

> the trade mark shall not entitle the proprietor to prohibit a third party from using, in the course of trade, indications concerning the kind, quality, quantity, intended purpose, value, geographical origin, the time of production of goods or of rendering of the service, or other characteristics of goods or services; provided he uses them in accordance with honest practices in industrial or commercial matters.

This defence has been transformed into all European laws examined in this context;[24] similar exceptions to trade mark infringement exist in Canada[25] and the US.[26] Under Swiss law there is no explicit provision to date. However, in view of the clear guidelines in European trade mark law and the Swiss legislature's expressed aspiration to bring the Swiss Trade Mark Act into line with European trade mark law,[27] it is evident that, under Swiss case, law third parties will also be able to rely on the concept of unauthorised permitted use of descriptive terms as a defence. This is further supported by the fact that the Swiss Federal Supreme Court has recently recognised other trade mark defences not expressly provided for in the Trade Mark Act.[28]

4.3   Unauthorised Permitted Use in a Multilingual Jurisdiction

The concept of unauthorised permitted use of descriptive terms also applies in

---

[24]   Article 13(6)(b) Benelux Trade Mark Act; s.11(2)(b) UK Trade Marks Act 1994; Article 37(b) Spanish Trade Mark Act.

[25]   s.20(1)(b)(ii) Canadian Trade-Mark Law.

[26]   Under US law such use is referred to as fair use or, more specifically, 'nominative fair use'; see *New Kids on the Block v New American Pub Inc.* (971 F.2d 302, 9th Cir 1992); Phillips, n.8.13.

[27]   See Message of the Federal Council of Switzerland (*travaux préparatoires*), BBl 1991 I 2, 7 and 58 et seq.

[28]   See Federal Supreme Court decision ATF 128 III 146 *Autohändler*, holding that use of another's trade mark in advertising is permissible if such use is clearly restricted to one's own offer; ATF 129 III 353 *Puls*, holding that the use of a trade mark is subject to the bounds drawn by unfair competition law.

multilingual jurisdictions. In such jurisdictions, however, the descriptive capacity of a sign is generally only understood by some of the relevant average consumers. Who is entitled to rely on such defence?

The concept of unauthorised permitted use of descriptive terms seeks to avoid situations where the trade mark owner can prohibit a third party from using a sign which it needs for the purpose of identifying its own products. Such need for using another's mark for the purpose of identification only emerges for third parties in whose own language the term is indeed descriptive. In this context, the interests of third parties in using a term which is descriptive in their own language in trade without restriction is to be valued higher than the trade mark proprietor's interest in exclusive trade mark usage. Third parties must accordingly be able to rely on the defence. If the sign is, however, not descriptive in the language of the third party seeking to use such a sign, such party lacks an interest in using the sign. In this context, the interest of the trade mark owner in exclusive trade mark usage is to be valued higher. The third party can, therefore, not rely on the defence if the use of a term is only descriptive in a language which is alien to such third party.

In multilingual jurisdictions one must, therefore, distinguish among the language groups in determining whether there is an exception to infringement: A third party may only rely on a defence if she or he speaks the language in which the mark has a descriptive capacity. She or he may, however, not rely on such defence if the mark is descriptive in a language which she or he does not speak.

5.   CONCLUSION

From a trade mark lawyer's point of view, multilingual jurisdictions are characterised by the following particularities:

- The number of signs understood as descriptive, immoral or deceptive increases with each additional language taken into account in trade mark examination. The number of registrable trade marks, therefore, decreases with each additional language. Even though the number of terms which are principally available as potential marks is comparatively large in multilingual jurisdictions, a trade mark applicant has in effect fewer terms available.
- A comparatively large number of signs are understood by the relevant average consumers as being descriptive. As the acquisition of trade mark protection more frequently depends on evidence of distinctiveness acquired through use, multilingualism leads in effect to a restriction in acquisition of trade mark protection.

- Since a higher number of signs are understood by at least some of the relevant average consumers and since marks consisting of descriptive and non-descriptive elements are distinctive if taken as a whole and can, therefore, be registered, the number of marks containing descriptive elements is higher in such jurisdictions. Because the trade mark owner may not prohibit the use of such descriptive terms, the scope of exclusive trade mark usage reserved to him is in effect reduced.
- The trade mark proprietor may not prohibit a third party from using a sign if such sign is descriptive in the third party's language. Because the number of signs which are understood as descriptive increases, the scope of such defence increases.
- From an overall assessment, one may say that the scope of exclusive trade mark usage reserved to the trade mark proprietor decreases with each additional language which has to be taken into account, whereas the sphere of signs available for unauthorised permitted use increases. To put it in a nutshell: the more languages, the larger the public domain.

18. Unauthorised use of another's trade mark: a view from Australia[1]

Jackie O'Brien

INTRODUCTION

Many Australian trade mark lawyers read the latest European decisions on third party use with interest but perhaps some antipodean bemusement. Their bemusement arises from the fact that many of the most interesting cases on trade mark infringement to emerge from European courts in recent years would be dealt with simply in Australia and not as a matter of trade mark infringement. Australians perceive that the difficulties associated with characterising third party use as infringing or non-infringing simply do not arise in their system. This chapter aims to test that assumption.

The primary reason why cases of descriptive use, use indicating product compatibility and comparative advertising do not greatly concern Australian trade mark lawyers is that such uses are not usually characterised as 'use as a trade mark'. Unlike legislation in Europe and the United States, Australian legislation expressly requires 'use as a trade mark' before third party use will be characterised as infringing.[2] Australian trade mark legislation also offers broader defences to infringement than its foreign counterparts, particularly in relation to comparative advertising.[3]

It would be wrong to assume, however, that the issues confronting European courts in relation to third party use do not arise in Australia. They do – but, rather than being dealt with as a matter of trade mark infringement, they arise in the context of the common law of passing off and consumer protection legislation such as section 52 of the Trade Practices Act 1974 (Cth). The Australian approach to unauthorised third party use is a pragmatic one, based in part on a legislative intention that the trade mark system should not be used

---

[1]   The author would like to acknowledge the invaluable assistance of Allens Arthur Robinson lawyer Alison Barnett, without whose assistance preparation of this chapter would not have been possible.
[2]   Section 120 Trade Marks Act 1995 (Cth).
[3]   Section 122(1)(d) Trade Marks Act 1995 (Cth).

as a secondary tool to tackle issues of unfair advertising and consumer protection. While many of the relevant considerations are ultimately similar to those in Europe, the regulation of such conduct lies outside the trade mark system and is not focused on protecting the mark or its owner.

AUSTRALIAN LEGISLATION ON TRADE MARK INFRINGEMENT

Section 120 of the Trade Marks Act 1995 (Cth) provides that a person infringes a registered trade mark by using *as a trade mark* a sign that is substantially identical with, or deceptively similar to, the trade mark in relation to goods or services in respect of which the trade mark is registered. Section 120(2) provides for infringement by using *as a trade mark* a sign that is substantially identical with, or deceptively similar to, the trade mark in respect of goods and services of the same description or that are closely related to goods or services in respect of which the trade mark is registered, unless the use is not likely to deceive or cause confusion.

Infringement under Australian law therefore requires an upfront consideration of whether the third party use complained of is use *as a trade mark*.[4] While this requirement was only made express in the Trade Marks Act 1995, the infringement provisions in Australian law have long been interpreted as making use as a trade mark necessary to establish infringement. Australian law on this point diverged from that in the United Kingdom from 1938 onwards, when the wording of the infringement provisions in the Trade Marks Act 1938 (UK) 'gave a clear foothold for a contention that the use referred to in the definition of the exclusive right was no longer limited to use as a trade mark'.[5] Australian courts continued to apply the older UK authorities such as *Irving's Yeast-Vite Ltd v F A Horsenail*[6] and to develop their own jurisprudence on the need for 'use as a trade mark' and what constitutes it.

In addition to the requirement that the mark be used as a trade mark, section 122 of the 1995 Act sets out various types of use which do not constitute infringement. Even without their specific exclusion, some of these acts would not constitute infringement because they would not be regarded as use as a trade mark. Relevantly, it is not trade mark infringement:

---

[4]   A trade mark is defined by section 17 of the Act as a sign used, or intended to be used, to distinguish goods or services dealt with or provided in the course of trade by a person from goods or services so dealt with or provided by any other person.

[5]   *Shell Co of Australia Ltd v Esso Standard Oil (Australia) Ltd* (1963) 109 CLR 407 per Kitto J at 424.

[6]   (1934) 51 RPC 110.

(a)   to use a sign in good faith to indicate the kind, quality, quantity, intended purpose, value, geographical origin, or some other characteristic, of goods or services: s.122(1)(b)(i); or
(b)   to use a trade mark in good faith to indicate the intended purpose of goods (in particular as accessories or spare parts): s.122(1)(c); or
(c)   to use a trade mark for the purposes of comparative advertising: s.122(1)(d).

AUSTRALIAN CONSUMER PROTECTION LEGISLATION

Section 52 of the Trade Practices Act provides that a corporation shall not, in trade or commerce, engage in conduct that is misleading or deceptive or is likely to mislead or deceive.

Section 53 sets out specific provisions regarding false or misleading representations in respect of goods or services, including representations in relation to

(a)   standard, quality, value, grade, composition, style or model: s.53(a) and (b);
(b)   sponsorship, approval, performance characteristics, uses or benefits: s.53(c) and
(c)   sponsorship, approval or affiliation: s.53(d).

Contraventions of sections 52 and 53 do not require an intention to mislead or deceive, or negligence.

Common law passing off is intended to protect the goodwill associated with the plaintiff's business or product, whereas relief under the Trade Practices Act is concerned with the public interest and consumer protection.

THE AUSTRALIAN APPROACH TO THIRD PARTY USE

When Australian lawyers approach questions of third party use of a trade mark, the following issues are fundamental:

(a)   Has the third party used the mark 'as a trade mark'? If not, there is no infringement.
(b)   Does the third party have a defence under any of the express exemptions from infringement in s.122 of the Act, for example in relation to descriptive use, intended purpose or comparative advertising? If so, there is no infringement.

(c)   If there is no trade mark infringement, can the third party's conduct be characterised as passing off or misleading or deceptive under s.52 of the Trade Practices Act?

This chapter considers the concept of 'use as a trade mark' and how it operates to take many instances of unauthorised use outside the realm of trade mark infringement and into the domain of consumer protection legislation. It then examines the Australian approach to the topical issues of product compatibility and comparative advertising.

USE AS A TRADE MARK

The issue of whether a third party is using a mark 'as a trade mark' has been described as a 'pivotal question' in relation to infringement in Australian trade mark law.[7] The issue was most recently considered by the Federal Court in *Christodoulou v Disney Enterprises Inc*,[8] where Crennan J held that the use of the mark THE HUNCHBACK OF NOTRE DAME by Walt Disney as the title of a film and in associated marketing did amount to use 'as a trade mark'. A recognised title of a version of a well-known story is used descriptively, not to indicate a relevant connection in the course of trade or to distinguish Disney's goods from those of other traders.

The leading case on the issue of use 'as a trade mark' is the High Court decision in *Shell Co of Australia Ltd v Esso Standard Oil (Australia) Ltd*.[9] Esso was the proprietor of registered trade marks for a caricature of a 'man' having a large head resembling a drop of fluid, large hands and a small body. It alleged that its marks were infringed by an animated 'oil drop' cartoon character that featured in televised advertisements for Shell's petrol. Was Shell's television presentation of those particular pictures of the oil drop figure a use of them 'as a trade mark'? Kitto J (with whom the majority agreed) stated the test as:

> whether, in the setting in which the particular pictures referred to were presented, they would have appeared to the television viewer as possessing the character of devices, or brands, which the appellant was using or proposing to use in relation to petrol for the purpose of indicating, or so as to indicate, a connexion in the course of trade between the petrol and the appellant. Did they appear to be thrown on to the screen as being marks for distinguishing Shell petrol from other petrol in the course of trade?[10]

---

7   *Johnson & Johnson Aust Pty Ltd v Sterling Pharmaceuticals Pty Ltd* (1991) 30 FCR 326 at 347 per Gummow J citing *Shell*, note 5.

8   [2005] FCA 1401.

9   (1963) 109 CLR 407.

10   (1963) 109 CLR 407 at 425.

The Court held that the oil drop figure did not appear as a mark chosen to serve the specific purpose of branding petrol in reference to its origin. Rather, it was being used to convey certain features of Shell's petrol. Since it was not used as a trade mark, there was no infringement.

Because infringement requires that the mark be used 'as a trade mark', descriptive use of a mark also does not constitute infringement in Australian law, even aside from the specific defences under s.122 of the Act. In *Pepsico Australia Pty Ltd v The Kettle Chip Company Pty Ltd,*[11] the Kettle Chip Company was the registered owner of the mark KETTLE and manufactured and sold potato chips. Pepsico began marketing a new product in their 'Thins' range, the packaging of which featured the words: 'THINS DOUBLE CRUNCH Kettle Cooked Potato Chips'. The Full Court of the Federal Court held that the appellants had used the mark not 'as a trade mark' but as a description of the method by which the chips were cooked.

The Australian approach to descriptive use differs from that in Europe and the United States. In Europe under Article 6 of Directive 89/104 a third party is entitled to use descriptive indications provided they are used in accordance with honest practices in industrial or commercial matters. In the US, a third party has a defence of fair use under s.33(b)(4) of the Lanham Act where the word was not used as a trade mark being used fairly, in good faith and only to describe goods or services.

In Australia, if the word has been used descriptively and not as a trade mark, there is no infringement in the first place. In Europe and the US, on the other hand, third party descriptive use will constitute trade mark infringement in the absence of honesty or good faith.

In *Johnson & Johnson Aust Pty Ltd v Sterling Pharmaceuticals Pty Ltd*[12] the respondent, the registered owner of the word mark CAPLETS, marketed tablets shaped like capsules. The appellant also began marketing tablets called 'Caplets'. It denied trade mark use, claiming that its use was descriptive and not distinctive. The Full Federal Court held that, since the word had been used descriptively rather than as a mark distinguishing the product from other products, there was no infringement despite a finding by the trial judge, not overturned on appeal, that there was an 'ulterior motive' on the part of the appellant to seek to make the trade mark generic through usage and, by doing so, to overcome the respondent's contention that the trade mark was distinctive and not descriptive.

In *Wingate Marketing Pty Ltd v Levi Strauss & Co*[13] Wingate imported and

[11]   (1996) 33 IPR 161.
[12]   (1991) 30 FCR 326.
[13]   (1994) 49 FCR 89.

supplied to retailers second-hand jeans originally manufactured by Levi Strauss and which still bore its trade marks. The jeans were in many instances modified by Wingate and an additional label added to the garments, bearing its own trade mark REVISE. The Full Court of the Federal Court held that Wingate did not use the Levi Strauss marks 'as trade marks' when they marketed the second-hand goods, despite the trial judge finding that Wingate's marketing strategy was to sell second-hand Levi's jeans, making it plain to the public that they were Levi's jeans with all the good-will and background of the Levi Strauss brand attached to them, some of the benefit of which would 'stick to' Wingate. Sheppard J (with whom Wilcox J agreed) observed:

> However relevant these matters may be to the causes of action for breach of s.52 of the Trade Practices Act (ie misrepresentation) and for passing off, it is not appropriate to approach the question of infringement of trade mark now under consideration in this way. I agree . . . that the question to be decided is whether Wingate is using the Levi Strauss marks as trade marks when it markets its product. . . . Again one feels drawn into the area of passing off principally because members of the public may be led to think that substantially altered jeans bearing the Levi Strauss label were originally Levi Strauss garments in the sense that they were, although second-hand and thus worn, altered Levi Strauss jeans. . . . But, in my opinion, it is properly dealt with in the context of misrepresentation and passing off and not in the context of infringement of trade mark.[14]

Gummow J added:

> It is generally accepted that the tort of passing off is concerned with the protection of the business goodwill of the plaintiff against damage by the misrepresentations made by the defendant. Neither protection of goodwill nor deceptive conduct are the primary concern of the action for trade mark infringement under the present legislation.[15]

Wingate was decided before the enactment of the Trade Marks Act 1995. However, this analysis of the different considerations involved in trade mark infringement compared to passing off and misleading and deceptive conduct remains relevant under the present Act, which makes 'use as a trade mark' an express requirement for infringement.

In contrast, when considering trade mark infringement, European courts are expressly required to determine whether the third party has complied with 'honest practices'. The condition of 'honest practice' has been defined by the European Court of Justice (ECJ) as the expression of a duty to act fairly in

---

14 *Wingate Marketing Pty Ltd v Levi Strauss & Co* (1994) 49 FCR 89
15 Ibid., at 218.

relation to the legitimate interests of the trade mark owner.[16] In determining whether the third party has complied with its duty, the Court will take into account whether the third party might be regarded as 'unfairly competing' with the proprietor of the trade mark.[17]

The difference in approach can be demonstrated by contrasting *Wingate* in Australia with *BMW* in the ECJ. In *BMW*, the BMW mark was used to indicate that the independent dealer was a specialist in the repair and sale of second-hand BMW vehicles. In Europe, a seller of second-hand goods may infringe a trade mark by selling goods bearing the original trade mark if that mark is used in a manner that either takes unfair advantage of the distinctive character of the trade mark or creates the impression that there is a commercial connection between the third party and the trade mark owner.

Wingate would probably be decided differently in Europe on the trade mark infringement point, because the Levi's mark on the second-hand jeans was found to be used in a way that was intended to create the impression that there was a commercial connection between Wingate and Levi's. In Europe that would be regarded as trade mark infringement while in Australia Wingate's conduct resulted in a finding that, while it had engaged in passing off and breached s.52 of the Trade Practices Act, there had been no trade mark infringement.

One area of Australian infringement law where considerations of 'good faith' are relevant is the express defences under s.122 of the Act, but the need for those defences only arises where the third party has used the mark 'as a trade mark'. The defences operate in a similar way to Article 6 of Directive 89/104. This means that, where a third party uses a mark 'as a trade mark' for the ulterior purpose of trying to gain a competitive advantage or to trade off the reputation of the owner of the registered trade mark, the conduct will be regarded as infringement for the purposes of Australian law.

In *Anheuser-Busch Inc v Budejovický Budvar*[18] Allsop J considered the meaning of 'good faith' for the purpose of s.122. While he did not make a finding of 'conscious dishonesty' or of a conscious and deliberate attempt to appropriate the goodwill of the applicant, he did find that it must have been evident to the respondent that there was the real possibility, depending on the strength of the applicant's BUDWEISER mark in Australia, that consumers would associate the word with the applicant's product. In circumstances where the respondent knew that confusion would arise, and in spite of a lack of

---

[16]   *Gerolsteiner Brunnen GmbH v Putsch GmbH (KERRY/GERRI)* Case C-100/02, [2004] ETMR 40 at [24]; *BMW v Deenik* Case C-63/97 [1999] ECR I-905, [1999] ETMR 339.

[17]   *Gerolsteiner* at [26].

[18]   [2002] FCA 390; (2002) 56 IPR 182.

conscious dishonesty, the Court held that the respondent had not used the word 'Budweiser' in good faith for the purposes of s.122.

The Australian and the European approaches to trade mark infringement are therefore not as divergent as they first appear. Both allow for considerations of whether the third party has used the mark in 'good faith' or in accordance with honest commercial practices. The Australian approach differs from the European approach, in the sense that considerations of 'good faith' only arise where there has been use as a trade mark.

PASSING OFF AND MISLEADING AND DECEPTIVE CONDUCT

Cases where it may be difficult for the registered trade mark owner to demonstrate that the third party has used the mark 'as a trade mark' are often argued on the basis of passing off and breach of s.52 of the Trade Practices Act, at least in the alternative to a claim of trade mark infringement.

In the European infringement cases considering 'honest practice', considerations similar to those in Australian case law on passing off and s.52 come into play, particularly that of whether the third party is trading off the reputation of the registered trade mark owner. There are some key differences, however. The test for 'honest practice' in the European cases is framed in terms of a duty to act fairly in relation to the legitimate interests of the trade mark owner and involves considerations of whether there has been a discrediting or denigration of the mark.[19] Passing off and s.52 cases in Australia are not considered in terms of the interests of the trade mark owner, but rather in terms of consumer protection and whether the third party's conduct is misleading.

This is a significant doctrinal distinction. Australian law provides for a separation between issues of trade mark infringement and those of consumer protection and trade practices. While fact scenarios often give rise to both types of claim, cases such as *Wingate* demonstrate that the considerations involved in relation to the two are significantly different.

PRODUCT COMPATIBILITY

Third party use for the purpose of indicating product compatibility has been a topical issue in Europe following the ECJ's ruling in *Gillette v LA-*

---

[19]   *Gillette v LA-Laboratories* Case C-228/03, [2005] ETMR 67; *BMW*; *Gerolsteiner*.

Laboratories Ltd.[20] This issue is dealt with in Australian law in a relatively simple way.

Use of a mark simply for the purpose of indicating compatibility with another product is not regarded in Australian law as 'use as a trade mark'[21] and is thus not infringement. There is no need for the third party to demonstrate that use of the trade mark is 'necessary' to indicate the intended purpose of the product. More specifically, and drawing on the test outlined in the ECJ's judgment, such use need not be the 'only means of providing the public with comprehensible and complete information on that intended purpose'. There is also no need for the third party to demonstrate that their use of the trade mark to indicate product compatibility conforms to 'honest practices in industrial and commercial environments'. Where the third party has only used the mark to indicate product compatibility, these considerations do not even come into play.

While it has long been assumed that use indicating product compatibility is not 'use as a trade mark' in Australian law, re-examination of the issue may possibly produce a different result. Use of a mark to indicate product compatibility may not be use to indicate the origin of the advertiser's product, but it must nevertheless be an indicator of origin as far as the other product is concerned.

This largely academic question rarely arises for consideration. This may be for the reason that, aside from the preliminary inquiry as to whether there has been 'use as a trade mark', there is also an express defence under s.121(1)(c) of the Act when a trade mark is used in good faith to indicate the intended purpose of goods (in particular as accessories or spare parts) or services.

In *Gillette Company v Pharma-Goods Australia Pty Ltd*[22] Burchett J examined a similar scenario to that recently considered by the ECJ. Gillette, proprietor of the SENSOR trade mark for razors, sought an interlocutory injunction to stop Pharma-Goods selling safety razor blade cartridges which bore, relevantly, the words '*No Frills Moving Blades are compatible with Sensor Razors'. The Court did not think a sufficient case had been made out to justify interim relief on the basis that Pharma-Goods had used Gillette's trade mark as a trade mark. In particular, Burchett J noted s.121(1)(c), which permits a party to use a mark in good faith to indicate the intended purpose of the goods.

If the third party has gone further than simply using a mark to indicate product compatibility, a Court might find it had used the mark 'as a trade mark'. In *Nokia Corporation v Mai*[23] Mr Mai had been selling after-market

20   Case C-228/03.
21   See *Interlego AG v Croner Trading Pty Ltd* (1992) 39 FCR 348; (1992) 25 IPR 65 per Gummow J at 110.
22   (1997) 38 IPR 509.
23   [2003] FCA 924; (2003) 59 IPR 413.

accessories including mobile phone covers and neck straps that displayed Nokia's trade marks. Nokia alleged that they were counterfeit accessories in the sense that the Nokia trade marks had been affixed to the products without Nokia's authority. Mr Mai submitted that he had not used Nokia's marks as trade marks, but rather to communicate that the accessories could be used in relation to a specific brand of product: he relied on the express defence under s.122(1)(c) of the Act. The Court rejected his argument, holding that his sale of goods prominently bearing Nokia's trade marks was use 'as a trade mark'. It gave the misleading impression that the mark NOKIA was a badge of origin of the goods indicating a connection in the course of trade between the goods and the person who applied it to the goods.

If the third party has used the mark solely to indicate product compatibility, the trade mark owner will have no remedy unless the use of the mark is misleading and sufficient to ground an action for passing off or breach of s.52 of the Trade Practices Act. In the *Gillette* interlocutory proceedings discussed above, Gillette argued that Pharma-Goods' reference to its blades being compatible with Sensor razors was misleading. It claimed that the less expensive competing product would be identified in the mind of the customer with the Gillette 'Sensor' and that some people might think that Pharma-Goods' product had been manufactured by Gillette as an unbranded product. Burchett J was not persuaded by this argument: consumers would simply interpret the word 'compatible' to mean that Pharma-Goods' cartridges fitted the Gillette razor.

COMPARATIVE ADVERTISING

Section 122(1)(d) provides that using a trade mark for the purposes of comparative advertising does not constitute trade mark infringement, thus expressing that which has been implicit in Australian trade marks law since the British ruling[24] that the use of a competitor's mark in comparative advertising does not constitute 'use as a trade mark' and is therefore not infringement. While this decision was regarded as unfair in the UK and its effect was nullified in 1938, the law in Australia did not change.

The current law on comparative advertising in the UK is contained in s.10(6) of the Trade Marks Act 1994. Australian law differs from s.10(6) in that it does not require that the use for the purposes of comparative advertising be 'in accordance with honest practices in industrial or commercial matters' before it cannot constitute trade mark infringement. Nor will use for

---

[24] *Irving's Yeast-Vite Ltd v F A Horsenail* (1934) 51 RPC 110.

the purposes of comparative advertising constitute trade mark infringement if it without due cause takes unfair advantage of, or is detrimental to, the distinctive character or repute of the trade mark. Rather, in Australian law, use of a mark for the purposes of comparative advertising is simply not trade mark infringement.

In Australia, if comparative advertising is misleading and deceptive, it is actionable under s.52 of the Trade Practices Act. If it is not misleading it is regarded as lawful and an appropriate form of competition. In this respect, the Australian approach resembles the unfair competition provision in s.43(a) of the Lanham Act in the United States.

The Australian analysis of comparative advertising is not as far removed from that in the UK as it might first appear, however. In both jurisdictions, the key consideration is whether the advertisement is misleading. In the UK, if an advertisement is significantly misleading it is not in accordance with honest practices for the purposes of s.10(6) of the 1994 Act.[25] In Australia, if an advertisement is misleading it will be in breach of s.52 of the Trade Marks Act.

The fundamental difference between the jurisdictions is that regulation of comparative advertising in the UK and Europe falls within the trade marks system, whereas in Australia it is expressly excluded from it. What is the rationale for the exclusion of comparative advertising from the Australian trade marks system? In the Second Reading Speech for the Trade Marks Bill 1995, the Minister indicated that the main thrust of the Bill was to implement the Government's response to the July 1992 report of the Working Party to Review the Trade Marks Legislation, *Recommended Changes to the Australian Trade Marks Legislation*.[26] That report states:

> The majority of submissions agree with the proposal that comparative advertising should not constitute infringement. Those not agreeing believe comparative advertising should constitute infringement, unless the consent of the relevant trade mark owner is first obtained. The Working Party believes that the issue of unfair comparative advertising could be appropriately dealt with under other legislation such as the *Trade Practices Act* and the States' *Fair Trading Acts*.[27]

---

[25]   *Barclays v RBS Advanta* [1996] RPC 307, [1997] ETMR 199; *Vodafone Group Plc v Orange Personal Communications Services Ltd* [1997] FSR 34; *O2 Limited v Hutchison 3G UK Limited* [2004] EWHC 2571, [2005] ETMR 61, 62.

[26]   Second Reading Speech to the *Trade Marks Bill 1995*, Mr Lee, Minister for Communications and the Arts and Minister for Tourism, Hansard Wednesday 27 September 1995, MC1910.

[27]   July 1992 report of the Working Party to Review the Trade Marks Legislation, *Recommended Changes to the Australian Trade Marks Legislation*, AGS, Canberra at 75.

It has been observed in the UK that there is some debate as to whether trade mark law is the appropriate doctrinal 'home' for what could be essentially advertising regulation, which has a related yet independent set of priorities and interests.[28] In Australia this debate has been simply resolved by removing the regulation of comparative advertising from the trade mark system. A misleading comparative advertisement does not equal trade mark infringement. Rather, a misleading comparative advertisement equals a misleading comparative advertisement and is directly actionable by a competitor as such.

CONCLUSION

While Australia has the threshold issue of trade mark use and the focus on consumer protection in matters of unauthorised use, it commonly achieves results similar to those being delivered in other jurisdictions. Australians, however, like to think that it is they who have found the correct doctrinal home for dealing with this issue.

---

[28] 'The Rise of the R: A Scoping Study of global Trademark Law', Dev Saif Gangjee, St Catherine's College, Oxford, April 2002, available at http://www.ip-institute.org.uk/res.html.

PART THREE

Looking to the future

19. Why is it better to brand so as not to rely on third party use?

Dawn Franklin

Previous chapters have explored how third parties may lawfully use a trade mark without authorisation. This may encourage us to assume that riding on established brands is an acceptable and reasonable business strategy and that, as long as the third party manages to avoid the most blatant forms of infringement that would result in certain legal action, 'all's fair in love, war and commerce'.

This chapter challenges that assumption and suggests that such an approach not only damages the brand owner but also works to the detriment of the consumer, of the economy and society and ultimately also of the third party.

CONSUMERS

Although we commonly refer to companies as brand owners because they are the legal owners of the trade marks and hold the value of the brands as company assets, it is important to recognise that brands actually belong to their consumers, who hold the ultimate power of determining whether the brand thrives or dies. Jeremy Bullmore of WPP has stated that '[brand] users will be totally and brutally unforgiving'.[1] CORONA soft drinks, KENNOMEAT dog food, RAWLINGS squashes, PEPSODENT toothpaste and RINSO washing powder, are some examples of once-popular and familiar United Kingdom brands that, having lost favour with consumers, have long since disappeared.

Brands that thrive and build a relationship of trust with their consumers carry a responsibility to provide consistent value and quality to continue to earn their consumers' loyalty. Consumers use the trade marks and brand cues as convenient signals to locate and confirm the identity of the trusted brand. Distinctiveness in the market place thus not only provides the trade mark owner with optimised trade mark protection under trade mark law but also is fundamentally important to the consumer.

---

[1] 'Posh Spice & Persil', The British Brands Group Lecture, Jeremy Bullmore 2001.

Competing companies, each seeking to establish in the minds of consumers their own distinctive brands with distinctive brand attributes, increase consumer choice. Increased competition among brands that compete fairly thus necessarily increases consumer power over the brands, because those brands must remain on their mettle if they wish to retain the trust and loyalty of their consumers in a highly competitive market. Thus a virtuous circle is established: the greater the distinctiveness of competing brands, the stronger the consumers' ability to differentiate between brands and to exercise easily their power of informed choice; the greater the consumers' power of choice, the greater the competition between brand owners to innovate in such a manner as to increase distinctiveness and differentiation among brands.

If third parties are encouraged to use the brands of others and thus to encroach on the protection accorded to others' trade marks, the distinctiveness of brands is eroded. This reduces the consumer's ability to exercise informed choice and, as the virtuous circle breaks down, results in a negative impact upon competition.

For example, while lookalike products may initially appear to offer cheaper options to established brands, they blur the distinctiveness of the copied brand and impair the consumer's ability to make an informed choice. The lookalike may resemble the brand but it comes with none of the guarantees and assurances of the brand as regards quality, consistency and value. Nor has it earned any of the trust that consumers place in the brand. Also, as own-label products do not have to compete in order to secure shelf-space, which is strictly limited for brands, an own-label lookalike will frequently displace a secondary or tertiary brand[2] which offered its own distinctive attributes and had earned its own brand loyalty, so the consumer has a reduced choice.

Similarly parallel goods that were produced and labelled for an export market but have been re-imported can generate distrust, since consumers are understandably suspicious of products that have been repackaged, over-stickered or relabelled, or which bear unfamiliar language. Such products will generally appear side by side and at the same price as the regular product and, by eroding trust, may cause the consumer to avoid the brand altogether, reluctantly accepting a less-favoured but familiar and reassuring alternative.

TRADE MARK OWNERS

Because major global brands and their famous trade marks are so well-known, it is easy to assume that branding is the prerogative of big companies and to

---

[2] Secondary and tertiary brands are those that occupy second and third place after the market leader.

forget that, since building brands is about building reputations, principles of good branding can apply to even the smallest companies that seek to differentiate themselves and their products and services in a competitive market. Statistics from WIPO in 2003 showed that 80 per cent of international applications for trade marks came from applicants with two or fewer trade marks, indicating a high use of the system by smaller companies.[3] Small companies in particular need the protection of robust trade mark laws and certainty in interpreting the law so that the law actively deters infringement. The cost and uncertainty of litigation means that small businesses with limited financial and management resources are frequently unable or unwilling to initiate legal action and are forced to tolerate even quite blatant infringement and to struggle against the resulting damage to their businesses. The same financial vulnerability should warn small businesses that it is as inadvisable to provoke litigation as to initiate it.

It is widely acknowledged in marketing that the ability to establish a distinctive position in the market and distinctiveness in the mind of the consumer is of vital importance to branded businesses. Reis and Trout identify the first three laws of marketing as

- being first into a market,
- being first in a new category and
- being first in the mind.[4]

Products that compete fairly will necessarily seek to supersede an existing brand in the mind of the consumer, but will do this by creating their own distinctive position and identity rather than by encroaching on the rights of existing brands.

It has been argued that third parties who encroach on trade mark owners' rights to erode distinctiveness merely act as an additional spur to trade mark owners to innovate and create new ways to differentiate their products. For smaller businesses lacking the resources and energy to keep changing to stay ahead of copiers, the task frequently proves overwhelming and they simply struggle to maintain their reputations and remain in business. To deter copying, larger companies are forced to divert resources into label and packaging redesign, anti-counterfeiting technology and legal actions from budgets that would otherwise be spent on innovation to provide real added-value to consumers. In short, such encroachment is merely wasteful, rather than an efficient spur to innovation.

3   *Intellectual Property: Source of Innovation, Creativity, Growth and Progress,* BASCAP and International Chamber of Commerce Initiative 2005.
4   *The 22 Immutable Laws of Marketing,* Al Reis and Jack Trout 1993.

The establishment of successful brands has a high failure rate and the cost of bringing new products to market is high. For example, figures from the Massachusetts Institute of Technology indicate that 75 per cent of new products are likely to fail within five years.[5] Gillette invested an upfront US$750 million on research and development to bring to market their 'Mach 3' razor, the world's first razor with triple blades;[6] the US Food and Drugs Administration quotes the current cost of bringing a new medicine to market as being as high as US$0.8 to $1.7 billion.[7] The upfront cost of product development and of marketing and advertising to establish their brands in the market and the cost of those products that fail in development or in the market place are costs that must be borne by the branded businesses. They can only continue to invest on this scale if they have a fair opportunity to recoup their expenditure and earn a sufficient reward for their efforts. Since copiers and others who trade on the reputation of established brands follow only the successes but none of the failures, they incur none of those costs but reap the rewards.

It is frequently suggested that a reduction in trade mark protection of brands, such as by imposing international exhaustion, rather than regional exhaustion within the EU, or by limiting protection against even blatant looka-likes, would reduce consumer prices and would ensure that brand owners could not abuse their responsibilities to consumers. In reality such proposals would merely transfer resources and rewards from the creators and innovators of brands to opportunist third parties who create no added value. It should be remembered that robust laws are already well established to deal with any brand owner who is in a position of market dominance and abuses that position, while competition among brand owners with differentiated brands, vying fairly against each other, strengthens the power of consumers and ensures that the markets themselves prevent abuse.

THE ECONOMY AND SOCIETY

Brands are a major part of the economy, driving economic growth, investment and employment. Tim Ambler of the London Business School has commented that 'brands are the essence of competition. They provide the identities that permit products to distinguish themselves from other products and therefore allow competition to take place'[8] and has even suggested that 'brands *are* the

---

5   'MIT, MA USA', cited in *Brand Strategy* Issue 194, July/August 2005.
6   Naomi Aoki, *The Boston Globe*, 31 August 2003.
7   *US Food and Drug Administration – Challenge and Opportunity on the Critical Path to New Medicinal Products* 2004.
8   *A Guide to Brands*, The British Brands Group.

economy'.[9] If competition depends on the distinctiveness of brands, it follows that erosion of that distinctiveness must reduce competition and damage the economy.

There is a correlation between the protection of intellectual property rights and national competitiveness. In 2004, the 20 countries that were perceived as having the most stringent intellectual property protection were classed among the top 27 in an index of growth competitiveness, while the 20 perceived as having the weakest regimes ranked among the bottom 36.[10]

Because brands owners have a relationship of trust with consumers on which they depend for their survival, they also have a high level of responsibility in maintaining and improving standards in environmental protection, corporate responsibility and consumer protection. As Jeremy Bullmore affirms: 'Brands were the first piece of consumer protection'.[11]

Although the anti-globalisation movement, as exemplified by Naomi Klein, would have us believe that the owners of major brands are capable of operating with impunity, contrary to laws protecting workers, the environment and consumers,[12] the opposite is in fact the case. The reputation and fame of such major brands means that any slip from the highest standard of behaviour would generate adverse publicity and put the brand at risk while their distinctiveness keeps them and their behaviour constantly in the public eye in every field of their activity. For example, clothing brands have been put under the spotlight because of poor working conditions and practices in some companies to which their manufacturing has been subcontracted.

THIRD PARTIES

Since a third party who manufactures lookalike products carries none of the development costs, incurs only limited packaging redesign costs and bears none of the risks of failure that have already been sustained by the owner of the successful brand, it must be accepted that he gains a financial benefit from doing so. However the advantage gained may only apply in the short term as

---

[9]   'Are Brands Good for Britain?' The British Brands Group Lecture. Tim Ambler 2000.

[10]   *The World Economic Forum Global Competitiveness Report 2004–5* cited in 'Intellectual Property: Source of Innovation, Creativity, Growth and Progress', BASCAP and International Chamber of Commerce Initiative 2005.

[11]   'Pro-Logo. Why Brands Are Good For You', *The Economist*, September 2001.

[12]   *No Logo – Taking Aim at the Brand Bullies*, Naomi Klein (HarperCollins 2000).

copying is not a sustainable business strategy. The copier can only compete on price and is therefore vulnerable over time to any other manufacturer with a lower cost base. Because retailers control the consumer price, communication with the consumer and access to the market, retailers selling lookalike products are able to increase pressure on the manufacturer of the lookalike to reduce his prices to them, whether or not they choose to pass on any cost saving to the consumer. As the manufacturer has not built a relationship with the consumer to enable him to generate a consumer demand for his product in preference to those of other manufacturers, he can be easily replaced. With pressure on his margins, he is less able to invest in his business and to attract and retain the best quality employees so his productivity will tend to suffer. Evidence from PIMS shows that 'unbranded FMCG businesses display lower capital productivity and employee productivity. Furthermore profitability is significantly lower in these businesses, to an extent that questions their long-term financeability.'[13]

Moreover, the copier's business is dependent on the decisions of the branded companies he copies. If the brand owner is able to invest sufficient resources to create further differentiation in the brand, the copier is forced to follow or to find another brand to imitate.

In choosing to follow others, the copier necessarily foregoes the advantage of legal certainty. The very existence of lengthy legal articles and books by learned legal experts arguing and counter-arguing the relative merits of interpretations of points of law demonstrates that the closer one works to the limits of trade mark law, the greater the risk of falling on the wrong side of an interpretation. Even though a legal advisor may confirm that an action is within the law, there will be no guarantee that the other party will receive the same advice nor any assurance that the other party will not pursue a legal action, even if the chances of success may be uncertain or limited. If the brand owner has been subject to concerted copying by others, he may choose to initiate legal action simply to make an example of one of the perpetrators or he may have had time and resources to gather compelling evidence, of which the defendant will be unaware, to provide substantiation for his case. Whatever the legal outcome, the management resources and energy inevitably consumed defending a legal action would be better employed within a business to produce added value to the business and to its customers.

A successful business strategy must focus on its customers' needs. Any business approach that takes a competitor's products and services as a starting point, be it copying, trading on the reputation of others, parallel trading or

---

[13]   'Brands, Innovation and Growth', PIMS Profit Impact of Market Strategy 2004.

using comparative advertising should be questioned because, especially over a longer term, these cannot be winning strategies. At best, the business can tag along as an also-ran behind the brands. None of these approaches allows the business to disassociate itself from the rest of the pack, to create clear space between itself and others through innovation and to soar to new heights. In other words, to be the best it can be.

CONCLUSION

Should we seek to explore the limits of trade mark protection? Of course we should, because new technologies, new media and new thinking are expanding and changing the ways in which brands can differentiate themselves and this differentiation needs to be encouraged and protected. We should resist attempts to weaken existing laws or limit trade mark protection and should perhaps consider strengthening some aspects of trade mark law to ensure that the law provides greater certainty, encourages the creation of distinctive brands and discourages the loss of brand distinctiveness.

20. Legal strategies for coping with unwanted third party use

Steven Warner

Every species of intellectual property confers a monopoly. The intellectual property owner is entitled to prevent third parties from encroaching on the sphere protected by that monopoly. It is equally true that all monopolies conferred by intellectual property are limited. In a competitive economy, the monopolies created by intellectual property rights are anomalous and will be tolerated only within certain boundaries. Trade mark rights in particular are circumscribed in a number of ways described in detail in preceding chapters and these limitations cannot be avoided.

Nevertheless, trade mark owners can use a variety of strategies to minimise the effect of these limitations on the trade mark monopoly. Some are obvious (but not necessarily simple), such as selecting inherently distinctive signs to serve as trade marks; others are, at least in theory, simple (but not necessarily obvious), such as relying on alternative intellectual property rights where trade mark rights cannot succeed. This chapter briefly considers some of the most important steps a brand owner can take to maximise its ability to prevent third parties from making unauthorised and unwanted use of its trade marks.

1. DEPLOY ALTERNATIVE INTELLECTUAL PROPERTY RIGHTS

A sign protected by a trade mark registration may also be protected by other intellectual property rights. This is because a trade mark may also be a copyright work[1] or a design that qualifies for protection.[2] Even a sign that merely

---

[1] For example, a logo trade mark may also be an artistic work within the meaning of section 4 Copyright, Designs and Patents Act 1988. See for instance *R Griggs Group Ltd and others v Evans and others* [2005] EWCA Civ 11, [2005] ECDR 12.

[2] For example, a logo trade mark may be new and have individual character and qualify for protection as either an unregistered or registered Community design under Council Regulation 6/2002. Thus the crest device used by Arsenal Football Club is

acts as a trade mark to identify the trade origin of the goods to which it is affixed may be able to ground not only an action for trade mark infringement, but also an action for passing off[3] (in jurisdictions modelled on the British common law) or unfair competition (in civil law jurisdictions).

While all species of intellectual property confer only a limited monopoly,[4] the limits to each are not coextensive. Third party use that will not infringe the rights conferred by a registered trade mark may nevertheless be unlawful when viewed from the perspective of a different species of intellectual property.

1.1 Passing Off and Unfair Competition

Passing off, a common law remedy, is intended to prevent one trader from illegitimately damaging the goodwill of another.[5] If a third party makes a misrepresentation in the course of trade which causes confusion resulting in damage to another's goodwill, that third party will be liable for passing off. Such a misrepresentation need not be (and rarely, if ever, is) express. A typical misrepresentation would consist in the third party using a sign that is in fact distinctive of the other party. The typical misrepresentation is the misuse by a third party of a trade mark, although there is no need for that mark to be registered and it is irrelevant to the cause of action if it is.

When the Trade Marks Act 1994 was enacted, some commentators predicted that passing off would rarely be required as a cause of action. The 1994 Act made possible the registration of signs that could not previously have qualified as trade marks and, since passing off is a relatively complex cause of action to litigate, it was thought that, once a sign was registered as a trade mark, the owner would focus solely on enforcing the rights conferred by that registration. This view underestimated the virtues of passing off. While there is no doubt that a trade mark infringement case is typically easier to make out,

---

registered in the UK both as a trade mark (no.2309100 and others) and as a design under the Registered Designs Act 1949, as amended to reflect Directive 98/71 (no.3001159).

[3]   See, for example, *Wagamama Limited v City Centre Restaurants plc and another* [1995] FSR 713, [1996] ETMR 23.

[4]   Most intellectual property is limited in two respects – there are limits on the *scope* of the monopoly conferred (that is there are certain uses to which the intellectual property may be put by third parties that the intellectual property owner cannot prevent) and there are limits on the *duration* of that monopoly (for example the rights conferred by a registered design cannot last beyond 25 years from the date of registration). Trade mark rights are limited only in scope: a trade mark can (in principle) remain validly registered in perpetuity.

[5]   Passing off plays a similar – albeit somewhat narrower – role to the unfair competition laws found in most other European jurisdictions.

there are two key features of passing off that may commend it to the trade mark owner faced with a difficult enforcement action.

First, the limits of passing off do not coincide with those of a registered trade mark. With certain exceptions, trade mark infringement requires that the defendant's use of the claimant's mark will cause confusion as to the trade origin of the goods to which that mark is affixed. In passing off, all that is required is that consumers be led to believe there is some connection between the defendant's goods and the products or business of the claimant. Provided that evidence of such confusion can be obtained, passing off may succeed in circumstances where trade mark infringement would fail.

Second, notwithstanding the wide range of signs that may be registered as trade marks under the 1994 Act, there will often be elements of a product's design or packaging that are not registrable (or certainly not readily registrable). Passing off by contrast is capable of protecting exclusivity in relation to an indefinite range of distinctive characteristics. Provided use by a third party of that characteristic amounts to a confusing misrepresentation, there is scope for preventing that use irrespective of whether the characteristic in question does, or even could, constitute a trade mark. If the brand owner's products not only bear a particular trade mark but also use a distinctive typeface, a distinctive colour scheme, packaging of a particular shape and consistent slogans or straplines, an action for passing off might be brought if a third party imitated these elements (or any distinctive combination of commonplace elements), even if any use of the brand owner's trade mark could not be prevented. In appropriate circumstances, an action in passing off might be brought even if the third party did not use the brand owner's trade mark at all.

For example, while it may not be possible to deploy trade mark rights to prevent a third party from labelling its products as being suitable for use as spare parts for the brand owner's goods, the brand owner may have a cause of action in passing off if the third party also imitated the 'get-up' or 'trade dress' of the genuine article. In some circumstances, establishing passing off may assist in making a case for trade mark infringement. Any defence to trade mark rights which requires the third party to be acting honestly, or in accordance with honest practices, will be denied to a third party that engages in passing off.

In the present context, passing off has a further virtue, albeit one that can appear to be a vice in other circumstances. Passing off is a highly flexible cause of action of uncertain scope. It is not clear quite where the boundaries lie between passing off and acceptable commercial behaviour.[6] In recent years,

---

[6]   See Christopher Wadlow, *The Law of Passing-Off: Unfair Competition by Misrepresentation, Third Edition* (London: Sweet & Maxwell, 2004), Ch. 7.

the boundaries have appeared to shift; and, with each shift, a wider range of activities has fallen within the scope of passing off.[7] There remains room for the scope of passing off to be expanded further over time. Although it would undoubtedly prove expensive to do so, brand owners, when confronted with a sufficiently damaging 'borderline' case may test – and perhaps expand – the limits of passing off.

The laws that govern unfair competition and unfair market practices in most civil law jurisdictions should be mentioned here. Although they are too many and too diverse to describe in detail, their application very frequently mirrors that of passing off law in situations in which an action for registered trade mark infringement may be brought. In jurisdictions in which such rights prevail, they may provide relief even where normal trade mark infringement action fails.[8]

1.2 Copyright Infringement

If a trade mark also qualifies as a copyright work, the availability of an action for copyright infringement can be a valuable addition to the proprietor's arsenal. Copyright infringement does not turn on use in the course of trade, let alone use 'as a trade mark'. No consumer need be confused by the third party's replication of a copyright work. The infringement is complete as soon as the third party commits one of the acts restricted by copyright – for example, copying the copyright work or issuing copies of that work to the public. There are limits to the monopoly conferred by copyright, just as there are limits to the monopoly conferred by a trade mark registration. However, because the underlying purpose of copyright (broadly speaking, to protect the results of creative endeavour) is different from that of trade mark rights (which is to offer a guarantee of the trade origin of goods or services), the limits to copyright protection are drawn very differently from those that apply to trade mark rights.

Not all trade marks are capable of attracting protection as a copyright work. Brand names and other word marks are unlikely to qualify as copyright works; no matter how inventive or distinctive, they are simply too short to qualify as

---

[7]   See Susie Middlemiss and Steven Warner, 'Is there still a hole in this bucket? Confusion and misrepresentation in passing off', [2006] *Journal of Intellectual Property Law & Practice*, 131–42.

[8]   Thus in *BVBA Kruidvat v Commission of the European Communities* Case T-87/92 [1997] ETMR 395 the Court of First Instance of the European Communities was prepared to recognise that an action for unfair competition might be brought to protect a selective distribution arrangement against the parallel importation of luxury goods in a situation in which the doctrine of exhaustion of rights would preclude an action for trade mark infringement.

literary works.[9] Save in the most unusual circumstances, slogans or straplines
are equally unlikely to qualify. To take advantage of the possibilities offered
by copyright protection, a brand owner should aim to include in its trade mark
portfolio (and to use as part of its core brand identity) one or more logo
devices and/or a bespoke typeface. Such logos and typefaces may qualify for
copyright protection as artistic works, provided they are original (in the sense
of not having been copied from pre-existing works). To serve a dual purpose
as both trade marks and copyright works, they will also need to be distinctive.
Although distinctiveness in the trade mark sense is not required for a logo to
attract copyright protection, a third party will infringe the copyright in that
logo only if it has copied the brand owner's work. If a logo is both distinctive
and original, the brand owner is likely to find it easier to establish to a court's
satisfaction that the third party is using an infringing copy of its logo rather
than a similar, but independently created, work of its own.

A brand owner must satisfy three essential prerequisites in order to take
advantage of the possibilities made available by copyright protection:

- *Ensure that copyright belongs to the brand owner.* Logos and bespoke
  typefaces will typically be designed by an independent creative agency.
  In the absence of any agreement to the contrary, any copyright that
  subsists in such works will be owned by the agency. The brand owner
  should ensure that it enters into written agreements with its design agencies and that these agreements expressly assign all copyright in the
  commissioned works to the brand owner.
- *Ensure the brand owner can evidence subsistence of copyright.*
  Copyright will subsist only if the work in question is original. Any
  assignment of copyright from the design agency will be effective only
  if the agency itself would otherwise own that copyright. The brand
  owner should ensure that it can demonstrate that the logo or typeface is
  an original creation rather than a copy of a pre-existing work and that
  those involved in its creation were either employed by the agency or, if
  working on a freelance basis, had themselves assigned all copyright in
  their work to the agency. Witness statements, proofs of design work
  from various stages and copies of employment or engagement contracts
  may be required in order to establish the subsistence of copyright and
  the agency's initial title to that copyright.
- *Ensure that the brand owner can evidence ownership of copyright.*
  Ownership of a trade mark registration which consists of or includes a

---

[9]   *Exxon Corporation and others v Exxon Insurance Consultants International
Limited* [1981] 3 All ER 241.

copyright work does not suffice to prove ownership of the copyright in that work. The brand owner should have readily available for immediate deployment sufficient evidence to demonstrate subsistence and ownership of copyright. Putting together a pack consisting of the evidence collected to demonstrate subsistence of copyright together with the assignment in favour of the brand owner will greatly assist the brand owner in enforcing its copyright against any infringing third party.

Copyright can be a very useful tool to prevent unauthorised use by third parties of logos and other stylised trade marks. When an agency is retained to develop a brand identity, it is easy to focus exclusively on the trade mark potential of that work. However, brand owners should be alert to the issue of copyright whenever creative work is undertaken for it by third parties. If the copyright is considered only when it becomes urgent to enforce it against a potential infringer, the brand owner may find itself either unable to obtain that copyright, or else having to pay a substantial sum to bolster its intellectual property portfolio in a way that could have been painlessly achieved earlier if addressed at the outset.

2.   REGISTER A STYLISED BRAND IDENTITY

As well as the potential for attracting copyright protection, logos and stylised typefaces may be more robust as trade marks than other signs when confronted with third party use at the limits of trade mark law.

In general, brand owners are advised to seek registration of word trade marks in plain text rather than in any stylised form or embedded in a logo or device. The principal reason for this is that a registration in plain text will typically give protection against third party use of that word in any form. All uses of the word mark will be uses of an identical mark. The monopoly conferred by a stylised registration is narrower. A third party that uses the word but not the style may be regarded as using only a similar (and not identical) sign, which makes enforcement more difficult. Moreover, if the stylisation is regarded as an essential element of the registered mark, a third party that departs from that stylisation may not even be using a 'similar' sign.

Nevertheless, when it comes to policing brands the protection of which lies at the periphery of trade mark law, a stylised version of a word mark or a device mark in which the brand name is embedded may be more useful than a plain text mark. For example, a third party may argue that it is entitled to use the NAME trade mark to indicate that its products are compatible with NAME brand products, or to draw comparisons between its own products and NAME brand products. A plain text mark is likely to be helpless to prevent such use (provided it is in accordance with honest commercial practices). However, the third party does not, in order to make such indications or comparisons, require the right to imitate the brand owner's distinctive stylised typeface or logos. To do so would risk infringing a registration for that stylised or device mark, even in circumstances in which there would be no infringement of a plain text registration.

Nothing can prevent a third party from exploiting the 'safe harbours' granted by trade mark law. However, a brand owner that holds a range of stylised and device trade marks in a portfolio can (provided it makes proper use of the relevant stylised typefaces and devices) compel a third party operating within one of these 'safe harbours' to do so in a way that clearly distinguishes official from unofficial products. While consumers who do not care about buying 'official' products (those who perhaps just look for the cheapest compatible product) may still be lost, the brand owner may be able to limit the 'leakage' of confused customers.

3.   THE MOST IMMEDIATELY ATTRACTIVE MARK MAY BE THE WORST MARK OF ALL

There is often a pronounced tension between what might be called 'marketing logic' on the one hand and 'trade mark logic' on the other. Marketing logic typically favours the adoption of brand names that immediately mean something to the potential consumer, that convey something of the nature and qualities of the products to which those names will be affixed. Trade mark logic, by contrast, looks for brand names to be as uninformative as possible (although not so uninformative as to be deceptive). Marketing logic advises that we exploit the meanings associated with established words or phrases. Trade mark logic applauds the use of neologisms that, other than identifying the brand owner, mean nothing.

There is no doubt that a well-chosen, descriptive name may help to sell a product. What it does not do is confer any immediate monopoly on the brand owner. To stand any chance of obtaining a trade mark registration, the brand owner will first need to educate consumers to identify the selected name as a trade mark. The brand owner must defeat the descriptive meaning of the chosen name and persuade consumers to recognise that NAME products are not merely name-type products, but products of that nature originating from a particular source. It takes time to educate consumers in this way. To achieve this result, the brand owner may need to be more successful than it needs to be to attract imitators into its market. If the imitators arrive before the education process is complete, it may be impossible for the brand owner to prevent those competitors from encroaching on what would otherwise have been the brand owner's legitimate monopoly. Once such imitators have arrived on the scene, trade mark protection may remain forever beyond the brand owner's reach. Even if the brand owner does manage to register the chosen name as a trade mark, the protection conferred by that registration is likely to be more limited – and more difficult and more expensive to enforce – than the protection conferred by an unambiguously distinctive mark.

4. SUCCESS BRINGS ITS OWN DANGERS

While the proposition may appear counterintuitive, the runaway success of a brand can prove damaging to the trade mark portfolio that protects that brand against imitation.

As well as tending to favour the adoption of descriptive, meaningful terms as brand names, marketing logic encourages a brand owner to celebrate when a brand name becomes so familiar to consumers that it is largely interchangeable with the product in relation to which it is used. Trade mark logic despairs at such developments. Even the most inherently meaningless, distinctive neologism will lose its power as a trade mark if it becomes just another (or, worse, the only) word by which to refer to the type of product. A name afflicted by 'genericity' will at least be more difficult – and therefore more expensive – to enforce. At worst, the name may cease to qualify as a trade mark at all.

It is easy to miss the fact that a mark is tending towards genericity because that process is often intimately connected with the increasing success and prominence of the brand in its field. The greatest danger to a trade mark may come not from the activities of infringers but from the success of the brand. Active policing of trade mark use is at least as important during the good times as during the bad. It is important to ensure that the trade mark is always treated as a trade mark, as a valuable asset. The brand owner's own personnel can inadvertently do lasting, even irreparable harm to the validity of the trade mark. Trade mark owners should establish clear guidelines for their own use of the mark and ensure that these are uniformly followed. In particular:

- *Distinguish the trade mark from surrounding text.* The brand owner should ensure that all communications properly identify its mark as a trade mark and do so consistently. For example, references to the mark may be in *italics*, in **bold**, in CAPITALS or at least should employ an initial capital letter. In addition, the mark might be accompanied by the symbols ® or ™ on at least one occasion in each document.
- *Designate an approved generic descriptor.* The trade mark should as much as possible be used in conjunction with a genuinely generic word

descriptive of the type of product in relation to which the mark is used. For example, the brand owner should refer to 'BRAND footwear' and not to 'a pair of BRANDs' or 'this season's BRANDs'. The designated descriptor should be used consistently.

- *Do not confuse the mark with the owner.* Distinguish references to the brand from references to the brand owner. Even if the owner of the BRAND trade mark is Brand plc, announcements, advertisements, labels and other documents issued by the brand owner should take care to separate the two. The BRAND mark should be used only as a trade mark.

As a brand becomes more successful and the trade mark more recognisable, it can be tempting to 'play' with the trade marks in a variety of ways to exploit that recognition factor and develop the brand image. For example, one may tease the consumer by using only part of the trade mark, leaving the consumer to infer the rest of the brand name. While occasional use in this way is unlikely to do much damage, a consistent and protracted pattern of such partial use may expose the brand owner to the risk that the mark is no longer being used as registered. In time, this can render the mark vulnerable to revocation. Another guideline that should be adopted by a prudent brand owner is, therefore, a general prohibition on cropping, distorting or otherwise manipulating the trade mark.

5. USE THE MARKS AND POLICE THE FIELD

There is a 'use it or lose it' element to most intellectual property regimes. In some cases (such as patents), third parties may claim licences of right (or compulsory licences) if the right-owner fails to use its intellectual property. In others (such as trade marks), failure to use the intellectual property can lead to the monopoly being lost. Unused trade marks are vulnerable to revocation. As a brand evolves over time, a large number of 'heritage' marks may be accumulated – marks reflecting older versions of the brand identity no longer in use. If there remains a market for products bearing such heritage marks, that market may come to belong entirely to the infringers if the brand owner fails to continue using those marks to some degree. Even if the brand owner itself is not interested in exploiting the market for such heritage products, licensing one official producer (perhaps on generous terms) should be sufficient to keep those marks alive and valid, at least in relation to some goods within the specification.

A brand owner must also enforce its trade marks when it encounters infringements or face losing the monopoly it has paid for. Failure to act quickly enough against a known individual infringer can result in the trade mark owner being ultimately unable to prevent that third party from using the trade mark. Of greater concern is that, in relation to trade marks, a pattern of such acquiescence can result in a loss of the trade mark monopoly against the world. A brand owner that concentrates solely on combating infringements in relation to widgets and ignores infringers producing gizmos may find itself unable to enforce its marks against any gizmo manufacturer in future. Enforcement against gizmo manufacturers can seem unduly expensive when the brand owner's business focuses on widgets. However, it can be far more costly to find, some years down the line when the brand owner's business plan has changed to include gizmos as a key product, that the trade marks have lost all power against the gizmo infringers. While no major brand owner is likely to be able to attack each and every infringement of its trade marks, any enforcement strategy should be forward-looking.

6. LIMIT THE RISK OF EXHAUSTION

Once a product is placed on the market in the European Economic Area (EEA) by the trade mark owner or with its consent, any trade mark rights within the EEA are exhausted. Indeed, all intellectual property rights that may subsist in that product will be exhausted and (subject to certain limited exceptions) none can be used to prevent the free movement of those goods across national borders within the EEA.[10]

However, goods first marketed outside the EEA may be prevented from entering any EEA territory protected by trade mark registrations, unless it appears that the trade mark owner consented to their importation into the EEA. Any trade mark owner with manufacturers or licensees based outside the EEA would be well-advised to ensure that the absence of any such consent is evident from the contractual arrangements with those manufacturers or licensees. The brand owner should ensure that all such contracts expressly state that the products in question are not to be imported into the EEA. If a given manufacturer is to be instructed to make goods for sale both in the EEA and elsewhere, procedures should be established (and set out in the contract) to distinguish batches bound for the EEA from those bound for other markets. While such procedures might involve some administrative inconvenience that could otherwise be avoided, the brand owner stands to gain more in terms of protection against grey market goods than it is likely to lose in additional expense and procedural complexity.

---

[10]   See Valentine Korah, *An Introductory Guide to EC Competition Law*, *Eighth Edition* (London: Hart Publishing, 2004), Ch. 10.

7.   CULTIVATE RELATIONSHIPS WITH THE CRIMINAL LAW ENFORCEMENT AGENCIES

Sometimes, there is no real doubt that a trade mark is valid or that a third party product infringes that trade mark. The problem facing a brand owner may not be the limits intrinsic to its trade mark monopoly, but the limits on its ability to police the infringements third parties produce. Each infringer may be too small to merit the costs of litigation, or products may be sold outside the usual retail channels with which the brand owner is familiar. A consistent stream of such infringing products can, if left unchecked, undermine the ability of the trade mark to function as a guarantee of trade origin and, in due course, can deal a fatal blow to the validity of the trade mark itself.

One fact that can easily be overlooked by a brand owner besieged by infringing products in this way is that others may be willing and able to help police the endangered marks. Misuse of trade marks can (provided the misuse is in relation to products rather than services) amount to a criminal offence as well as a civil infringement. By enlisting the assistance of trading standards officers and other enforcement agencies, a brand owner can gain a valuable ally in its fight against infringers. Enforcement agencies may be able to police venues (such as street markets, ports and airports) that the brand owner is unable to monitor. Counterfeit products may be seized, thereby taking them off the market immediately, and the vendor or importer may be subject to criminal sanctions, which may prove a greater deterrent than the risk of civil liability alone.

8.   CONCLUSION

There is no doubt that the monopoly conferred by a trade mark registration is limited in a number of important – and frequently frustrating – ways. However, there is equally no doubt that brand owners can adopt a number of strategies to help minimise the exposure created by those limits. While unwanted third party use can never be eliminated, the harm such third parties are capable of inflicting on the value and integrity of the brand can be diminished if the brand owner takes the right steps at the right time.

21. Non-traditional trade marks: unauthorised but permitted use

Karin Cederlund and Petra Hansson

1. INTRODUCTION

This chapter considers, from the perspective of the proprietor, the issue of non-traditional trade marks and how they are affected by unauthorised but permitted use in Europe. Although a number of issues relating to unauthorised but permitted use of a trade mark have been clarified through the emerging case law of the ECJ,[1] the extent to which that case law affects non-traditional trade marks remains unclear.

2. NON-TRADITIONAL TRADE MARKS

Words and logos have long been seen and accepted as trade marks by the public, registration authorities and courts throughout Europe and beyond. However, innovative brand creation and an increasingly competitive marketplace have created new types of trade marks that no longer consist of words or logos or a combination of both, but of features such as colours, shapes, sounds, scents, tastes and sometimes entire concepts. These new types of trade marks are often referred to as 'unconventional' or 'non-traditional' trade marks.

A difficulty with non-traditional trade marks is that, as a genre, they normally lack inherent distinctiveness.[2] The average customer is simply not

---

[1]   See for example *Bayerische Motorenwerke AG (BMW) and BMW Nederland BV v Ronald Darel Deenik*, Case C-63/97[1999] ETMR 339, [1999] ECR I-905; *Gillette Company, Gillette Group Finland Oy v LA-Laboratoires Ltd Oy*, Case C-228/03 [2005] ETMR 67; *Gerolsteiner Brunnen GmbH & Co v Putsch GmbH*, Case C-100/02, [2004] ETMR 40; *Pippig Augenoptik GmbH & Co. KG v Hartlauer Handelsgesellschaft mbH and Verlassenschaft nach dem verstorbenen Franz Josef Hartlauer*, Case C-44/01 [2004] ETMR 5 and *Toshiba Europe GmbH v Katun Germany GmbH*, Case C-112/99, [2001] ECR I-7945, [2002] ETMR 26.

[2]   See for example *Libertel Groep BV v Benelux-Merkenbureau* (colour), Case C-104/01 [2003] ECR I-3793, [2003] ETMR 63 and *Koninklijke Philips Electronics*

accustomed to perceiving non-traditional trade marks immediately as identifiers of the origin of goods or services. It is therefore only through extensive use and considerable market investment that most non-traditional trade marks can acquire distinctiveness. However, once a non-traditional trade mark has acquired distinctiveness, it can constitute a very valuable trade mark due to its often attention-grabbing capacity with significant brand awareness as a result.

Another difficulty with non-traditional trade marks is that they will, at least as indicated by the limited case law available, only be awarded a limited scope of protection.[3] Consequently, it is uncertain to what extent the proprietor of a non-traditional trade mark is able to defend the trade mark in relation to use of marks that are not identical but similar to the non-traditional trade mark.

Since the public is not accustomed to perceiving non-traditional trade marks as immediate identifiers of the origin of goods or services, non-traditional trade marks are normally used together with a traditional trade mark, that is a word mark or a logotype. This dualistic approach may also be due to the audio and visual limitations of non-traditional marks.

3. RIGHTS CONFERRED BY A TRADE MARK

Article 5(1) of the Trade Mark Directive[4] deals with the exclusive rights conferred by a registered trade mark, and states

> The proprietor shall be entitled to prevent all third parties not having his consent from using in the course of trade:
>
> (a) any sign which is identical with the trade mark in relation to goods or services which are identical with those for which the trade mark is registered;
> (b) any sign where, because of its identity with, or similarity to, the trade mark and the identity or similarity of the goods or services covered by the trade mark and the sign, there exists a likelihood of confusion on the part of the public, which includes the likelihood of association between the sign and the trade mark.

Article 5(2) of the Trade Mark Directive adds that the proprietor of a trade mark with a reputation may also be given a right to prevent the use of an identical or similar mark for dissimilar goods or services.

NV v Remington Consumer Products Ltd (shape), Case C-299/99[2002] ECR I-5475, [2002] ETMR 81.

[3]   See for example 'In defence of magenta: German dispute explores the enforcement of colour marks', 2002 *Trademark World* 166, p. 16 concerning the German case *Deutsche Telekom AG v Mobilcom AG* and the Northern Ireland case of *BP Amoco Plc v John Kelly Ltd*, CA (NI), 2 February 2001.

[4]   First Council Directive 89/104 of 21 December 1988 to approximate the laws of the member states relating to trade marks.

These provisions illustrate that the rights of the proprietor of a trade mark are extensive, even when considering the important general limitation that there must be use 'in the course of trade' before an act is considered to infringe.[5] It is therefore generally accepted that it is necessary to have exceptions to rights in trade marks in order to reconcile the fundamental interests of trade mark protection with those of free movement of goods and freedom of competition.[6] As a consequence, use of another's trade mark that is not authorised by the trade mark proprietor will be permitted in certain circumstances under Article 6 of the Trade Mark Directive as well as under Article 3a of the Comparative Advertising Directive[7].

4. UNAUTHORISED BUT PERMITTED USE

4.1 Article 6 of the Trade Mark Directive

Article 6(1)(a) of the Trade Mark Directive permits the use by a third party of his own name or address. Article 6(1)(b) additionally permits the use of indications concerning the kind, quality, quantity, intended purpose and other characteristics of goods or services. Finally, Article 6(1)(c) permits the use of another's trade mark which is *necessary* to indicate the intended purpose of a product or service, in particular as accessories or spare parts. In relation to all the exceptions to the rights of the trade mark proprietor under Article 6, it is a prerequisite that the use has been in accordance with *honest practices* in industrial or commercial matters.

Since the use of one's name and address will, as a general rule, mean the use of one or more words, the exception in Article 6(1)(a) of the Trade Mark Directive will be of little or no relevance in relation to non-traditional trade marks. This exception will therefore not be discussed further.

In contrast to Article 6(1)(a), Articles 6(1)(b) and 6(1)(c) are both of interest in relation to non-traditional trade marks. These articles have been

---

5   This requirement has been discussed in some detail in a number of cases including *BMW* and *Arsenal* [2002] ECR I-10273, [2003] ETMR 19. In *BMW* the ECJ took the view that the use of a trade mark to inform the public that the advertiser was specialised in, inter alia, repair and maintenance of the trade mark proprietor's products constituted use in the course of trade mark under Article 5(1)(a) of the Trade Mark Directive. Further, in *Arsenal* the ECJ held that the unauthorized use of another's trade mark as a 'badge of loyalty' does not exclude that the said use also constitutes trade mark use. See also *Hölterhoff* [2002] ETMR 917, [2002] ECR I-4187.

6   See for example *BMW*, para. 62, and *Gillette*, para. 29.

7   Council Directive 97/55 of the European parliament and of the council of 6 October 1997 amending Directive 84/450 concerning misleading advertising.

interpreted by the ECJ in a number of cases including *Gerolsteiner*,[8] *BMW*[9] and *Gillette*.[10] However, none of these cases concerns the use of a non-traditional trade mark.

4.2 How are Non-traditional Trade Marks Affected by Unauthorised But Permitted Use Under the Trade Mark Directive?

4.2.1 The 'necessary' requirement

The lawfulness or otherwise of use of another's trade mark under Article 6(1)(c) of the Trade Mark Directive depends on whether that use *is necessary to indicate the intended purpose of a product or service*.[11] A use is necessary in order to indicate the intended purpose of a product or service marketed by that third party, if such use constitutes the only practical means of providing the public with comprehensive and complete information on that intended purpose in order to preserve the undistorted system of competition in the market for that product.[12]

When assessing whether a use has been necessary within the meaning of Article 6(1)(c), one must determine whether other means of providing such information exists, for example the possible existence of technical standards or public norms. If they do, the use of another's trade mark will not be considered necessary.

It is clear that the 'necessary' requirement should not be understood to mean that the use of another's trade mark must be absolutely necessary in the true sense of the word. Instead, it is sufficient that there is a clear legitimate interest to use another's trade mark in order to provide information as to the intended purpose of a product or service.[13]

The question whether the use of a non-traditional trade mark can be considered 'necessary' remains unanswered. If a non-traditional trade mark is capable of providing information as to the intended purpose of a product or service it is hard to see why the use of such a trade mark should not be capable of being considered as necessary within the meaning of Article 6(1)(c). However, as discussed in relation to the Comparative Advertising

---

[8]   *Gerolsteiner Brunnen GmbH & Co. v Putsch GmbH*, Case C-100/02.
[9]   *Bayerische Motorenwerke AG (BMW) and BMW Nederland BV v Ronald Darel Deenik*, Case C-63/97.
[10]   *Gillette Company, Gillette Group Finland Oy v LA-Laboratoires Ltd Oy*, Case C-228/03.
[11]   See *Gillette*, para. 39.
[12]   See *BMW* para. 60, *Gillette* para. 39.
[13]   Judgment of the Svea Appeal Court 5 June 2001 in Case T 191–99 (this case constituted a Swedish parallel to *Gillette*); see also Pawlo in NIR 2002 p. 437.

Directive and the concept of indispensability under section 4.4.1 below, it could be argued that it can never be 'necessary' to use a non-traditional trade mark if it has been an alternative to use a word mark that is used together with the non-traditional trade mark in neutral writing.

4.2.2 The condition of 'honest practice'

The condition of use in accordance with 'honest practice' constitutes the expression of a duty to act fairly in relation to the legitimate interests of the trade mark proprietor.[14] Further, it is clear that the use of another's trade mark will *not* comply with the honest practice condition if

- it is done in such a manner as to give the impression that there is a commercial connection between the third party and the trade mark proprietor;
- it affects the value of the trade mark by taking unfair advantage of its distinctive character or reputation;
- it entails the discrediting or denigration of that trade mark; or
- if the third party presents its product as an imitation or replica of the product bearing a trade mark of which it is not the proprietor.[15]

Despite the ECJ's clarifications and explanations regarding the interpretation of the condition of honest practice, it is still unclear whether the use of another's non-traditional trade mark such as a colour mark or a shape mark will be considered in accordance with honest use.

Taking into account that non-traditional trade marks are normally used together with a traditional trade mark, it could be argued that even if the use is considered to be 'necessary', it is *not* in accordance with honest practices for a third party to use a non-traditional trade mark, on its own or together with a traditional trade mark, when it would be possible to use a traditional trade mark on its own. Such use of another's non-traditional trade mark is more likely to exceed the mere provision of information and enter the area of unlawful suggestion of a commercial connection with the proprietor of the non-traditional trade mark since the origin of the product would not be so clear. It may additionally be argued that, since the public is not so accustomed to perceiving non-traditional trade marks as identifiers of the origin of goods or services, such marks are, as a general rule, more sensitive to dilution.

The argumentation above seems to be supported by a judgment by a

---

14   *BMW* para. 61 and *Gillette* para. 41.
15   *BMW* and *Gillette*.

Swedish Appeal Court[16] in a parallel Swedish dispute to *Gillette*. In the Swedish dispute Gillette claimed that the Swedish supermarket chain Kooperativa Förbundet (KF) infringed Gillette's SENSOR trade mark by the use of the trade mark on the packaging of its razor blades. KF sold its razor blades on the Swedish market under KF's device mark and the trade mark FLEXRAKBLAD. The back of the packaging of KF's razor blades stated in neutral writing: 'Also compatible with Personna and Sensor razors'. The Swedish Appeal Court held that, since KF had marked its razor blades prominently with its own trade marks and had only presented the Gillette trade mark in small, neutral letters on the back of the packaging, KF's use of the SENSOR trade mark had been in accordance with honest practices and the Swedish implementation of Article 6(1)(c) of the Trade Mark Directive was therefore applicable. A reasonable conclusion from the Swedish Appeal Court judgment seems to be that, had KF *not* used the SENSOR trade mark in small neutral letters but employed for example a logotype, or indeed used a non-traditional trade mark held by Gillette, such use would *not* have been in accordance with honest practices.

4.3 The Comparative Advertising Directive

The 13th recital of the Comparative Advertising Directive recognises the rights of the proprietor of a trade mark under Article 5 of the Trade Mark Directive. Having asserted this main rule, the 14th recital of the same preamble continues that 'it may, however, be *indispensable*, in order to make comparative advertising effective, to identify the goods or services of a competitor, making reference to a trade mark or trade name of which the latter is the proprietor' (emphasis added). According to the 15th recital, such use of another's trade mark, trade name or other distinguishing mark does not infringe the exclusive rights of the trade mark proprietor if it complies with the conditions specified in the Comparative Advertising Directive, as long as the intended purpose of the comparative advertising is to *distinguish* between the products and therefore to highlight differences objectively.

Using an attractive and memorable trade mark is one of the easiest ways to attract the attention of prospective customers. For a manufacturer of a new product, without a well-known brand of his own, the use of a competitor's well-known brand may facilitate a fast and inexpensive launch of the product on the market. For this reason advertisers are often eager to mention the trade marks of their competitors in comparative advertising.

---

[16] Judgment of the Svea Court of Appeal in Case T 191–99 dated 5 June 2001, see also NIR 2002 p. 430.

The conditions for permitted comparative advertising are found in Article 3a(1) of the Comparative Advertising Directive. As regards unauthorised but permitted use of a trade mark in comparative advertising, the conditions set forth in Article 3a(1)(d) ('no confusion'), (e) ('no discrediting') and (g) ('no taking unfair advantage of the reputation') are of particular relevance.[17]

In this context it should be borne in mind that it does not follow from the Comparative Advertising Directive that references to another's trade mark which does not comply with the Comparative Advertising Directive will necessarily be regarded as trade mark infringements: such use will require proof of a likelihood of confusion before liability may be established.[18]

The rules on comparative advertising under the Comparative Advertising Directive have been interpreted by the ECJ in two cases, *Toshiba*[19] and *Pippig*.[20] Neither of those cases however concerned the use of non-traditional trade marks.

4.4 How are Non-traditional Trade Marks Affected by Use in Comparative Advertising?

4.4.1 The concept of indispensability

As mentioned above, one of the characteristics of non-traditional trade marks is that they are normally used in combination with traditional trade marks. Due to this characteristic, the interpretation of the concept 'indispensable' set forth in the 14th recital of the preamble to the Comparative Advertising Directive is of particular importance. Although not explicitly mentioned among the conditions laid down in Article 3a(1), it is at least arguable that a prerequisite for permitted use of a competitor's trade mark should be that the comparison is

---

[17] 'Comparative advertising shall, as far as the comparison is concerned, be permitted when the following conditions are met:

(d) it does not create confusion in the marketplace between the advertiser and a competitor or between the advertiser's trade marks, trade names, other distinguishing marks, goods or services and those of a competitor;

(e) it does not discredit or denigrate the trade marks, trade names, other distinguishing marks, goods, services, activities, or circumstances of a competitor; . . .

(g) it does not take unfair advantage of the reputation of a trade mark, trade name or other distinguishing marks of a competitor or of the designation of origin of competing products . . .'

[18] See Jeremy Phillips, *Trade Mark Law: a Practical Anatomy*, p. 252. See also Annette Kur, 'Die vergleichende werbung in Europa: Kurz vor dem pyrrhus-sieg?', *Vennebog till Mogens Koktvedgaard*, p. 436.

[19] *Toshiba Europe GmbH v Katun Germany GmbH*, Case C-112/99.

[20] *Pippig Augenoptik GmbH & Co. KG v Hartlauer Handelsgesellschaft mbH and Verlassenschaft nach dem verstorbenen Franz Josef Hartlauer*, Case C-44/01.

272

impaired if there is no reference to the trade mark.[21] If the Comparative Advertising Directive were to be interpreted in that way, use of non-traditional trade marks would not be permitted when the comparison could be made by a reference to for example a word mark in neutral writing.

National laws show some variation in this regard.[22] In *Pippig* the ECJ did not consider Article 3a(1)(e), regarding discrediting and denigration, as an obstacle to the reproduction of a competitor's logotype and shop front in comparative advertising. This ruling might be said to indicate that it is permitted to use any kind of trade mark, including a non-traditional trade mark, in comparative advertising, even though it would have been possible to use a word mark in neutral writing instead without impairing the comparison. However, the ruling of the ECJ is limited to the question whether Article 3a(1)(e) as such prevents the use of a competitor's logotype and shop front in comparative advertising and deals, in this regard, with none of the other conditions in Article 3a(1). The extent to which non-traditional trade marks may be used in comparative advertising must therefore be considered an open question, when it is possible to identify the competitor by the use of a more neutral trade mark without impairing the comparison.

The refusal to give advertisers a free choice to use any of a trade mark proprietor's trade marks in comparative advertising may be explained in several ways. Limiting permitted use to the most neutral use possible, without impairing the comparison, would be in accordance with the principle that exceptions to exclusive proprietary rights should be interpreted narrowly. Such limitation of permitted use would not conflict with the purpose of the exception to the exclusive right provided by the Comparative Advertising Directive, that is to enable effective comparative advertising. Furthermore, such limitation would be compatible with the provisions for permitted use under Article 6(1)(c) of the Trade Mark Directive, in particular the requirement that use must be necessary and in accordance with honest practices.[23] It remains to be seen whether the ECJ will stick to the approach taken in *Pippig* or whether the court will take an approach that is more advantageous to the trade mark proprietors.

---

[21] See for example the Opinion of the Advocate General in *Toshiba*.

[22] Cf. Ingerl/Rohnke, Markengesetz, 2nd edition, 2003, §14, para. 153, Oberlandesgericht Frankfurt am Main, GRUR 2000, 621 et seq. – Magentafarbener Pfeil, *O2 Ltd, O2 (UK) Ltd v Hutchinson 3G UK Ltd, High Court of Justice* (Chancery Division) Pumfrey J, 9 November 2004 [FN1].

[23] See interpretation of necessity and honest practices in the BMW case and the Gillette case.

4.4.2   The concept of 'distinguishing'

The Comparative Advertising Directive applies not only to the use of 'trade marks' and 'trade names', but also to 'other distinguishing marks'.[24] This concept was discussed in *Toshiba*, both by the Advocate General[25] and the ECJ. The Advocate General mentioned the shape and the colour of a product as examples of other distinguishing marks and held that, in order to avoid a situation where the development of comparative advertising gives free rein to parasitic business conduct, it is essential that the concept of distinguishing marks is interpreted very broadly. However, in its ruling the ECJ referred to its own previous trade mark case law[26] and concluded that, with regard to the distinctiveness of a mark, the national court must make an overall assessment of the greater or lesser capacity of the mark to identify the goods and services for which it has been registered as coming from a particular undertaking, and thus to distinguish those goods or services from those of other undertakings. The ECJ questioned whether Toshiba's product numbers were to be considered as 'other distinguishing marks' since 'they are in fact combinations of numbers or of letters and numbers and it is questionable whether they would be identified as product numbers of an equipment manufacturer if they were not found, as in the present case, in a column headed OEM product number'. The ECJ also wondered whether those combinations would enable the manufacturer to be identified if they were not used in combination with his trade mark.

As previously stated, to prove that a non-traditional trade mark is identified as coming from a particular undertaking may be difficult and will depend on the overall presentation of the comparative advertising and the degree of awareness and distinctiveness of the trade mark. Trade dress and packaging designs that have acquired distinctiveness will probably also be identified as coming from a particular undertaking when used in comparative advertising. However, a colour that has acquired secondary meaning with respect to certain goods and services, and which is used as background colour in a comparative advertising, will not necessarily be perceived as a sign coming from a particular undertaking when used in that context. However, if the same colour is used on a packaging design, it may be more probable that it will be perceived as coming from a particular undertaking. The assessment must be made by the national courts on a case-by-case basis.

---

[24]   15th recital of the preamble and Article 3a(1)(d), (e) and (g).
[25]   Opinion of Advocate General Léger, 8 February 2001.
[26]   *Lloyd Schuhfabrik Meyer & Co. GmbH v Klijsen Handel BV*, Case C-342/97 [1999] ECR I-3819, [1999] ETMR 690.

4.4.3   Taking unfair advantage of the reputation under Article 3a(1)(g)[27]

The concept of 'unfair advantage' may be understood in the light of interpretations of equivalent provisions of the Trade Mark Directive and the Council Regulation 40/94 (the 'CTM Regulation'. According to the ECJ,[28] use of distinguishing marks within the meaning of Article 3a(1)(g) of the Comparative Advertising Directive enables the advertiser to take advantage of the reputation attached to those marks only if the effect of the reference to them is to create, in the mind of the persons to whom the advertising is directed, an association between the competitor and the advertiser, in that those persons associate the reputation of the competitor's products with the products of the advertiser. In order to determine whether that condition is satisfied, the ECJ states that the overall presentation of the advertising at issue and the type of person for whom the advertising is intended shall be taken into account.

The fact that the trade mark in question is a non-traditional trade mark constitutes part of the overall presentation of the advertising. Provided that a non-traditional trade mark is deemed to have a distinguishing capacity in a particular comparative advertisement, the strong brand awareness and eye-catching capacity of such a mark, compared to a word mark in neutral writing, may increase the risk of association between the trade mark proprietor and the advertiser. However, if use of the non-traditional trade mark is indispensable in order to make the comparison effective,[29] such use is not considered to take unfair advantage of the reputation of the trade mark regardless of whether the use would actually lend an aura of quality to the advertiser or his goods and services.[30] The advantage obtained under those circumstances is not 'unfair'. If, on the other hand, use of a non-traditional trade mark is not indispensable, for example due to the availability of a parallel word mark, it seems more likely that a court would consider the use contradictory to the condition in Article 3a(1)(g). Although the concept of indispensability would not be given the interpretation discussed above, the possibility of an advertiser identifying the competitor by a neutral word mark without impairing the comparison could, as such, render the obtained advantage from such use unfair. Otherwise there will be a significant

---

[27]   A similar assessment could be made with respect to Article 3a(1)(e) regarding confusion. However, it will often be difficult to claim confusion, since the very purpose of the comparative advertisement is to distinguish between the compared products. As regards trade mark infringement and comparative advertisements, see Annette Kur, 'Die vergleichende werbung in Europa: Kurz vor dem pyrrhus-sieg?', *Vennebog till Mogens Koktvedgaard.*

[28]   See *Toshiba.*

[29]   That may for example be the case if the word-mark of a company name is known to the public.

[30]   See *BMW* and *Toshiba.*

risk that the Comparative Advertising Directive will open a possibility for advertisers to disguise advertisements that as a matter of fact take unfair advantage of the reputation of a trade mark as comparative advertisement.

Extensive use of a trade mark in comparative advertising may be harmful to the distinctive character of the trade mark. This risk is of significant relevance to non-traditional trade marks, due to their low inherent distinctiveness. By way of example, if a well known packaging design is frequently used by competitors in comparative advertising, there is a considerable risk that the packaging design will lose its exclusive character, its capacity to attract attention and, in the end, its acquired distinctiveness. It is therefore remarkable that the Comparative Advertising Directive does not explicitly mention that the comparison must not be detrimental to the distinctive character of the trade mark as a condition for permitted comparative advertising in Article 3a(1), at least if the comparison concerns a trade mark with a reputation protected under Article 5(2) of the Trade Mark Directive.[31] It remains to be seen to what extent the courts will take this risk into account in their assessment of whether use of a non-traditional trade mark in comparative advertising is permitted.

4.4.4 Discrediting and denigration under Article 3a(1)(e)

In *Pippig* the national court referred to the ECJ the question whether the condition in Article 3a(1)(e) of the Comparative Advertising Directive was to be interpreted as meaning that the information on the identification of the competitor must be restricted to the extent absolutely necessary and whether it therefore was not permitted, in addition to the competitor's name, to use its company logo and its shop front. When answering this question, the ECJ referred to the 15th recital in the preamble to the Directive and concluded that use of another's trade mark, trade name or other distinguishing mark does not breach the exclusive right in cases where it complies with the conditions laid down by the said Directive. Article 3a(1)(e) did not therefore prevent a party from, in addition to citing the competitor's name, reproducing its logo and a picture of its shop front in comparative advertising, if that advertising complies with the conditions for lawfulness laid down by Community law. As concluded above, it remains to be seen to what extent this approach will also apply to Articles 3a(a)(d) and (g). Although it may be correct that identifying a competitor by using pictures of his shop front with his company logo is not in itself sufficient to discredit the competitor since discrediting is attributable more to the content and presentation of the comparison and not the use as such,[32] it cannot be excluded that the mere use of such signs may take unfair

---

[31] The UK Trade Marks Act 1994, s.10(6) takes this risk into account.
[32] The opinion of the Advocate General in *Pippig*.

advantage of the reputation of the trade mark and possibly also give rise to confusion.

5.   FINAL REMARKS

A number of questions relating to unauthorised but permitted third party use of non-traditional trade marks remain to be answered. An underlying issue of particular importance is the interplay between the Trade Mark Directive and the Comparative Advertising Directive. Although this issue has been addressed in the preamble of the Comparative Advertisement Directive as well as in *Toshiba*, there is still considerable room for argument as to what third party use of a non-traditional trade mark the proprietor of the mark can and can not prevent. This is unsatisfactory for proprietors of non-traditional trade marks and third parties wishing to use such trade marks alike.

Finally, it is unclear to what extent copyright and design rights, if applicable, can be used in order to protect non-traditional trade marks when trade mark law is of little or no use the proprietor of a non-traditional trade mark. If the proprietor of a non-traditional trade mark can rely on copyright or design rights to protect his non-traditional trade mark against third party use that is otherwise permitted under the Trade Mark Directive and the Comparative Advertising Directive, there will be an obvious conflict between national copyright and design legislation and said directives. It is an open question how this conflict will be solved. However, it has been proposed that a principle analogue to the ECJ decision in *Dior*[33] should be applied. In that case, the ECJ refused to allow the proprietor of copyright in an artistic work, which was also a trade mark, more control over the use of the mark than he would have had as a trade mark proprietor.

---

[33]   *Parfums Christian Dior SA v Evora* Case C-337/95 [1998] ETMR 26.

Conclusion: Where do we go from here?

Jeremy Phillips

The assiduous reader, having followed the threads of thought through the labyrinths of permitted but unauthorised use, may be entitled to pause at this point and ask, 'so what?' A cynic might say that this book has demonstrated a small number of propositions that could have been deduced with ease from a handful of recent cases and news cuttings:

- Trade mark owners possess a powerful legal right to stop others using their registered trade marks;
- Several identifiable groups, including consumers, competitors, manu-facturers of compatible goods and those members of the public who are environmentally and morally conscious, have an interest in being able to refer to those marks and to make use of them even where the trade mark owner objects;
- The law provides for both specific instances and general classes of unauthorised use that will not constitute trade mark infringement;
- Those rules that tolerate unauthorised use are not always easy to apply on the facts of cases that fall to be decided by a court of law.

This cynical view does not however take into account the dynamics of a world which is far more complex than a classical model of trade mark enforcement. The marketplace is constantly developing new devices through which the goodwill in a brand may be exploited, and situations persist in arising in which new pitfalls appear. Some of these issues have not been developed in this book because they are too new; others have been considered but will require constant revisiting as their satisfactory resolution become more important. For example

- Product placement has become an increasingly attractive means of promoting the desirability of a brand, as leading trade mark-protected products are featured prominently in films and even in literary works such as novels. But is the trade mark owner entitled to protection against the use of his products by the villain? BMW may be pleased to pay for the highly visible placement of its product as the hero's getaway car, but

277

could Mercedes complain if one of its own vehicles is driven by the evil
and greatly detested persona of the driver who gives chase?

- The sale of trade marks as key words for internet searches has attracted
legal analysis and substantive litigation in the United States and Europe,
as has the use of trade mark search terms as triggers for pop-up or listed
advertisements on search results pages or target websites. Does the fact
that an internet search company charges a fee for a third party to use a
popular or attractive trade mark mean that it is something that should be
prohibited in the absence of the trade mark owner's permission, or is it
no different to the position of a waiter who, when asked for a COCA-
COLA, responds by asking his customer if he wouldn't fancy a PEPSI
instead? The internet is still very much a developing medium and little
legislative thought has been devoted to issues wider than that of whether
the use of trade marks as key words, metatags or anything else constitutes an infringement of the law as it stands.

- Several commentators in this volume have mentioned the need to
preserve to third parties the right to make use of terms that are descriptive of their own goods or services, or of those of others. As the test of
registrability of largely descriptive signs as trade marks becomes easier
to satisfy, and as trade mark registration increasingly comes to protect
product shapes and packaging, the need of third parties to rely upon
what Susie Middlemiss refers to as the descriptive defences will
increase. It may well be that, just as trade mark law has extended the
scope of protection, it will need to provide an equivalent degree of
protection for honest uses by third parties too.

- Although it is well established as a phenomenon in the United States
and is also legitimated by European Union law, comparative advertising
is still treated with acute suspicion in many parts of Europe, where the
use of another's mark is often viewed by courts and commentators as an
undesirable practice. It is highly likely that, if pan-European comparative advertising campaigns are found to be lawful in some countries but
not in others, further references will be made to the European Court of
Justice for preliminary rulings as to the parameters of legitimacy of such
practices.

- Much the same point may be made in regard to referential use of
another's trade mark so as to indicate that the third party's products are
compatible with those of the trade mark owner. In this instance, discussion in Europe has turned greatly on whether that use is 'necessary'
rather than whether it is fair in itself. One wonders whether this discussion is ultimately productive, since commercial conduct – particularly in
terms of an action for unfair competition – is predicated on conditions
of fairness, not necessity.

- Readers may have noted that some of the European contributors have taken the position that, since defences to trade mark infringements are exceptions to the principle that the use of another's trade mark is an infringement unless it is specifically permitted, those defences should be narrowly construed. This is not because they act on behalf of trade mark owners (even the biggest trade mark owners are also unauthorised but licit users of the trade marks of others), but because the principle that an exception is construed narrowly is one which has a long and respected tradition within European jurisprudence. But there is another way of looking at it (as Jacob J did in the RoHo cushion case (*Hodgkinson & Corby Ltd v Wards Mobility Services Ltd* [1994] 1 WLR 1564)): the basic principle is that a trader can do whatever he wants unless the law clearly prohibits it. This being so, the trade mark right, which constitutes such a prohibition, is then the exception to the general principle and its parameters should be construed narrowly; the defences, which are there to protect the general principle, should then be construed with generous width.

These issues, and many more like them, will remain a central feature of discussion concerning trade mark law and practice over the coming decade. This book cannot pretend to provide the answer to them all. If however it has provoked and retained the interest of those participating in that discussion, it will have done its job.

Index of trade marks, trade names and geographical indications

Subject index